FREE WILL

To Marty —
Enjoy! With respect
for the work you do.
Warmly, Laura Ekstrom

FREE WILL

A Philosophical Study

Laura Waddell Ekstrom

COLLEGE OF WILLIAM AND MARY

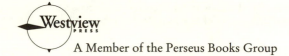

A Member of the Perseus Books Group

Focus Series

Copyright © 2000 by Westview Press, A Member of the Perseus Books Group

Published in 2000 in the United States of America by Westview Press, 5500 Central Avenue, Boulder, Colorado 80301-2877, and in the United Kingdom by Westview Press, 12 Hid's Copse Road, Cumnor Hill, Oxford OX2 9JJ

Find us on the World Wide Web at www.westviewpress.com

Library of Congress Cataloging-in-Publication Data
Ekstrom, Laura Waddell.
  Free will : a philosophical study/Laura Waddell Ekstrom.
    p. cm.—(Focus series)
  Includes bibliographical references and index.
  ISBN 0-8133-9094-x (hc)—ISBN 0-8133-9093-1 (pb)
  1. Free will and determinism. I. Title. II. Focus series (Westview Press)
BJ1461 .E45   1999
123'.5—dc21   99-048181

The paper used in this publication meets the requirements of the American National Standard for Permanence of Paper for Printed Library Materials Z39.48-1984.

10   9   8   7   6   5   4   3   2   1

To my husband,
Mark Edward Ekstrom,

and my daughter,
Kristen Grace Ekstrom

CONTENTS

PREFACE

Among the other great philosophical issues—the nature of truth, the foundation of ethics, the existence of God, the source of political authority, the possibility and scope of human knowledge, and the nature of meaning, causation, and consciousness—the problem of free will takes its place prominently as one both vigorously debated through philosophical history and to this day largely unsolved. Philosophers continue to debate not only the empirical question of whether or not we have free will, but also certain deeper and more fundamental theoretical questions: What is the essence or nature of a free act? Is our having the ability to act freely consistent or inconsistent with certain other propositions about the nature of the supernatural and the natural world? Would our having free will be, in fact, a good? And if so, what kind?

This book is designed both to highlight central issues in recent discussions of free will and to propose a particular indeterminist account of its nature. Various developments of the consequence argument for incompatibilism and the consequent debates over the properties of power necessity have been for many philosophers the centerpiece of free will theory during the past two decades. Discussion of the issues relevant to assessing the incompatibilist arguments thus takes a prominent place in this book. But it is also important to set out and examine directly the differing conceptions of free action itself underlying the arguments for incompatibilism and the compatibilist responses to those arguments. Hence I spend some time, following discussion of the arguments, making explicit and critically evaluating not just one compatibilist and one incompatibilist understanding of the nature of freedom, but rather a number of particular versions of each type of account, culminating in the proposal of a particular libertarian theory. This theory makes appeal, as libertarians traditionally have, to agent causation but proposes, contrary to tradition, that the notion is *reducible* to purely event-causal terms.

But why *care* about free will and hence about its consistency or inconsistency with certain other doctrines, such as scientific determinism, in the first place? What values would the possession of free will secure for us? The book begins by considering these questions, motivating the discussion of arguments concerning the metaphysics of freedom by making clear what is at stake. The final two chapters turn to discussing pivotal issues in the voluminous literature on the connection between free will and moral responsibility. In particular, I address competing views, not generally made explicit, of the function of moral responsibility ascriptions, along with leading compatibilist accounts of responsibility and Frankfurt-type counterexamples to the principle of alternative possibilities.

The writing of this book was supported by a summer stipend from the National Endowment for the Humanities for summer 1998, as well as by the pretenure leave program at Bates College for spring 1997. I gratefully acknowledge the support of both institutions. A portion of Chapter 6 appeared as "Protecting Incompatibilist Freedom" in *American Philosophical Quarterly* (vol. 35, July 1998); it is reprinted by permission of the editor.

The comments of Robert Kane, Keith Lehrer, Mark Okrent, David Robb, Scott Davison, Tom Senor, and Michael Bratman led to some specific improvements in one or another of various chapters; I thank each of them. Alfred Mele, Timothy O'Connor, and Eleonore Stump generously read the manuscript in full and provided a number of very useful critical comments. Sarah Warner at Westview Press provided excellent editorial supervision. My thanks to the students in an advanced seminar in free will at the College of William and Mary and to the students in Alfred Mele's senior colloquium on motivation, freedom, and responsibility at Davidson College, who studied the book in manuscript form.

I am grateful, as well, to those philosophers who were especially influential in my philosophical education: Robert Cummins, Joel Feinberg, Alvin Goldman, Keith Lehrer, and John Pollock at the University of Arizona; Alvin Plantinga at the University of Notre Dame; and Michael Bratman, Stuart Hampshire, and John Perry at Stanford University. I also would like to express thanks to my father for inspiring a love of argument and to my mother for her encouragement to become anything I wanted (a philosopher, of all things!).

Finally, I am grateful to Beverly Williams, Joy Hayes, Kim Decker, and my husband, Mark Ekstrom, for the provision at various times of loving child care, without which the writing of this book would not have been possible.

Laura Waddell Ekstrom
Williamsburg, VA

CHAPTER ONE

The Problem
of Human Freedom

The problem of free will is one of the most subtle and fascinating of all philosophical problems. Its complexity is not worn on its face. Rather, like finally untangling the varied aspects of a profound personality in an intimate relationship, appreciation comes only with directed effort through time. Occasionally someone, usually an introductory student, will pronounce the matter simply solved: "What's so hard about free will? Either we have it, or we don't. What's there to talk about?" Reflection on certain facts frequently induces appropriate humility.

The issue of free will has concerned scholars through the centuries, including such significant philosophical talents as Aristotle, Augustine, Aquinas, Descartes, Hume, Locke, Leibniz, Kant, and Sartre, among others. That the problem continues to generate volumes of print in both academic monographs and contemporary scholarly journals, with the lack of an emerging consensus, attests to the fact that we have neither resolved the issue nor finished plumbing its intricate depths. The contemporary philosopher Robert Nozick remarks:

> Over the years I have spent more time thinking about the problem of free will—it felt like banging my head against it—than about any other philosophical topic except perhaps the foundation of ethics. Fresh ideas would come frequently, soon afterwards to curdle ... this [the problem of free will is the] most frustrating and unyielding of problems.[1]

What makes the problem so unyielding? Even this question has no simple answer. A number of strands comprising "the problem of free will" must, first, be disjoined. That is, as a number of philosophers have pointed out, the problem of free will is not one problem but many.[2] The empirical question—Do any of us ever act freely?—is but one concern, although the driving one. Its resolution for us depends upon our answer to the distinct question of whether or not we have good *reason to believe* that we do at times enjoy freedom in our activities. And both the existence problem and the epistemological problem are logically parasitic on the question of what *constitutes* a free act, in other words, on the theoretical matter of establishing what it is (or would be) to act freely, or of one's own free will.

Think for a minute about this latter question. Often the immediate thought is of the relative lack or availability of political freedoms. So the term 'free will' may bring to mind the observation, for instance, that many women in our day and part of the world are free to leave the home and work for compensation outside of the home. In past generations, in many places, this is something that women were not so free to do. The example concerns something that most women are now socially and politically *allowed* to do.

But the question of free will is not a question of what persons are socially, politically, or legally allowed to do. Philosophers interested in the topic of free will are concerned with a deeper question. Of course, there are certain actions that we all are politically and legally free to do (such as, if one is an American citizen over the age of eighteen, vote and marry a person of the opposite sex) and others that none of us are politically or legally free to do (such as murder another person or, at the time of this writing, marry a person of the same sex). And there are actions that some of us are legally, politically, or socially allowed to do (such as convene a special session of Congress or call to order a courtroom) that others of us are not. If none of us is legally free to murder another person, then what does it mean to say that someone murdered another of his own free will? In what sense, if any, did Moses, for example, commit a free act in murdering an Egyptian man?

While the example of a woman's ability to earn wages for work outside the home is more pertinent to the topic of political freedom than to the topic of freedom of the will, it is nonetheless instructive for seeing both the beginnings of an account of free will and the difficulty of refining it. For we said that her freedom in that case is a matter of what the political world, or her social and legal circumstances, *allow* her to do. The deeper question of interest to free will theorists is whether or not, in leaving the home to work as she is politically free to do, a woman acts freely in the sense of being fully *self-directed* in her action. And another way of expressing this question is this: Does the way the world is—including its past events, its current natural (and perhaps supernatural) circumstances, and its physical laws—*allow for* us to act freely in a deep sense, such that our actions are truly attributable to our selves rather than to something external to us, such as social conditioning, genetic and neurophysiological programming, brainwashing, or some other external coercive force? Do reigning metaphysical conditions allow us to be the masters of our own fates, the captains of our own ships, the directors of our lives' directions? In short, is what we think and do and say ultimately *up to us*?

Analyzing what it is for an act to be "up to oneself" is no elementary task, as it requires an account both of who *we* are as agents—or what it is to be a genuine self—and of the nature of the requisite *control* over action. Securing legal and political freedoms is important to our establishing control of some kind over certain areas of our lives. But political, social, and legal freedoms do not exhaust the kinds of freedom that are of genuine concern. Many such freedoms may exist in a particular society, while there remains from a philosophical point of view the possibility that no one in that society ever acts sufficiently of his or her own accord, and not as the result of heteronomous factors, to count as acting freely, or with free will. The use of the term 'free will', then, signifies that our topic is the metaphysics of freedom: the issue of how much control over our own actions, and so over our own lives, the extrapolitical world—the natural (and perhaps also the supernatural) world—affords us.

Skepticism Regarding Free Will

Some philosophers question whether the term 'free will' can be given an accurate analysis at all, as they doubt that there is a coherent concept of it. Richard Double, for instance, argues in two provocative recent books, *The Non-Reality of Free Will* (1991) and *Metaphilosophy and Free Will* (1996), that free will cannot exist, as the term 'free will' fails objectively to refer. The second of Double's books extends the argumentation of the first to emphasize the dependence of philosophical theories, in particular theories concerning the nature of free will, on metaphilosophical factors, such as views concerning what philosophy in general is *for* (conversational enjoyment, for instance, or making us better persons). These meta-level stances, according to Double, are only non-truth-valued subjective facts about us, incapable of being proved objectively better or worse than any others. Not only, then, is there no coherent concept of free will or free action, but the deep relevance of meta-level factors to a person's judgment of the plausibility of various accounts of free action, on Double's view, makes "argumentation about free will wildly relativistic" and talk about free will only "so much verbiage, a kind of A. J. Ayer-like boohing and hurrahing."[3]

But one need not be so pessimistic as Double about the possibility of reasoned, meaningful, and persuasive argumentation about the nature of free action, nor need one accept the proposition that views about the goal of free will theorizing are mere non-truth-valued subjective stances unsusceptible to rational evaluation. For in fact any view, meta-level or not, motivated by desire or not, is liable to assessment with regard to justifiedness and plausibility.[4] Thus the appropriate response to another's views concerning the nature of free will is not a shrug of detached amusement. Instead, it is possible and appropriate to enter into reasoned dialogue with the potential for the change of our own or the other's account on the basis of theoretical considerations.

A Fundamental Source of Difficulty

I noted above that the notion of acting of one's own free will may be explicated roughly as being allowed by the world to act in a way that is fully self-directed. Indeed, it is a deep-rooted and pervasive aspect of our sense of ourselves as persons that we are capable of being self-directed in our affairs. The task in free will theorizing, then, is to illuminate this important part of our self-conception.

But if this is right—if the goal in elaborating a free will theory is to explicate a salient aspect of our self-conception—then a fundamental difficulty is that various aspects of our conception of ourselves push us in different theoretical directions. We are impressed and persuaded by success in psychological, neurophysiological, and genetic studies to view much (or all) of our selves and our behavior as physically set. We observe in the natural world that events have causes, and that those causal events themselves have causes, and so we naturally come to view the world as lawlike, regular, and, should we know enough about the circumstances and the natural laws, wholly predictable. Possible indeterminacy at the quantum level notwithstanding, usual events at the macrophysical level display regular deterministic order. Yet, our internal lives, and in general the unfolding of the sequence of events comprising our lives, seem wholly unpredictable, and not merely from lack of information. There seems to be some genuine randomness in the direction our lives take, or at least some room for *agency* not accounted for in a purely deterministic picture.

Thus, should we begin in characterizing ourselves with our most sober scientific outlook on the behavior of persons? Or, rather, should we reflect on our own first-person perspectives of ourselves as free agents, leaving aside temporarily the matter of the reconciliation of our self-image with a scientific viewpoint? In other words, should we start with an internal perspective or an external one?[5] What takes precedence in settling our self-conception?

Hence, rather than stemming from differences in conception of what engaging in philosophy is all about—whether in theorizing we are merely verbally entertaining ourselves or trying to better the world or aiming to say the truth about some aspect of reality—the difficulty in characterizing the nature of free will, it seems to me, derives primarily from the apparently conflicting data concerning the nature of our selves. In giving a theory of free will, the goal is clear: to provide an account recognizable as capturing certain prominent intuitions about ourselves and other persons as self-directed agents. But the problem is how exactly to do this.

C. A. Campbell once remarked that "to 'account for' a 'free' act is a contradiction in terms," for, he thought, "free will is *ex hypothesi* the sort of thing of which the request for an explanation is absurd."[6]

Certainly, though, we want to do better in giving a free will theory than this. It is difficult indeed to see how an act can be *intelligible* rather than random, genuinely attributable to a self acting for reasons of his or her own, if the act has no explanation whatsoever. Regarding the multidimensional problem of free will, which Susan Wolf calls "arguably the most difficult problem in philosophy,"[7] we may conclude at the outset only this: An answer easily arrived at is almost certainly an answer supported by thinking that is of insufficient depth.

The Significance of Free Will

While the difficulty of the problem of free will takes some time to uncover, its significance, on the other hand, is for most of us readily apparent. Generally we care whether or not we have free will, and we care what it would *be* to have it, even if we can exactly characterize neither our inchoate conception of it nor our sense of why it matters. Occasionally one hears of a philosopher who claims to have "absolutely no interest in the problem of free will." This sentiment is, frankly, difficult to understand. (A low level of general mental curiosity is likely not the right diagnosis.) Perhaps the proponent of the sentiment views the issue of free will as excessively anthropomorphic. The question, after all, is one about *our* powers, *our* abilities as persons in the face of certain prospective foes of our agency. Yet the same could be said of a number of the classic philosophical problems of perennial interest: the possibility of epistemically justifying our beliefs, the nature and function of our rights claims, the nature of our (and other sentient creatures') mental states. Set theory and inquiry into the nature of objectivity may be instances of more abstract intellectual pursuits, but they are for many individuals, precisely in virtue of that fact, significantly less pressing than the matter of self-direction.

Self-direction is, in fact, evidently something we strive valiantly to attain and protect. The early North American colonists, Southerners during the U.S. Civil War, Lithuanians, Ukrainians, and Soviet Georgians are among those who have fought for the ability to be self-determining, in a political sense, in their affairs. And illustrations of the importance of individual self-direction pervade literature. Though Vronsky suffers politically for refusing the post at

Tashkent, he is satisfyingly self-determined in resigning and, instead, traveling with Anna Karenina. Likewise, although your parents may not fully endorse your choice of career, it is, after all, *your* choice: A career is something you (ordinarily) want to be initiated and directed by yourself.

But that we do care does not explain our interest. Why exactly is it important to so many of us whether or not we can be self-directed, not just politically but also metaphysically? In certain philosophical contexts, such as some discussions of the problem of evil, the high value of free will is taken as an undefended premise.[8] And attempts to support it are sometimes less than persuasive. For instance, it has been argued that free choice is required for rationality, for learning, and for cooperation, and that therefore it is significant.[9] But, on the contrary, there seems to be nothing in the notion of a rational (or a warranted or a justified) belief that depends upon the belief's being freely acquired. And if learning is the acquisition of information, then it is, at least in principle, not reliant on free choice. Cooperation, likewise, is arguably engaged in by creatures (carpenter ants, for instance) not generally thought to possess free will. If having free will is valuable, then its value apparently must either be intrinsic or derive from its enabling goods other than these.

Moral Responsibility

The most widely recognized source of interest in free will is concern for the appropriate assignment of moral responsibility. Many of our reactions to the behavior of ourselves and others are governed by a concern for whether or not that behavior was free. Thus, when you smash your grocery cart into mine, I react with anger and indignation, until I discover that you were pushed. When I have betrayed a friend by revealing a delicate secret, I feel remorse if I view the revelation as my own free act. But if I divulged the secret under torture or force, then the attitude I take toward myself is one more of pity than contempt. Furthermore, underlying our assumption of the *appropriateness* of such patterns of intra- and interpersonal attitude adoption is the belief that persons are the appropriate subjects of such attitudes only when they are morally responsible for what they do; and they are morally responsible for what they do only when they commit their acts of their own free will.[10]

Distinguishing free acts from unfree ones is important not only to our judgments of the appropriateness of various attitudes, but also to our judgments of the appropriateness of certain practices and institutions (which, on one view, have as their point the expression of our personal attitudes). The practices at issue are those of blame and praise, and the institutions are the accompanying ones of punishment and reward. A person's being appropriately praised or blamed, as well as rewarded or punished, on the basis of some act is normally thought to depend upon his being genuinely morally responsible for what he did, where this depends upon his doing it freely.[11] If a person did not act of his own free will, for instance, in violating the moral and legal prohibition against stealing (perhaps because he was pushed into it by another person, or perhaps because he was compelled by severe hunger), then, many have thought, it is inappropriate to either blame or punish him. Likewise, the doer of a good deed—for instance, the donor of a large sum of money to a charitable cause—who did not perform the act of her own free will, is not an appropriate candidate for praise or reward. If the donor *had* to give the money, then why should we praise her for giving it?

So closely are the notions of free will and moral responsibility linked by many, that some philosophers take the meaning of the term 'free act' to be equivalent to that of the phrase 'an act for which the actor is morally responsible'. But whether the terms are in fact coextensive remains an open issue and is, I think, unlikely.[12] Nonetheless, an interest in free will is driven naturally by an interest in moral responsibility. In the following sections, however, I want to emphasize that the significance of free will does not derive *exclusively* from concerns about moral responsibility.

The Paradise Island Scenario

In order to bring to the fore intuitions concerning free will's importance, consider the following scenario. Imagine that you wake up one morning and find yourself on a tropical island. Everywhere you look is beauty: turquoise water, palm fronds waving in the breeze, an expansive beach of fine white sand, petite pastel-painted houses, flowering shrubbery. Sea turtles and French angelfish swim among the coral reefs just offshore. The aroma of grilling fish, coconut, and pineapple drifts past. Smiling people pass by giving you a friendly wave. Over the next days, you find that your every basic need is met: for food, drink, companionship, shelter. You have somehow been transported to what is apparently paradise.

But now suppose that, unbeknownst to you, this pleasing new existence is one entirely without freedom of choice. You got to the island not by choice, and, little do you know, you could not leave if you tried. In fact, you could not try to leave even if you wanted to. But you do not want to leave, and you never will want to leave. It is determined that you will always want to stay; all of your desires must be exactly what they are.

Sure, you are aware that you arrived on the island not by will, but you have no idea of the extent of your lack of control over your own life now. Unlike life as we know it, on the island you routinely get what you need and want (and in this, and many other respects of circumstance, island life is an improvement). But the truth is that, once you're on the island, your desires and ideas themselves are not ones that you have of your own volition. You could not possibly have any different desires or thoughts than the ones you do have. For instance, one night at dinner in the restaurant where you customarily eat, you find yourself envisioning some steamed swordfish with papaya for dinner. Shortly, it arrives at your table. But, unbeknownst to you, the only entree in the restaurant's kitchen was swordfish with papaya. You could not possibly have had a different dinner, nor could you have wanted anything different.[13] It was all a setup, as is everything about your life on the island. In the morning when you find yourself wanting to ask a certain attractive person for a date later in the day, that was determined, too: at precisely that time, you would form just that desire regarding precisely that person. At the time, you could not have desired anything different instead. As it turns out, everyone on the island is in the same situation as you: delicately and elaborately controlled. Were you to become aware of the "rigged" nature of your life, you might conclude that you are like a marionette on strings: happy, yes, but free, no.

Now consider these questions: Is life on Paradise Island an existence you would want for yourself? In lacking the ability to be fully self-directed, is the life we have envisioned missing anything of value? If so, what value is missing?

One might object to the depiction of Paradise Island life as always positive, wholly happy. A life without any negative events—setbacks, losses—would not allow for full appreciation of, or robust joy over, the good things of life. On this basis, one might argue, island life compares unfavorably to life elsewhere. But one need not think of the island life as entirely without suffering. Bad things might happen on the island: occasional sickness, a tropical storm. The crucial point is that none of these come about as the result of free choice, and neither are they reacted to freely. Nothing on the island comes about by free will, since on the island there is no free will.

Dignity

Here is a natural reaction: If my life is controlled by way of control of my desires, as depicted in the Paradise Island scenario, then I am only a puppet. But if I am just a puppet, then my life is trivialized. I do not have dignity or significance as an agent. Without free will, I am a plaything, a passive toy. To find out that this is true of me would lead to a sense of despair and hopelessness. Life would not seem to mean anything, one might think, if I did not possess the sense of dignity deriving from knowing that at least some aspects of the direction and outcome of my life owe themselves directly to me.

Consider dignity to be worthiness of respect from oneself and others as a being who is especially valuable. And consider a sense of dignity to be a sense of oneself as being worthy of respect. The connection between human dignity and free will, as well as that between a personal sense of dignity and the belief that one has free will, is supported by a number of philosophers. Kant, for instance, argued that rational beings should be treated as "ends in themselves" because they are "the ultimate creators of their own ends."[14] Robert Kane, speaking of persons' "unquenchable thirst for individuality and personhood," contends that "belief in free will is a higher order expression of that thirst in response to the seditious influences of the world" and that "the thirst goes with the territory of self-reflectiveness and is connected to higher aspirations in human beings toward a *worth* for their existence that transcends transitory satisfactions."[15]

In more specifically characterizing this worth, the special kind of value had by agents with free will, Robert Nozick uses the notion of *originative* value, or value deriving from the ability to be the source of novel goods. Originative value is "a function of the value [a being] introduces into the world, the new instrumental or intrinsic value it introduces that was not presaged by or already fully counted in previous instrumental value."[16] Free will enables its possessors to introduce evils into the world, but conversely, it allows them to introduce goods that would not otherwise exist, such as instances of artistic creativity and acts of charity and kindness. Nozick's thought is that, if we were determined to commit such acts, then we would not be the originators of the goods, but instead mere conduits of value. One's action being necessary to produce a certain value, without one's being the original source of the value, indeed gives one some kind of value, what Nozick terms *contributory* value. Yet, "a puppet can have contributory value," Nozick writes, and "although that is value indeed, it is not value enough, of the right sort. We want it to be true that in that very same situation we could have done (significantly) otherwise, so that our actions will have originatory value."[17]

Nozick's notion of personal worth in virtue of the capacity for new value introduction is one way of making sense of the idea that the inhabitants of Paradise Island lack dignity. While their lives may be pleasurable, they seem in some way frivolous. Of course, the island inhabitants are conscious, reasoning, emotional, and social beings, and on that basis they may be defended as worthy of respect. But as one imagines oneself in the island existence, lacking the ability to direct one's life on one's own, having no ability to act of one's own accord on genuinely authentic preferences and convictions, it is natural, I think, to have difficulty shaking the feeling that one would, in such a situation, be in some measure trivialized and undignified. Nozick gives one way of explicating this intuition: Lacking the ability to do or to think or to desire otherwise than they do, the island inhabitants can at best be conduits of value—the tools through which something of value is produced. As their actions, thoughts, and desires happen of necessity, they lack the ability to be the originators, or source points, of value.

The connection between dignity and free will is undergirded by the pervasive conviction that dignity attaches only to the sort of being who can face both success and hardship without being necessitated to respond in any particular way. Likewise, a sense of dignity results commonly from believing that one's accomplishments were freely achieved and that one's brave and honest dealings with struggles were done of one's own accord.[18]

Personal Relationships

As attractive as the island scenario is in many respects, one source of disvalue in it is in the nature of the personal relationships among islanders. Since the inhabitants are wholly without free will, one might contend that something is defective in their relationships with each other. The problem is that their interpersonal interactions seem ungenuine. As an inhabitant of the island, it is not in any deep or ultimate sense up to oneself to choose with whom to spend time, whom to hate, whom to love. But if I am not in control of whom I like and love and detest, and others are not in control of their interpersonal attitudes and actions either, then it appears that our relationships with each other are not grounded in any real emotion, commitment, or desire. When we befriend someone on the island, have dinner with another, or help someone to carry an excess load of shells, that is exactly what we must want and do at the time (perhaps as part of an elaborately detailed plan for island society's functioning).

But, concerning at least certain of our personal relationships, crucial to our sense that they are genuine is the assumption that the participants are free in adopting whatever emotional stances they take, including their commitment, or lack of it, to each other. To suppose that human beings are wholly without free will seems naturally to require that we give up some of the satisfaction we derive from our relationships, since a view of persons who act, but never freely, entails that our speech, thoughts, emotions, and bodily motions never count as free expressions of ourselves. One type of relationship especially illustrative of this dependence of a sense of genuineness upon an assumption of free will is the romantic sort of personal relationships. One philosopher has given expression to the thought in this way: "It is an essential part of our most intimate relationships that we view our love as a 'freely given gift.' If I learn that my spouse loves me only because this 'love' is the inevitable product of some childhood experience then the whole relationship takes on a strange and dark colour."[19] If it is true that there is a connection between the genuineness of personal relationships and the personal possession of free will, and if the reality and quality of our personal relationships matter to us, then free will is significant.

Satisfaction of Desire

One source of the significance of free will is so ordinary as to be sometimes overlooked, yet it is one made plain by the Paradise Island scenario. That is, most basically, we care about being free because we naturally care about satisfying our desires. If you want some chocolate cake, then you can be satisfied in this desire only if you are free to have some chocolate cake. But our being able to get what we want depends not only upon a lack of obstacles to getting what we want. It also depends upon a lack of manipulation of our desires themselves, so that what we try to get to satisfy our desires is something that *we* genuinely want. Suppose that you want some chocolate cake only as the effect of a posthypnotic suggestion telling you to seek chocolate cake when you next feel hunger. Your seeking chocolate cake in that instance fails to fulfill the natural drive to fulfill desires of *one's own*. Less fancifully, perhaps your desire for chocolate cake traces back to the many mouthwateringly tempting depictions of such cakes on the television advertisements you have recently seen. Or perhaps your desire to have a physique of a certain sort results from the saturation of your culture's media with glorified images of that physical type. A concern with free will derives immediately from a concern for being able to get what one wants and being able to have one's wants authentically.

Thus, I would venture, it is a natural drive to be concerned with freedom of action. The concern is fundamental to us as desiring creatures. If we are free to do as we choose, and free to choose as we like, and free to like whatever we please, then we can get what we genuinely want. One source of the value of free will is that it enables our satisfying our desires.

Self-Concept

The final source I will discuss from which the issue of free will gains significance is a concern for knowing the truth about ourselves as agents. Think again about the inhabitants of the island described above. They are lucky to enjoy beautiful surroundings. But the poor souls are deluded. If any of them ever think about it—and it is a thought that readily occurs to a reflective person—they will think that their life is their own, that they enjoy free will, that they are in control of what they think, desire, and do. But their thought will be untrue.

Are our thoughts about ourselves as free agents similarly falsehoods? Adopt for a moment the perspective of your facing a dilemma and deciding what to do. As you deliberate practically, standing at a point in time and looking forward into the future, it seems ordinarily (at least sometimes) that a number of possible courses of action are open to you and that it is up to you to choose which course to pursue. An aspect of one's self-conception, the part easily accessed by adopting the practical deliberative point of view, is that one is a being with the power to act freely, or of one's own free will.

Interest in free will is driven, then, by concern to know whether this aspect of one's conception of oneself is correct. Am I, and are we all, "cogs in a machine," or are we the originators of courses of action? One reason to care about whether or not we have free will is in order to have an *accurate* self-concept. The significance of free will derives in part from an interest in the truth regarding what sorts of powers we have. Knowing the truth is intrinsically valuable, and knowing the truth about oneself is, for most of us, both valuable and gripping.

Challenges to Free Will

No one in the Paradise Island scenario described above has free will. But none of *us* (except the fortunate reader presently on a tropical island) thinks that he or she is possibly in such a situation. Thus, since free will is valuable in virtue of securing for us a number of recognizable goods, why not simply conclude that we do in fact possess free will and declare the matter resolved? What would make a reasonable person think that it remains an open question whether or not we are free agents?

The answer is this: Although it is obvious that we are not (with the exception noted) inhabitants of the odd Paradise Island, it is not so obvious that certain other situations of threat to our free agency do not, in fact, obtain. In particular, certain theological and scientific doctrines may well accurately describe reality, and if they do, then our ability to act freely is cast under suspicion.

Divine Foreknowledge

Consider first a challenge from the theological domain. Part of the theistic conception of God is that God is essentially omniscient (which implies infallibility in what God believes) and eternally existing. But if God always exists, knows everything, and cannot be wrong, then God knows everything about you, including what you do and think at every moment of your life. And if God knows this, then supposing that you make a trip to the bookstore later today, God presumably knows before the event occurs what book you will select from the shelf. Thus while you look forward to browsing in the bookstore and assume that it will be open to you to select from among the options, say, a book on free will, a collection of the works of van Gogh, or a biography of Martin Luther, God already knows exactly which book you'll choose: the one on free will. But if God already knows that you will choose the book on free will, then how could it be open to you to choose the biography? If you were able to select the biography, then that would seem to imply that you are able to cause God to have a mistaken belief. But God, being God, cannot have a mistaken belief, and so you cannot possibly cause God to be incorrect. But then it seems that you must not really be free to select the biography, or for that matter anything other than the book on free will.

The reasoning governing this mundane example extends easily to more significant situations in which we routinely think that the outcome is up to us: our choice of university or college, our choice of spouse, our choice regarding whether or not to adopt a child, our choice of career field, our decisions regarding what political stances to adopt. If God foreknows in each instance exactly what we will do, then our freedom in acting seems seriously undermined.[20]

Divine Providence

Trouble for human freedom derives from an additional feature of theistic metaphysics: the doctrine of divine providence, or control over the universe. God as traditionally conceived is omnipotent and sovereign. In other words, God can do anything and has authority over all creation. But if God is in fact in control of *everything*, then how could you or I be in control of *anything*? The writer of the biblical Book of Proverbs declares that "the Lord works out everything for his own ends."[21] And, after a period of banishment from the royal palace of Babylon, King Nebuchadnezzar proclaims: "I praised the Most High . . . His dominion is an eternal dominion . . . He does as he pleases with the powers of heaven and the peoples of the earth. No one can hold back his hand or say to him: 'What have you done?'"[22] Each of these gives expression to the idea that nothing happens outside of the divine will, that God in God's sovereignty orders and controls all that occurs.

But God's controlling everything that occurs seems at least as potentially damaging to our ability to do anything of our own free will as does God's knowing exactly what will occur. For if God controls everything in the created world, then God must be in control of *us* and our actions, as well, making even our actions work out God's purposes. The problem is especially acutely felt when the doctrine of divine sovereignty is applied to the area of human salvation: If it is up to God's sovereign will who is saved and who is not—if it is true that "those God foreknew he also predestined to be conformed to the likeness of his Son"[23]—then what room does this leave for us to turn in faith toward, or to reject, God of our own free will? Divine sovereignty and predestination threaten to undercut the belief in our ability to act freely.

Scientific Determinism

A third significant challenge to our having metaphysical freedom comes from a different direction: a doctrine about the nature of the physical universe. The doctrine of scientific (or causal) determinism maintains that every event is causally necessitated by a previous event, so that every event stands in a chain of events stretching backward into history, the links of which are deterministic causal connections. An alternate way to put the doctrine is this: At any particular moment, there is, given the actual past and the laws of nature, exactly one way the world could go. As Peter van Inwagen expresses the matter, there is at any instant, according to determinism, exactly one physically possible future.[24]

The tension, or at least the apparent tension, of this doctrine concerning the working of the natural world with the supposition of our having free will is fairly straightforward. According to determinism, every event is the necessary outworking of the laws of nature and the events of the past. At no point in time, holding fixed the circumstances, the past, and the natural laws, could the future unfold in a multiple number of ways. But a natural and intuitively attractive way of looking at ourselves as free agents in relation to the future is as beings standing at points from which diverge multiple branching paths, paths representing alternatives in our power to make actual. The forking-paths model of the future must be inaccurate if determinism is true, and thus insofar as the model is a component of our concept of free will, free will and determinism are in conflict.

But whether in fact the truth of scientific determinism and persons' possession of free will are mutually exclusive has been the subject of much highly interesting philosophical debate. It is this debate concerning the scientific challenge to free will that this book will go on to examine in detail, leaving aside, for purposes of focus, the challenges from the theological direction.[25]

Many philosophers have contended that, despite initial appearances to the contrary, determinism is, in fact, *compatible* with our acting freely. Such theorists reject incompatibilists' claims that living in a deterministic world would be like having the life of an automaton—a highly complex and interesting life, perhaps, but an automatic and unfree one nonetheless. Compatibilists reject such contentions as confused. Daniel Dennett, for instance, labels incompatibilist analogies for human life on the assumption of determinism (such as that it would be like being in prison, being paralyzed, being an animal, a puppet, or a plaything) "bugbears" and "bogeymen," contending that "the free will problem *is* the family of anxieties . . . [encapsulated in] the analogies and intuition pumps."[26] Dennett's plea "please don't feed the bugbears" is cleverly designed to get us to set aside incompatibilists' concerns.

But Dennett's dismissive attitude is too quick. For the problem of free will does not dissolve without the analogies—they are simply vivid pictures designed to help us to feel the pull of the philosophical problems concerning free agency. In order to assess the debate between compatibilists and incompatibilists concerning free will and determinism, we need to seek an understanding of what exactly incompatibilists use the analogies to illustrate, and we must examine directly the positive philosophical arguments for incompatibilism, along with compatibilist replies to such arguments. I turn to the arguments at the heart of the debate between compatibilists and incompatibilists in the following chapter.

Notes

1. Robert Nozick, *Philosophical Explanations* (Cambridge, MA: Harvard University Press, 1981), p. 293.

2. See, for instance, "On Giving Libertarians What They Say They Want" in Daniel Dennett's *Brainstorms* (Montgomery, VT: Bradford Books, 1978), pp. 286–299, in a footnote of which Dennett distinguishes several different questions constituting the free will problem. See also Robert Kane, who, in *The Significance of Free Will* (New York: Oxford University Press, 1996), differentiates several facets of the free will problem (pp. 12–13). Immediately below I distinguish from one another the existence question, the epistemological question, and the definitional question. But there are many other questions commonly taken as constituting part of "the problem of free will," such as the questions to be discussed in this and subsequent chapters concerning the compatibility or incompatibility of free will with certain scientific and theological doctrines, and the question of whether or not free will is required for moral responsibility (and if so, then what sort of free will).

3. Richard Double, *Metaphilosophy and Free Will* (New York: Oxford University Press, 1996), p. 13. Galen Strawson supports the incoherency of the notion of free will from a different direction in his *Freedom and Belief* (Oxford: Clarendon Press, 1986), chap. 2.

4. For Double's defense of the unprovability of metaphilosophies, see his *Metaphilosophy and Free Will*, pp. 33–39.

5. Thomas Nagel presses this difficulty for free will theory in *The View from Nowhere* (New York: Oxford University Press, 1986), chap. 7.

6. C. A. Campbell, "Has the Self 'Free Will'?" in *On Selfhood and Godhood* (London: Allen and Unwin, 1957), pp. 158–165, 167–179.

7. Susan Wolf, *Freedom Within Reason* (New York: Oxford University Press, 1990), p. vii.

8. In his treatment of a related problem, the problem of divine hiddenness, Michael J. Murray relies implicitly on the high value of free will by suggesting that God must maintain a certain amount of epistemic distance from human agents in order to be noncoercive in his interactions with them. See his "Coercion and the Hiddenness of God," *American Philosophical Quarterly* 30, 1993, pp. 27–38.

9. See, for instance, W. S. Anglin, *Free Will and the Christian Faith* (Oxford: Clarendon Press, 1990), pp. 11–24.

10. Peter Strawson argues that the "reactive attitudes" (for instance, love, resentment, gratitude, hatred, and the like) need not depend for their appropriateness upon human possession of free will. Rather, he thinks, the attitudes are justified in virtue of being natural; we could not succeed in suspending these attitudes even if we tried. But the naturalness of an attitude (or even its necessity for maintaining life as we know it) is no clear indication of the attitude's justifiedness, as the examples of racist and sexist attitudes show. (See Peter Strawson, "Freedom and Resentment," *Proceedings of the British Academy* 48, 1962, pp. 1–25. Reprinted in Gary Watson, ed., *Free Will*, Oxford: Oxford University Press, 1982; also reprinted in John Martin Fischer and Mark Ravizza, eds., *Perspectives on Moral Responsibility*, Ithaca: Cornell University Press, 1993.) Galen Strawson has questioned the elder Strawson's unsuspendability claim with respect to the reactive attitudes in his *Freedom and Belief* (Oxford: Clarendon Press, 1986).

11. Some theorists take a person's moral responsibility to be *constituted* by his proneness to the reactive attitudes and the accompanying practices of praise and blame. Competing views of the function of moral responsibility ascriptions are discussed in Chapter 5.

12. Contrary to the views of Susan Wolf in *Freedom Within Reason* and Paul Benson in "Freedom and Value" (*Journal of Philosophy* 84, 1987, pp. 465–486), although it is perhaps plausible to believe that objectivist normative competence is required for moral responsibility on a certain (metaphysical) conception of moral responsibility ascriptions, it is implausible to believe that the same is required in order for an act to be sufficiently self-directed to be done freely. An act might reveal and be directed by the values or preferences of the self without that self's having a full and right appreciation of the True and the Good. In other words, there is no good reason, in my view, for thinking that only morally enlightened individuals can act of their own free will. Thus the right account of morally responsible action may have further (epistemic and normative) conditions than does the account of free action.

13. We need not envision that the dinner you get is the *same* one every night. One night, the restaurant may be serving steamed swordfish; the next night, turtle; the next, grilled salmon. But on each night, there is only one dinner you could possibly get, even though it is the one you want, and only one dinner you could possibly want. Change in general is not precluded in this scenario, only change that is genuinely up to you.

14. Immanuel Kant, *Foundations of the Metaphysics of Morals*, trans. L. W. Beck (Indianapolis, IN: Bobbs-Merrill, 1959), p. 52.

15. Kane, *Significance of Free Will*, p. 101, emphasis added.

16. Nozick, *Philosophical Explanations*, p. 311.

17. Ibid., p. 313.

18. That most of us have a sense of dignity, as well as a belief in the reality of human dignity, is attested to by our emotionally indignant and acute physiological responses to poor treatment of ourselves and other human beings. A sense of personal dignity shows itself in one's regard for one's own health, tastes, talents, and peace of mind.

19. Anglin, *Free Will and the Christian Faith*, p. 21.

20. One solution to this dilemma is to take God's eternality as consisting in God's existence *outside of time* rather than at all times, past, present, and future. On this construal of eternality, God's knowledge of what you do could not accurately be described as *fore*knowledge. Some philosophers take this solution to generate certain other difficulties, such as how an essentially eternal God so conceived could act in the created world in time.

21. Proverbs 16:4.

22. Daniel 4:34–35.

23. Romans 8:29.

24. Peter van Inwagen, *An Essay on Free Will* (Oxford: Clarendon Press, 1983), p. 3.

25. For excellent discussions of various solutions to the dilemma of divine foreknowledge and free will, see John Martin Fischer, *The Metaphysics of Free Will: An Essay on Control*, Aristotle Society Series, vol. 14. (Cambridge, MA: Blackwell, 1994), chap. 6; and William Rowe, *Philosophy of Religion* (Belmont, CA: Wadsworth, 1993), chap. 11. Other notable readings on foreknowledge and freedom include St. Augustine, *On the Free Choice of the Will* (Indianapolis, IN: Bobbs-Merrill, 1964); and Nelson Pike, "Divine Omniscience and Voluntary Action," *Philosophical Review* 74, 1965, pp. 27–46. For a very interesting recent discussion of the problem of reconciling divine sovereignty and human freedom, see Hugh McCann, "Divine Sovereignty and the Freedom of the Will," *Faith and Philosophy* 12, 1995, pp. 582–598.

26. Daniel Dennett, *Elbow Room: The Varieties of Free Will Worth Wanting* (Cambridge, MA: MIT Press, 1984), p. 18.

CHAPTER TWO

Arguments for Incompatibilism

Although widespread philosophical agreement on any topic is rare, there is broad-based support among philosophers for the claim that a person's having free will requires that he at least sometimes have the ability to act otherwise than he does. To appreciate the point of the condition, consider the many acts and series of acts you carry out each day, from tying your shoes to phoning your friend to deciding whether to purchase the white shirt or the black one to composing a philosophical argument. Suppose that not only these actions but *all* of the actions you ever performed in your lifetime were such that they were, at the time you did them, *the only acts you could have done*. A natural reaction is: Then I do not have any free will. For if what I do is always the only thing I can possibly do, how could I have any free rein in conducting my life?

Alternative Possibilities

Many philosophers from diverse periods make explicit note of this "alternative possibilities" condition of free will. Aristotle apparently requires the condition when, in his discussion of the voluntary in *Nicomachean Ethics*, he observes that "where it is in our power to act it is also in our power not to act" (1113b6).[1] David Hume defines liberty as "a power of acting or not acting according to the determinations of the will; that is, if we choose to remain at rest, we may; if we choose to move, we also may."[2] Thomas Reid proposes that the "power to produce any effect implies the power not to produce it" (1983: 523). Kant likewise maintains that for an act to be truly free, "the act as well as its opposite must be within the power of the subject at the moment of its taking place" (1960: 45).

The thought echoes among contemporary thinkers. According to A. J. Ayer, "When I am said to have done something of my own free will it is implied that I could have acted otherwise."[3] Bernard Williams describes the claim that free will exists as consisting in "something to the effect that agents sometimes act voluntarily, and that when they do so they have a real choice between more than one course of action; or more than one course is open to them; or it is up to them which of several actions they perform."[4] Similarly, Peter van Inwagen writes: "When I say of a man that he 'has free will' I mean that very often, if not always, when he has to choose between two or more mutually incompatible courses of action—that is, courses of action that it is impossible for him to carry out more than one of—each of these courses of action is such that he can, or is able to, or has it within his power to carry it out."[5]

Hence it has become a philosophical commonplace that the possession of free will requires sometimes being able to do otherwise. Of course, how exactly to *interpret* the requisite ability is not uncontroversial, and in particular whether causal determinism precludes or does not preclude a person's ever having the ability rightly understood is a matter vigorously contested. We need not require that every free act is one for which the agent has at the precise time of acting multiple available options for acting in order to generate the question at the center of the controversy. For if it is true, as is plausible and prevalently supposed, that a person has no free will (or no power ever to act freely) if she cannot *ever* in her lifetime act otherwise than she does, then the question arises as to whether the alternative possibilities required for the possession of free will are or are not compatible with the truth of causal determinism.

Let us say that an agent has free will only if some of the actions she performs during her lifetime are such that she can do (or could have done) otherwise with respect to them. I will call *the minimal supposition of human free will* the thesis that, for some human person, this necessary condition—the ability at some time to act otherwise—is met. Thus if no human person can ever do otherwise than act precisely as he or she does act, then the minimal supposition of human free will is false. The minimal supposition requires that at least on occasion what some human person *can* do is not exhausted by what she *does* do.

The Compatibility Question

Does the truth of determinism imply the falsity of the minimal supposition of human free will? Causal determinism is the doctrine that there is at every instant exactly one physically possible future. Put differently, the doctrine maintains that, for every instant, a proposition expressing all of the facts about the universe at that time, together with a proposition expressing all of the actual laws of nature, entails every truth as to what happens after that time. According to the determinist, the laws of nature are wholly deterministic, and every event is covered by or falls under a law. Thus, according to determinism, the prevailing laws of nature are such that there do not exist any two "possible worlds" that are exactly alike up to some time, that differ thereafter, and in which those laws are never violated.[6] If the minimal supposition of human free will and the thesis of determinism are compatible, then there is no logical contradiction in supposing them both to be true at once. If they are incompatible, then at most one of the claims can be true.

The compatibility question has been the centerpiece of free will debates for the past twenty-five years. Lining up on the side of incompatibilism are van Inwagen (1975, 1983), Ginet (1966, 1990), Wiggins (1973), Lamb (1977), Kane (1985, 1996a, 1996b), and Fischer (1983, 1994),[7] with kindred-minded philosophical ancestors in (arguably) Aristotle, Aquinas, Leibniz, Kant, John Bramhall, Thomas Reid, and C. A. Campbell. On the other side, compatibilism—the position that if determinism is true, it does not rule out persons' having free will—has been recently defended by Lehrer (1966), Davidson (1973), Lewis (1981), Dennett (1984), and Wolf (1990), with historical support from such figures as Hobbes, Spinoza, Hume, Mill, Jonathan Edwards, and Moritz Schlick. This chapter examines arguments for incompatibilism: Why would a person think that *either* the thesis of determinism is true *or* persons have free will, but not both?

Simple Arguments for Incompatibilism

I will begin with a simple version of an argument for the incompatibilist position and proceed to arguments for the view that are more complex. I will then examine the major lines of response to incompatibilist arguments and assess what one should conclude after considering the metaphysical issues pertinent to free will.

Clashing Images of Personal Life

Consider first a straightforward line of reasoning in favor of incompatibilism. Here is the argument: A deep-rooted and pervasive understanding of ourselves as agents with free will assumes two things. First, it assumes that we are disengaged from the past in a way that makes us not "pushed" into doing precisely what we do by previous events or states of affairs. The thought that all of my behavior is the causally necessary outcome of my genetic blueprint, environment, and social conditioning—in short, the thought that I am pushed into doing what I do by what has come before me—undermines the idea that some of the acts I perform are genuinely "up to me," determined by a self with some causal autonomy from the past. Second, the understanding assumes a forking-paths model of the future (representing a natural interpretation of "the ability to do otherwise") that may be represented as follows:[8]

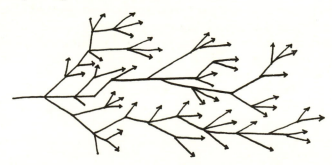

FIGURE 2.1   Forking-Paths Model of the Future

On this model of the "path of life" of a free agent, as one lives through time facing various choices about what to do, one has open to oneself at a number of points in time multiple possible futures, multiple options for what to decide. As depicted in Figure 2.1, if one is a free agent, then as time proceeds from left to right and as one lives one's life traversing a path from left to right, there are at various junctures "forks in the road"—a number of alternative ways one might choose that, once chosen, alter the course of one's life from that point on. We might think, for instance, of your choice of spouse. The assumption that you have free will regarding whom to marry incorporates a forking-paths model of the future according to which there are a number of possible ways your life might unfold, depending upon exactly which among the several persons under consideration you actually choose. Which person you choose alters your life path significantly, and at the juncture of choice it was in your power to make actual any one of several possible futures.

But both of these aspects of the common understanding of ourselves as free agents are rather straightforwardly at odds with the thesis of scientific determinism as defined above. The doctrine of determinism maintains that every event occurs as the necessary unfolding of events of the past. But if so, then nothing we think or prefer or do (each instance of these being an event) is sufficiently "disengaged" from the past. Again, determinism claims that there is at every instant exactly one physically possible future. Yet the picture inherent in the practical deliberative point of view under the assumption of free agency is of a future involving multiple accessible branching paths. The following diagram makes the point clear. If determinism is true, then the course of events composing the history of the world and its future can be represented as shown in Figure 2.2.

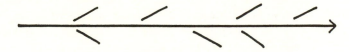

FIGURE 2.2   Deterministic Model of the Future

As Figure 2.2 illustrates, there may be *apparent* "forks in the road" from the perspective of a person living in a deterministic universe, but exactly one of the "alternatives" is one that an agent can actually take, since there is only *one* way, given the past and the natural laws, that the course of events can proceed. From the point of view of the agent, there may at times appear to be available options for acting at the next moment. Yet if the thesis of causal determinism is true, then the agent cannot *get to* any of the alternative paths from the path he is on. But this model of the path of one's life through time is incongruous with the model incorporated into the assumption of agential free will. Hence, it cannot be true both that we have free will and that the doctrine of determinism is correct. One or the other of the suppositions is false.

The above is one way of putting the intuitive case in favor of the position of incompatibilism. It represents a very natural way of thinking about the matter of free will and determinism. In fact, by far the most common reaction among those first hearing of the compatibility problem is an incompatibilist reaction. A large number of compatibilist philosophers, however, have alleged that lines of reasoning leading to incompatibilism are flawed, a charge I will examine further on in this chapter.

The Consequence Argument

Consider a different and more succinct way of expressing a simple argument for incompatibilism. In the most sustained recent defense of the incompatibilist thesis, *An Essay on Free Will* (1983), Peter van Inwagen presents three arguments for incompatibilism, each a proposed refinement of a certain basic line of reasoning. The basic line of reasoning, which van Inwagen calls "the Consequence Argument," is as follows:

> If determinism is true, then our acts are the consequences of the laws of nature and events in the remote past. But it is not up to us what went on before we were born, and neither is it up to us what the laws of nature are. Therefore, the consequences of these things (including our present acts) are not up to us.[9]

Since only acts that are "up to us" are free, the argument shows that, if determinism is true, then we can never act freely. A natural initial reaction to this informal argument is the following: There must be something wrong with the argument because obviously our present acts *are* (contrary to the conclusion of the argument) "up to us." A present action seems the epitome of something that is "up to oneself," as opposed to, say, what the weather is today, to which parents you or I were born, what someone unknown and unrelated to me in another country decides to do today (for instance, whether a Pakistani political leader acts to escalate a nuclear arms race with India). These latter events and states of affairs are not at all up to me; they are beyond my sphere of influence, out of my control. But what I do today—how I think, how I react emotionally, what I plan to accomplish, what overt actions I commit—unless I unwittingly am manipulated from the outside or I let someone else control me, is up to me and not up to anybody else, or so it is natural to believe.

But, of course, this reaction does not necessarily impugn the consequence argument itself. Instead, it simply underscores the intuitive implausibility of an alleged result of supposing determinism to be true. The consequence argument is meant obviously to focus our attention on the *implications* of the doctrine of determinism. That doctrine maintains that every event is the causally necessary outcome of previous events, so that a chain of deterministically linked events stretches backward into history. We can envision the matter this way: Suppose that determinism is true. Then pick any past event in roughly your space-time region. From that past event, given determinism, one can trace a line forward in time through necessarily linked events up to each present event, including the events of your own acts. But then the consequence argument just states what seems intuitively compelling: Since past events are now out of your control and the laws of nature are out of your control, what happens now as the necessary outcome of those events and laws is also out of your control, if determinism is indeed true.

One can discern even before this argument is made more precise that the reasoning involved in it employs some sort of inference rule concerning what is under our control (what is "up to us," what we have the *power* to do, what we are *able* to do). Namely, if something is the necessary result of factors that are not under our control (not "up to us," not *within our power*, or factors such that we are not now able to affect them), then that result itself is likewise not under our control (not "up to us," not within our power, or something that we are not now able to affect). And it is at the point of the argument's reliance on this sort of inference rule that many compatibilists focus their attack on arguments for incompatibilism. Incompatibilists, for their part, defend the "transference of power" inference rules as impeccable and thus take the consequence argument, or at least one of the several alternate ways of setting out the line of reasoning that the consequence argument roughly embodies, as demonstrating the inconsistency of supposing both that persons have free will and that scientific determinism is true.

Detailed Arguments

As a consideration of two informal arguments has shown, incompatibilists urge that it is clear on a little reflection that the hypothesis of determinism's truth undercuts the initial judgment that one's acts are up to oneself in a sense sufficient for those acts to be freely performed. I turn to examining several attempts to make the reasoning in support of the incompatibilist position more precise. Although the technical material in the arguments to follow may initially strike one as overly complex, readers will come to appreciate the usefulness of the technicality in enabling the relevant principles of reasoning to be made explicit. In what follows, the '$\equiv$' symbol represents 'if and only if'; the '$\neg$' symbol signifies 'it is not the case that'; and the '$\supset$' symbol is a conditional sign, such that '$p \supset q$' is to be read 'if p, then q'.

What Is Beyond One's Control

We might make the consequence argument more explicit in the following way. Let us say that it is *up to* agent S at t whether or not it is the case that P (which I will abbreviate as $U_{S,t}$ P) just in case S is able at t to make it the case that P and S is able at t to prevent its being the case that P. We can represent this notion in the following way, where '$A_{S,t}$ P' represents 'S is able at t to bring it about that P is the case' and '$A_{S,t}$ ($\neg P$)' represents 'S is able at t to prevent its being the case that P':

$$U_{S,t}\, P \equiv A_{S,t}\, P \text{ and } A_{S,t}\, (\neg P).$$

Then it is *not up to* S at t whether or not it is the case that P just in case either S is not able at t to make it the case that P ($\neg A_{S,t}\, P$) *or* S is not able at t to prevent its being the case that P ($\neg A_{S,t}\, (\neg P)$). Consider some sentence P expressing a true proposition. The notion of its being *beyond the control of* S at t that P, may be defined as follows:

$B_{S,t} P \equiv P$ and $\neg A_{S,t} (\neg P)$.

Now consider the following transfer rule:

Transfer Rule T: If $B_{S,t} P$ and $B_{S,t} (P \supset Q)$, then $B_{S,t} Q$.

If something (some actual event or state of affairs) is completely out of one's control, and it is beyond one's control that a second thing (event or state of affairs) is a consequence of the first, then, it seems highly reasonable to believe, the second thing (event or state of affairs) is also beyond one's control. For instance, if it is beyond my control that the temperature in Paris is over seventy degrees Fahrenheit today, and it is beyond my control that (if the temperature in Paris is over seventy degrees Fahrenheit today, then the temperature in Paris is over sixty degrees Fahrenheit today), then it is beyond my control that the temperature in Paris is over sixty degrees Fahrenheit today.

Likewise, consider the following examples in support of rule T. First, let S represent *me* and let t be *right now*. Let P represent: The surgery is badly performed today. Let Q represent: My loved one dies today. If it is right now beyond my control that the surgery is badly performed today, and it is beyond my control that (if the surgery is badly performed today, then my loved one dies today), then it is beyond my control that my loved one dies today.

Second, let S be *you*, and let t be *noon today*. Let P be: There is an earthquake of great magnitude in the San Francisco Bay area next December. Let Q be: The San Francisco Bay area sustains damage next December. If it is at noon today beyond your control that there is an earthquake of great magnitude in the San Francisco Bay area next December (and at noon today beyond your control that if there is an earthquake of great magnitude in the San Francisco Bay area next December, then the San Francisco Bay area sustains damage next December), then it is at noon today beyond your control that the San Francisco Bay area sustains damage next December.

Now, using transfer rule T, we might spell out a detailed argument for incompatibilism in the following way. Let P abbreviate a sentence expressing the state of the universe at a past moment, $t0$, before the existence of human beings. Let L stand for the sentence expressing the conjunction of all the laws of nature. Let A abbreviate a sentence expressing the proposition that agent S performs a certain act at time t. The symbol '$\square$' represents 'broadly logical necessity', so that the term '$\square P$' is to be read 'it is logically necessary that P'. The argument—call it the "Beyond Control Argument"—may be put as follows: If determinism is true, then

1. $\square\,((P \text{ and } L) \supset A)$
2. $B_{S,t}\,P$
3. $B_{S,t}\,L$
4. $B_{S,t}\,(P \text{ and } L)$
5. $B_{S,t}\,((P \text{ and } L) \supset A)$
6. $B_{S,t}\,A$

The above argument relies upon, in addition to transfer rule T, the following highly plausible inference rules, the first in arriving at 5 from 1, the second in deriving 4 from 2 and 3:

Inference Rule A: If $\square\,P$, then $B_{S,t}\,P$.
Inference Rule C: If $B_{S,t}\,P$ and $B_{S,t}\,Q$, then $B_{S,t}\,(P \text{ and } Q)$.

(In fact, given that rule C is derivable from rule A and rule T, the argument most basically relies upon two inference principles.)[10]
The first premise of the argument above corresponds to the first premise of the informal consequence argument *(if determinism is true, then our acts are the consequences of the laws of nature and events in the remote past)*. The second, third, and fourth premises above set out what is stated in the second premise of the informal consequence argument *(but it is not up to us what went on before we were born, and neither is it up to us what the laws of nature are)*. Rule A, premise 5, and rule T then show the reasoning leading to the conclusion of the consequence argument *(therefore the consequences of these things, including our present acts, are not up to us)*. Hence if the thesis of causal determinism is true, then what we do is beyond our control and thus our actions are not freely done.

The No Choice Operator

Not all arguments for incompatibilism use the same "transference of power" principles, as not all of those arguments employ the same ability, or power, operator. An argument quite similar to the one above, but reliant upon a different modal operator, is the third argument for incompatibilism in van Inwagen's *An Essay on Free Will*. The argument (call it "van Inwagen's Third Argument") makes use of the following "no choice" operator:[11]

'Np' = df. p, and no one has, or ever had, any choice about whether p.

Let $P1$ abbreviate a sentence expressing the way the universe was at an instant in the very distant past. Let L stand for the sentence expressing all the laws of nature conjoined. For P one may substitute any sentence expressing a true proposition. Van Inwagen's Third Argument runs as follows. Suppose that determinism is true. Then:

1. $\square((P1 \text{ and } L) \supset P)$
2. $\square(P1 \supset (L \supset P))$
3. $N(P1 \supset (L \supset P))$
4. $NP1$
5. $N(L \supset P)$
6. NL
7. $NP.$

This argument relies on the following two inference rules:

Inference Rule α: If $\square p$, then Np.
Inference Rule β: If Np and $N(p \supset q)$, then Nq.

Consider the premises of the argument. Premise 2 is deduced from 1 by elementary modal and sentential logic. Premise 3 results from an application of rule α to 2. From premises 3 and 4, premise 5 follows by rule β. And premise 7 follows from premises 5 and 6, again by rule β. Premises 4 and 6 are introduced and defended as plausible: $P1$ expresses a proposition about the remote past (say, before the existence of human beings), and L expresses the proposition that the laws of nature obtain. Surely no one has any choice about whether $P1$, and no one has any choice about whether L. If sound, the proof shows that if determinism is true, then no one ever has any choice about anything.

Rule β has proved to be the most controversial element of van Inwagen's Third Argument. Further on I will consider some proposed counterexamples and examine whether or not those counterexamples work against transfer rule T, used in the Beyond Control Argument.

Before turning to compatibilist replies, however, let me continue to set out some of the most influential recent positive arguments for the incompatibilist position. The relations between these various arguments are interesting in themselves. The central point, however, in setting out a *number* of detailed arguments for incompatibilism is to make explicit that there is not only *one* argument for the incompatibilist thesis, but rather a variety of them and that, together, they constitute a formidable body of arguments worthy of careful consideration and response.

Van Inwagen: The Fixity of the Past and the Laws

Consider another of van Inwagen's refinements of the consequence argument, the first detailed argument for incompatibilism in *An Essay on Free Will* and the most widely discussed. I will examine a slight modification of that argument. Here free will is construed as a power or ability, which van Inwagen for purposes of expressing the argument puts in terms of the ability to render certain propositions false. Determinism is defined as follows: (1.) For every instant, there is a proposition that expresses the state of the world at that instant; (2.) If p and q are propositions that express the state of the world at some instants, then the conjunction of p with the laws of nature entails q.

The argument (together with commentary explicating and defending these seven propositions) is as follows: Suppose that a certain judge, call him Judd, needs only to raise his hand at a certain time in order to grant clemency to a particular criminal; if Judd does not raise his hand at the appointed time, then the death penalty will be carried out. Now suppose that Judd does not raise his hand at the appointed time and that he refrains from raising it after careful reflection (not as the result of hypnosis, pressure, drugs, excessive fatigue, or anything of that sort). Judd's ability to have done otherwise at the time may be expressed in van Inwagen's proposed terminology as Judd's having the ability to render false the proposition that his hand was not raised at the appointed time. Now let $t1$

be a time prior to Judd's birth. Let J denote the agent, Judd. Let $P1$ denote the proposition expressing the entire state of the world at $t1$. Let A denote the proposition that Judd's hand is left unraised at $t2$ (where A is one conjunct of the more complex proposition $P2$ expressing the state of the world at $t2$, a time at which Judd's hand *is not raised*). Let L stand for the conjunction of all the laws of nature. It is important to note that these variable letters are rigid designators: $P1$, for instance, is the name of the proposition that in fact expresses the state of the world at $t1$.

1. If determinism is true, then ($P1$ and L) entails A.
2. If J could have raised his hand at $t2$, then J could have rendered A false.
3. If J could have rendered A false, and if ($P1$ and L) entails A, then J could have rendered ($P1$ and L) false.
4. J could not have rendered $P1$ false.
5. If J could have rendered ($P1$ and L) false, then J could have rendered L false.
6. J could not have rendered L false.

Therefore,

7. If determinism is true, then J could not have raised his hand at $t2$.

According to this argument, if determinism is true, then Judd could not have done otherwise than what he did at $t2$. Since the argument can be generalized to cover any agent and any act at any time, the argument, if sound, shows that no agent can ever do otherwise than what he in fact does, on the assumption of determinism. But persons have free will only if they can sometimes do otherwise than what they in fact do. Thus if the argument is sound, then determinism is incompatible with the minimal supposition of human free will: One of the two hypotheses can be true, but not both.

Consider the premises of the argument. Premise 1 follows from the truth of determinism and the designation of the variable letters. According to premise 2, if J could have raised his hand at t, then J could have done something that made A false. By stipulation, at $t2$ J's hand is not raised, and A is the name of the proposition expressing the fact that J's hand is left unraised at $t2$. So it is not possible for J's hand to be raised at $t2$ and for A to be true. J's ability to do otherwise than leave his hand unraised is translated into van Inwagen's terminology as the ability to render false the proposition that his hand is left unraised at $t2$. Premise 3 is an instance of the following general principle:

> Principle (P^*): If S can render r false, and if q entails r, then S can render q false.

Van Inwagen thinks that principle (P^*) is "a trivial truth."[12] The idea is that if S can produce $\neg r$, then S can produce $\neg q$, given that q entails r. If there is some state of affairs (or 'arrangement of objects') that S can produce that is sufficient for the falsity of r, then there is some state of affairs (or 'arrangement of objects')—that is, the very same one—that S can produce that is sufficient for the falsity of q. Premise 3 is one of the more controversial of the argument; I will return to it.

Premise 4 asserts that J could not have done anything to make $P1$ false. Since $P1$ concerns the distant past—it describes states of affairs that obtained before Judd was even born—the claim is highly plausible. Premise 5 follows from premise 4 and the general truth that if S can render the conjunction of p and q false, and S cannot render p false, then S can render q false. If S has the power to falsify a certain conjunction, then since it takes the falsity of at least one of the conjuncts for a conjunction to be false, S has the power to falsify at least one of the conjuncts; and in this case, since P concerns matters prior to his existence, it must be that J can render L false. Premise 6 says that nothing J could do would make false the natural laws. This is a particular case expressing the general idea that no one can falsify a law of nature, given what a law of nature *is*. That is to say, whatever precisely the laws of nature are, we do not have any *say* over them: It is not up to us to set or to change them. Laws of nature are not under our control—they are set before we are born and obtain independently of what we do or wish.

The conclusion of the argument is that J could not have done otherwise than leave his hand down at the appointed time, assuming causal determinism. Generalizing, if determinism is true, then for each agent, all acts but one act are ruled out at each moment by the past and laws of nature. Hence determinism and free will are incompatible.

Return for a moment to premise 3. Principle (P^*), of which premise 3 is a particular instance, may be restated as follows, using the operator '$R_{S,t}$' to represent 'agent S at t can render false':

Principle (P^*1): If $R_{S,t}(r)$ and q entails r, then $R_{S,t}(q)$.

Notice that it is *not* equivalent to the above principle to assert the following:

Principle (P^*2): If $R_{S,t}(q)$ and q entails r, then $R_{S,t}(r)$.

(Since q is sufficient but not necessary for r, the ability of S to render false q does not imply an ability of S to render false r. Hence principle (P^*2) is false.) Alternately, we might represent van Inwagen's principle (P^*) as follows, where '$P_{S,t}(r)$' represents 'agent S has at t the power to make proposition r the case':

Principle (P^*3): If $P_{S,t}(\neg r)$ and q entails r, then $P_{S,t}(\neg q)$.

Principle (P*3) is equivalent to the following principle:

Principle (P^*4): If $P_{S,t}(q)$ and q entails r, then $P_{S,t}(r)$.

Stating the inference rule relied on in van Inwagen's first argument as principle (P^*4), makes clear that it is a "power transference" principle—a principle claiming that an agent's power can be transferred through logical entailment. (The operator $P_{S,t}$, in other words, is closed under logical entailment.) This sort of principle, as mentioned above, has been controversial. It should be evident that much turns in the evaluation of incompatibilist arguments on the precision of the representation of notions of power and ability. Consider one other way of representing those notions.

Fischer: Power Necessity

John Martin Fischer employs an alternate power operator, '$N_{S,t}(p)$', used to stand for: It is power necessary for S at t that p (in other words, p obtains and S is not free at t to perform any action such that if S were to perform it, p would not obtain). If p is power necessary for S at t, then S is powerless at t over the fact that p obtains.

The generation of an argument for incompatibilism using this operator requires the following way of putting the thesis of determinism: For any given time, a complete statement of the facts about that time, together with a complete statement of the laws of nature, entails every truth as to what happens after that time.

Suppose that at a certain time, call it $t2$, you perform some act b, such as tucking your baby in bed for the night. From the fact that this is an act you routinely perform, it does not follow that it is an act you perform unfreely. Ordinarily, we would think that you are free to tuck your baby in bed at the time and are free to do something else instead (keep the baby up longer, say, or take the baby into your own bed, or get yourself a snack while someone else puts the baby to bed). Now suppose that causal determinism is true. It follows that a complete statement of the conditions at an earlier time, call it $t1$, together with a complete statement of the natural laws, entails that you do b (in this case, tuck the baby in bed) at $t2$. Call the complete statement of the conditions at the earlier time E. Since you have no control over the past—since, in other words, you are powerless over the fact that any past fact obtains—it is the case that:

1. $N_{you,t2}(E)$.

Furthermore, given that the natural laws are out of your control, it is true that:

2. $N_{you,t2}$(If E at $t1$, then you do b at $t2$).

Now Fischer defends the following as "a very attractive and reasonable principle":[13]

> *Principle of the Transfer of Powerlessness:*
> If: (i) $N_{S,t}(p)$, and (ii) $N_{S,t}$(If p, then q),
> then: (iii) $N_{S,t}(q)$.

And by the principle of the transfer of powerlessness, it follows from premises 1 and 2 that:

3. $N_{you,t2}$(you do b at $t2$).

Here, then, is the argument visible in one glance:

1. $N_{\text{you},t2}(E)$.
2. $N_{\text{you},t2}(\text{If } E \text{ at } t1, \text{ then you do } b \text{ at } t2)$.

Therefore,

3. $N_{\text{you},t2}(\text{you do } b \text{ at } t2)$.

We can generalize the argument to cover any agent at any time. But if, given the assumption of determinism, one is powerless over what one does, then determinism and free will are incompatible.

Summary: The Family Case

There is strength in numbers. Recall that the point in setting out a variety of arguments for the incompatibilist thesis was to show that, although related, there are a number of *different* arguments for the position of incompatibilism. Hence an objection to one or another of those arguments, even if successful against it, need not topple all the rest. Other closely related prominent arguments for incompatibilism include those formulated by Carl Ginet and David Wiggins. Ginet's argument relies on the notion of what is *open to* an agent at a time, using the operator '*OstP*', which reads 'it was open to S at t to make it the case that P' (1990: 101). Wiggins's argument uses a notion of what is *historically inevitable* at a time to reach by similar reasoning the incompatibilist conclusion.[14] Rather than surveying a further array of incompatibilist arguments, however, let us allow the case for incompatibilism to rest with the arguments set out above, including both the loose informal arguments and the more detailed ones. In my view and in the view of a growing number of philosophers, these arguments for incompatibilism are convincing and strong. In order to deny the conclusion of the arguments, one would have to deny a principle with very high plausibility.

Compatibilist Replies

Compatibilists have, of course, not been without their replies to this family of arguments for incompatibilism. Each of the compatibilist responses falls into one of four different categories: (1.) compatibilism founded on challenge to transference principles; (2.) local miracle compatibilism; (3.) multiple pasts compatibilism; (4.) "new" compatibilism.

Challenges to Transfer Principles

Consider first compatibilism founded on suspicion of transfer of power (or transfer of powerlessness) principles. Some compatibilists have, indeed, gone beyond suspicion of the principles to provide detailed arguments against one or another of them. Of course since, as we've seen, the transference rules employed by incompatibilists *vary*, compatibilism based on counterexample to one or another of the particular principles is vulnerable to defeat by the existence or development of an additional incompatibilist argument reliant upon a different particular rule (or perhaps upon no "transfer" rules at all). I want to focus on two particular recent cases for compatibilism based on challenge to transfer inference rules.[15]

First Case. Thomas McKay and David Johnson present a counterexample to rule β, the rule employed by van Inwagen's Third Argument.[16] Recall rule α: If $\Box p$, then Np; and rule β: If Np and $N(p \supset q)$, then Nq. The McKay and Johnson argument proceeds by the derivation of a simple principle, "the principle of agglomeration," from rule α and rule β and by the presentation of a convincing counterexample to the principle of agglomeration. Since rule α is indisputable, and since α and β together entail the principle of agglomeration, which is shown false by the counterexample, McKay and Johnson conclude that rule β must be false. The principle of agglomeration is as follows:

Principle of Agglomeration: If Np and Nq, then $N(p$ and $q)$.

Consider the following counterexample to the principle of agglomeration. Let p represent: The coin does not fall heads. Let q represent: The coin does not fall tails. Suppose that I do not toss the coin in question, but I could have. McKay and Johnson argue that agglomeration fails for this case since Np is true and Nq is true yet $N(p$ and $q)$ is false.

One might react in this way. The proponents of the counterexample are mistaken, since neither Np nor Nq is true. It is false that no one has, or ever had, any choice about whether p (the coin does not fall heads); I could make it the case that the coin does not fall heads simply by refraining from tossing the coin at all. Likewise, I have a choice about whether the coin does not fall tails; I can make this the case by refraining from tossing the coin.

However, by 'p, and no one has, or ever had, any choice about whether p', van Inwagen evidently does not mean 'p, and no one can, or ever could, make it the case that p'. For in his response to a different proposed counterexample, this one directly to rule β (in which p represents: Alfred throws a six; and q represents: Alfred plays dice), van Inwagen writes: "Strictly speaking, Alfred does have a choice about whether he throws a six. . . . He can avoid throwing a six by avoiding playing dice."[17] This suggests that 'Np' should be read as 'p and no one can, or ever could, avoid p's being the case.' On this reading, it is not clear that either Np or Nq for the proposed counterexample is false.

McKay and Johnson are right in pointing out that the phrase 'no one has or ever has had any choice about p' is unclear. Does it mean 'p, and no one can or could make p false'? Does it mean 'p, and no one can control whether p is true or not'? McKay and Johnson contend that van Inwagen intends 'Np' to stand for 'p, and no one can or could (choose to) make p false', which corresponds to 'p and Mp'. (*Mp*: Every ability of x's is such that after some exercise of that ability, p. That is, no matter what x does, it might be the case that p.) But rule β fails on this interpretation, given the counterexample to the principle of agglomeration. And if rule β fails, then van Inwagen's argument for incompatibilism reliant upon it is invalid.

Second Case. Tomis Kapitan proposes that an agent S is *strictly able* to bring about P just in case S is able to act upon a reliable strategy for bringing about P (where acting upon a reliable strategy entails that the agent has a conception of both the result and a strategy for producing that result).[18] Now define the notion of *unavoidability* with the operator N, so that NP is true just in case the state of affairs P obtains and S is strictly unable at t to prevent P from obtaining.

Now Kapitan argues against the transfer principle 'If NP and $N(P \supset Q)$, then NQ' in the following way: Let W be the proposition that Sam's office window is closed throughout the twenty-minute interval t. Let H be a complete description of a past state of the world and L be a conjunction of the laws of nature. Now consider the following instance of the transfer principle under consideration:

If $N(H$ and $L)$ and $N((H$ and $L) \supset W)$, then NW.

Kapitan alleges that the antecedent of this conditional is true but that the consequent is false. If so, then there is a successful counterexample to a transfer principle. The antecedent, '$N(H$ and $L)$ and $N((H$ and $L) \supset W)$', is true because both 'H and L' and '$(H$ and $L) \supset W$' obtain, and Sam is strictly unable to prevent either. But, Kapitan argues, it is false that Sam is strictly unable to prevent W: "Sam may well be able to do something that he correctly understands would reliably result in the window's being opened, namely, grasping the sash handle and pulling upwards until the window opens" (1996: 427).

Rejoinder.   One difficulty for compatibilism based on a challenge to the transfer of power (or powerlessness) inference rules is, as I alluded to above, the possibility of a successful argument for incompatibilism unreliant upon any sort of transfer principle. Fischer, for instance, has what he calls a "basic version" of an argument for incompatibilism that he does not think relies upon any type of transfer inference rule. The basic argument rests on the idea that every possible pathway into the future that a person can take is one that is an extension of the actual past. Van Inwagen has a similar additional argument.[19] If there *are* successful arguments for incompatibilism independent of any sort of transfer principle, then the type of compatibilism under consideration is undercut.

But suppose just for the sake of the argument that every argument for incompatibilism *does* rely upon some sort of transfer of power (or powerlessness) principle. Still, neither of the above compatibilist challenges is successful in undercutting incompatibilism. Consider first the Kapitan argument. The described case contravenes a reasonable requirement that van Inwagen places on acceptable counterexamples, namely, that they not beg the question by presupposing the falsity of incompatibilism. But the Sam case is a counterexample to the transfer principle to which it purports to be a counterexample only assuming the truth of compatibilism. True enough, during the interval t, Sam may have the *skill* needed to open the window (including a conception of how to go about doing so). However, given the truth of the conditional '$(H$ and $L) \supset W$', it is necessitated that Sam *will not exercise* that skill during the interval t. To claim that Sam is able to bring it about that the window is opened within time interval t is to violate the condition on ability of physical possibility. Given that the window's remaining closed during the interval t is causally necessitated by the past and natural laws, the window's being open during that interval of time is physically impossible. But what is physically impossible at a time is decidedly not something a normal human agent can be rightly asserted to have the ability to bring about.[20]

Consider next the McKay and Johnson challenge to a transfer principle. The proposed counterexample to the principle of agglomeration (and so to rule β) supposed that P represented: The coin does not fall heads; and that Q represented: The coin does not fall tails. Notice that the example does *not* work against rule C (If $B_{S,t}$ P and $B_{S,t}$ Q, then $B_{S,t}$ (P and Q)), used in the Beyond Control Argument, which I set out above. For, given the definition of the modal operator, although $B_{S,t}$ P is true and $B_{S,t}$ Q is true, $B_{S,t}$ (P and Q) is also true. That is, it is true that it is now beyond my control that the coin does not fall heads ($B_{S,t}$ P), since I am not now able to make it the case that $\neg P$. In other words, I cannot make the coin fall heads (assuming that if I try, I genuinely *toss* the coin rather than deliberately placing it, so that the coin counts as *falling* heads). Likewise, it is true that it is now beyond my control that the coin does not fall tails ($B_{S,t}$ Q), since I am not now able to make it the case that $\neg Q$. In other words, I cannot make the coin fall tails. Now, whereas the falsity of $B_{S,t}$ (P and Q) would show rule C to be violated, $B_{S,t}$ (P and Q) is not false but is, like $B_{S,t}$ P and $B_{S,t}$ Q, *also true*.

Recall that $B_{S,t}$ (P and Q) is true if and only if the following is true: (P and Q) and $\neg A_{S,t}$ ($\neg (P$ and Q)). In the example, I do not toss the coin, but I could have. So the first conjunct (P and Q) is true. The second conjunct is true as well, since I am unable to prevent its being the case that the coin does not land heads and the coin does not land tails. The coin *might* land on end (in spinning position) or get stuck on end in a crevice or be intercepted midair by another person after I toss it; I am unable to prevent this. Thus, while I am able to make it the case that (P and Q) by refraining from tossing the coin, I am *not* able to make it the case that $\neg (P$ and Q), because I cannot control all outside agents and circumstances that might lead to the coin's not falling either heads or tails even after I *try* to make $\neg (P$ and Q) true by tossing the coin. Hence the example fails to be a successful counterexample to rule C.

McKay and Johnson themselves present the following rejoinder to their own counterexample: Reinterpret '*Np*' as '*p* and *Vp*'. (*Vp* signifies that every ability of *x*'s is such that after every exercise of that ability, *p*. That is, no matter what *x* does, it would be the case that *p*.) Then '*Np*' is to be read '*p* and no one can or could (choose to) do anything that *might* lead to *p*'s being false'. On this interpretation, the premises *Np* and *Nq* for the proposed counterexample to agglomeration are not true. For I can toss the coin, which might lead to the coin's falling heads. And I can toss the coin, which might lead to the coin's falling tails. On the reinterpreted version of *Np*, a corresponding rule to rule β (rule β4) may be constructed:

Inference Rule β4: If *p*, *Vp*, *p* ⊃ *q*, and V(*p* ⊃ *q*), then *q* and *Vq*.

Rule β4, McKay and Johnson claim, is a valid principle, and, given the supposition of determinism, it licenses inference from the true premises '*V(P1)*', '*V(L)*', and '*V((P1* and *L)* ⊃ *P)*' to the conclusion '*VP*'. But if so, then, given determinism, no one can ever do otherwise.

Compatibilism based on challenge to transfer faces the difficulty that leading arguments for incompatibilism are put in terms of differing vocabulary, use different modal operators, and rely on different, although similar, inference rules. Some operators are better defined than others. Hence it may be that a particular way of developing an argument for incompatibilism falls to considerations against which others are immune. It is for this reason that I have treated the various proposed incompatibilist lines of reasoning as distinct *arguments*, all of which, of course, have the same goal: to establish the truth of incompatibilism.

I have argued that neither of the above compatibilist challenges to a particular principle of the transfer of power (or powerlessness) succeeds in undercutting incompatibilism. Furthermore, I conclude, in general, that a challenge to one or another transfer principle is not a particularly promising strategy for a compatibilist to take in responding to arguments for incompatibilism.

Lewis: Local Miracle Compatibilism

David Lewis, in his intriguing paper "Are We Free to Break the Laws?" (1981), replies to van Inwagen's First Argument (which, recall, concerned the abilities of a hypothetical free determined agent, the judge we called Judd). Lewis claims that van Inwagen's argument relies on an ambiguity. There is no single construal of the phrase 'can render false', contends Lewis, on which both premise 5 of the argument—if *J* could have rendered (*P*1 and *L*) false, then *J* could have rendered *L* false—and premise 6—*J* could not have rendered *L* false—are true.

Lewis supports this claim by distinguishing two senses in which one might be said to be able to render a proposition false (or to violate a law of nature). In the *strong sense,* one is able to render a proposition *P* false just in case one can do something such that, if one did it, then *P* would be falsified by one's act itself or by an event caused by that act. Thus if one can, in the strong sense of ability, violate a law of nature, then one is able to *break* a law (by one's act itself or by an event caused by that act). By contrast, in the *weak sense*, one is able to render a proposition false just in case one is able to do something such that, if one did it, the proposition would have been falsified somehow or another, but not necessarily by one's own act or by an event caused by one's act. Hence if one can, in the weak sense of ability, violate a law of nature, then one can do something such that, if one did it, the law would be broken.

To illustrate the distinction, consider an ability to break a window. Most of us have this ability in the *strong* sense: We are able to do something—such as throw a rock at the window with sufficient force—that either *is* itself, or *causes,* a window-breaking event. To claim that any of us has an ability to break a law of nature in the strong sense would be, likewise, to claim that one of us can do something—such as throw a rock so extremely hard that it travels faster than the speed of light—that either is itself or causes a law-breaking event. This would, indeed, be quite an incredible ability. However, the compatibilist need not attribute this incredible power to the free determined agent, Lewis argues. While it is true that, if the free determined agent had done otherwise, then the proposition *L* reporting all of the actual laws of nature would have been false, this truth claim reports, on one construal, only a counterfactual relation and does not attribute any causal power over the laws to the agent. The weak sense of ability to render false a proposition is *distinct* from the strong sense, just as the claim that, if your grandmother had graduated from college, then she would have (had to have) enrolled in college is not equivalent to the claim that, if your grandmother had graduated from college, then her graduating from college would have caused her enrollment in college.

Notice that Lewis's reply to the first van Inwagen argument does not rely on the claim that, if a free determined agent had done otherwise, then something would have been both a law and broken. Such a claim, says Lewis, is indeed "a contradiction in terms if, as I suppose, any genuine law is at least an absolutely unbroken regularity." Rather, Lewis's position is that, if a free determined agent had done otherwise, then a law of nature would have been violated in the following sense: "something that is in fact a law, and unbroken, would have been broken, and no law." It would, he says, have been at best "an almost-law."[21]

Thus, the response to the incompatibilist argument is this: If we take the weak sense of the ability to render a proposition false throughout van Inwagen's First Argument, then Lewis denies premise 6. But if we take the strong sense, then Lewis denies premise 5—for all that follows from the antecedent of the conditional in premise 5, according to Lewis, is that J could have rendered L false in the weak sense.

Lewis, then, points out that there is a sense in which one can have "power" over the laws of nature: One can have a counterfactual power over them; that is, one can do something such that, if one did it, then the laws would have been (would have had to have been) different. But there is also a sense in which we do not have power over the natural laws: We cannot *change* the laws; that is, we cannot cause them to be different from what they in fact are. According to Lewis, one who admits to our having counterfactual power over the laws is not committed to the claim that, if determinism and the supposition of human free will are both true, then we have *causal* power over them. The counterfactual sense of power over laws, Lewis thinks, is harmless, and the distinction between it and the causal sense of power over the laws can be used to block the incompatibilist conclusion.

Now this is an intriguing move against the van Inwagen argument. But the fact that *Lewis* makes this move against the argument is initially surprising. For, in response to the question of what it means to say that one event *causes* another event, Lewis proposes a certain sort of analysis, according to which, roughly, if the first event had occurred, then the second event would have occurred, and if the first event had not occurred, then the second event would not have occurred. That is, Lewis proposes a *counterfactual* theory of the nature of the causal relation. Consider, for instance, the causal claim that *my flicking the pen caused the pen to move across the table*. This statement is to be analyzed, on a counterfactual account of causation, as follows: If I had flicked the pen, then the pen would have moved; and if I had not flicked the pen, then it would not have moved.

However, this view about the nature of the causal relation appears to create a problem for Lewis's reply to the first van Inwagen argument for incompatibilism. If causal dependence between two events can be analyzed in terms of the holding of counterfactual dependence between them, then, it seems, the distinction between a free determined agent's counterfactual power over the laws and her causal power over them *collapses*. Lewis relies on precisely this distinction in his proposal for blocking the conclusion of the incompatibilist argument. How, then, does Lewis uphold his position?

The answer is that on Lewis's account, causal dependence—in terms of chains of which causation itself is analyzed—requires the appropriate patterns of counterfactual dependence among propositions reporting the occurrence of *particular events*. If c and e are two distinct particular events, then event e causally depends on event c just in case the family of propositions $O(e)$, $\neg O(e)$ counterfactually depends on the family of propositions $O(c)$, $O(c)$; that is, if and only if it is true that, if c had occurred, then e would have occurred, and if c had not occurred, then e would not have occurred.[22] According to Lewis, one is able to cause a change in the laws only if there is some *particular* law-breaking event that counterfactually depends upon one's doing otherwise.

But Lewis denies that there is any such particular event. This is because, if one did otherwise, then the law of nature would have been violated, but the law's violation *might have come about in a number of different ways*. Suppose, for instance, that I had dressed my daughter in a green shirt this morning (when, in fact, I did not). Then—holding fixed the past prior to the moment when I put something other than a green shirt on her—the laws would have been violated, by some divergence miracle or another. But this pattern of counterfactual dependence does not suffice for causal dependence, since the occurrence of some miracle or another is not a particular event. If the distinction between a free determined agent's counterfactual power over the laws and her (nonactual) causal power over them can be upheld, then the first van Inwagen argument for incompatibilism is unsuccessful.

Multiple Pasts Compatibilism

Multiple pasts compatibilists exploit Lewis's distinction between strong and weak senses of the ability to render a proposition false, applying it, rather than against the inviolability of the natural laws, against van Inwagen's premise that one cannot render false a proposition concerning the past. Put another way, the multiple pasts compatibilist endorses the distinction between a counterfactual and a causal power while adopting a differing analysis of counterfactuals.

Lewis's theory of counterfactuals is a *miraculous analysis,* since, on this view, a world in which a local divergence miracle occurs and almost all of the past is the same as our past, is *closer* to the actual world than is a world in which the natural laws are exactly the same as our laws. On a competing theory of counterfactuals, the closest worlds share our natural laws but have a past that differs at each moment of time back to the beginning of history. The multiple pasts compatibilist endorses this competing *nonmiraculous analysis* of counterfactuals and argues on the basis of it that it is false that the free determined agent could not have rendered false a proposition $P1$ about the distant past.

The free determined agent could have rendered $P1$ false, according to this line of reply to the incompatibilist's argument, in the sense that she had counterfactual power over the truth of $P1$: She could have done something such that, if she had done it, then $P1$ would have been falsified (somehow or another, but not necessarily by the agent's own act or an event caused by that act). Hence, according to multiple pasts compatibilists, there *are* multiple pasts, in a sense. There are pasts that would have had to have been the case if the free determined agent were to have done otherwise than she in fact did.

Rejoinder: Countering Lewis

One way to argue against Lewis's reply to the incompatibilist argument—whether that reply is conjoined with a *local miracle* or a *multiple pasts* analysis of counterfactuals—is to make use of the notion of disjunctive events. Take the case of my not dressing my daughter this morning in the green shirt but dressing her in something else instead. Suppose that I could have done otherwise with respect to this action: that I could have put the green shirt on her. Then, given determinism, I had a counterfactual power over the laws (or the past): I could have done something such that, if I had done it, then the laws would have been violated (or the past would have been different). This counterfactual power does *not* amount to a causal power, according to Lewis, because there is no distinct divergence miracle (or no distinct past event) that depends upon my doing otherwise.

But consider the disjunction of the ways in which my dressing my daughter in a green shirt this morning might have come about— for instance: my not looking as I reached in the closet for a yellow shirt, grabbing the green one instead; *or* my being moved by her pleas for a green shirt today; *or* my remembering the note from her teacher requesting that she wear the team color (green) on this particular day; and so on. Why is the disjunction of these events not itself a particular event? If it is, then there *is* a particular law-breaking (or past-changing) event, the disjunctive one, the occurrence of which counterfactually depends upon my doing otherwise: If I had put on the green shirt, then this event would have occurred; and if I had not, then this event would not have occurred.

To be sure, the described event is one of an odd sort. But intuitively we ought to allow some cases of events that are disjunctions, and Lewis himself does admit them. (He gives the example of a stamping event that is a disjunction of one event that is essentially a stamping of the right foot and another that is essentially a stamping of the left foot.) Lewis, in fact, thinks that disjunctive events count, provided that the disjuncts are not too "miscellaneously varied."[23] But once this is allowed, the difficulty lies in setting the appropriate limits for allowable variation and, furthermore, in showing that the law-breaking disjunctive events counterfactually dependent upon free determined agents' otherwise acts do *exceed* those limits.

Regarding the first difficulty, some disjunctive events in which the disjuncts are quite varied seem intuitively as if they ought to count. For instance, Kadri Vihvelin presents a case in which my pushing a button causes the disjunctive event of (either *A*'s doorbell ringing or a bomb going off in *B*'s house).[24] The varied nature of the disjuncts seems irrelevant to the status of the disjunctive happenings as an event caused by the pushing of the button. If I push the button, then I cause something to happen: a noise. If I had not pushed the button, then the noise would not have occurred. But if, as the button pusher, I have a causal power over the noise, then it seems analogously that, as a free determined agent, given the counterfactual analysis, one has causal power over the laws (or the past).

Lewis and other compatibilists endorsing his position might rule out all disjunctive events, but then certain cases of causation are left out of the account. Alternatively, disjunctive events may be allowed, but then the "weak" counterfactual sense collapses into the "strong" causal sense of ability to violate a law (or to render a proposition false). For if Lewis drops the ban on overly varied disjunctive events, then on his analysis of causation, an agent's doing otherwise is a cause of some particular law-breaking event (the disjunctive one); thus the agent's power over the laws of nature, given determinism and the free will thesis, is *causal*. This is a victory for the incompatibilist, since an agent's having causal power over the past or laws, given both determinism and the free will thesis, is absurd. So either determinism or the minimal supposition of free will is false.[25]

Suppose that this appeal to disjunctive events is countenanced. Even so, for an incompatibilist to take the above line of reply to Lewis saddles her with a difficulty. The difficulty is that the incompatibilist apparently must endorse a counterfactual account of causation, in order to uphold the claim that Lewis's distinction between counterfactual power and causal power over the laws (or past) *collapses*. But there are well-known problems for the counterfactual approach to analyzing causation, such as the problems of overdetermination, preemption, and directionality.[26]

This difficulty is, perhaps, surmountable: The incompatibilist might endorse some theory of causation that both (i.) entails that the counterfactual dependence between two events *suffices* for causal dependence between those events and (ii.) explains this fact, without the account itself being a reductionist counterfactual theory. The discussion of Lewis's reply to the first van Inwagen argument reveals the tactical benefit to an incompatibilist of endorsing either a counterfactual theory of causation or some theory meeting the two conditions specified in the preceding sentence.

Nonetheless, a perhaps even more powerful way of arguing against Lewis is as follows: Suppose we grant Lewis's distinction, in the sense that we admit to being able to *see* the distinction he draws between being able to break a natural law and being able to act such that the law would have been broken (somehow or another). But why should we think that anything *follows* from the drawing of this distinction about the incompatibilist argument?

It seems clear that van Inwagen intends what Lewis calls the *strong* reading of the ability to render false a proposition. Lewis says that, on this reading, he *agrees* that premise 6 (*J* could not have rendered *L* false) is true. And, regarding premise 5 (if *J* could have rendered [P1 and *L*] false, then *J* could have rendered *L* false) Lewis grants the antecedent, stating: "Indeed it is true both in the weak sense and in the strong sense that I [or the free determined agent] could have rendered false the conjunction [P1 and *L*] of history and law."[27] But to assert that premise 5 is false, since it does not follow from the antecedent that *J* could have rendered *L* false in the strong sense is deeply puzzling and ad hoc. The only factor recommending a switch in reading to the weak sense of ability to render false for the consequent of the conditional in premise 5 is, it seems, a prior commitment to compatibilism.

Notice that it is a deep-seated feature of a widespread conception of the past that, once they occur, events of the past are set and are not malleable as a result of what we do in the present. Some theorists, such as Fischer, refer to this feature of our conception of the past as *the present strict fixity of the past*. Likewise, it is an essential aspect of our concept of natural law that the laws of nature are what they are independently of us—they were fixed prior to our existence, and we cannot do anything to alter them. Call this *the present strict fixity of the natural laws*.

Certainly any compatibilism that denies the present strict fixity of the past or the present strict fixity of the natural laws is suspect. The compatibilist who follows Lewis is committed to the claim that the truth of causal determinism is consistent with the following situation: Given all of the events of the past and the natural laws, an agent is able at some time to act in such a way that, if he so acted, either the laws of nature would be violated or the past would be different from what it actually was. But to claim that a human agent *can* now do something that has the effect that the laws of nature are violated (or that the past is different from the actual past), even if this violation (or difference) occurs merely "somehow or another" and is not directly produced by the agent's act, is to violate a powerful intuitive conviction concerning the nature of the past and the natural laws. We must keep in mind that, at the moment of the act of which the freedom is in question, the past is over and done, and the natural laws are what they are—they are fixed, set. We may grant that, if a free determined agent had acted otherwise, then the laws (or the past) would have been different. But from this fact it does not follow that, given the laws as they are and the occurrence of past events up until the present moment, what an agent now *can* do includes something that either itself abrogates or entails the abrogation (somehow or another) of the laws or the past.

The compatibilist is thus in a quite awkward position. A challenge to one or another of the various transfer of power principles is vulnerable to defeat by an argument for incompatibilism reliant either upon a different transfer principle or upon no transfer principle at all. The compatibilist might, alternately, deny either the present strict fixity of the past or the present strict fixity of the natural laws, but this is extremely implausible. In light of this difficult compatibilist situation, Fischer has recently presented a "new compatibilism" as one possible compatibilist position.[28]

New Compatibilism

"New compatibilism" relies on a combination of the view that all truths are world indexed (and there is a complete catalog of such indexed truths at each time and in each possible world) and the view that there is no single, unique actual world—that each possible world is real and actual relative to itself (a view termed *indexical possibilism*). Since, on this view, there are no index-free statements about what happens (or obtains) and since in each possible world there is a true set of statements about what obtains in all of the possible worlds, the new compatibilist can assert that a free determined agent's hypothetical otherwise act (such as Judd's raising his hand) does *not* entail an ability to act so that the past would be different from what it actually was. For the past, conceived as the complete catalog of world-indexed truths, *does not change* in going from world to world: The world-relativized truths are the same in all possible worlds. Furthermore, given indexical possibilism, the free determined agent in doing otherwise does not have any sort of power over a fact about the past concerning which world is "the actual world."[29] Of course, if Judd, for instance, does not raise his hand at $t2$ in $W1$, then it is necessarily true that Judd does not raise his hand at $t2$ in $W1$; and if "Judd" does raise his hand at $t2$ in $W2$, then it is not the Judd of $W1$ who does this, but his "counterpart."

By endorsing certain rather peculiar metaphysical views, then, the compatibilist may consistently uphold his position against incompatibilist arguments. New compatibilism, however, has extremely implausible consequences. As Fischer himself points out, the view makes *all* truths into *necessary* truths. But to abandon our distinction between what is contingent and what is necessary is surely a hefty price to pay for maintaining a belief in our ability to do otherwise in a deterministic universe.[30] The new compatibilist is committed to a modal collapse, and this, I would think, is sufficient for the support of new compatibilism itself to be judged flattened.

Conclusion

Introspection reveals a decisionmaking process that operates on the assumption of multiple available options. As I sit at my desk, I believe that I can pick up a nearby binder clip or leave it still; that I can get up, or intentionally knock over my clock, or move a book to the right or the left or the back of the desk. I believe that I will do only one of these things if I do any of them, at the next moment, but I believe that at the present moment, I am free to do each of them. In other words, it is within my power at the present moment to actualize any one of several possible futures, or at least so it is natural and common to believe.

The arguments for incompatibilism show that, if determinism is true, then this natural and widespread assumption about ourselves is false. If determinism were in fact demonstrated to be the case, then our belief that we have free will would be shown to be incorrect, for as we've seen (as one way of putting the case), determinism rules out the forking-paths model of the future integral to the notion of freedom.

I have argued that the case for incompatibilism is potent and convincing. The reader might wonder, however, what positive arguments are offered on the opposing side. Before judging the issue conclusively settled, of course, we must consider those arguments. Positive arguments for the compatibilist position and corresponding compatibilist conceptions of free will are the subjects of the following chapter.

Notes

1. Richard McKeon, ed., *Introduction to Aristotle*, 2nd edition (Chicago: University of Chicago Press, 1973), p. 395. For a provocative libertarian reading of Aristotle, see Richard Sorabji, *Necessity, Cause and Blame* (Ithaca: Cornell University Press, 1983). A reply is Gail Fine, "Aristotle's Determinism," *Philosophical Review* 90, 1981, pp. 561–579.

2. David Hume, *An Inquiry Concerning Human Understanding* (Indianapolis, IN: Bobbs-Merrill, 1977; originally published in 1748), sec. 8.

3. A. J. Ayer, *Philosophical Essays* (London: Macmillan, 1954), p. 271.

4. Bernard Williams, *Making Sense of Humanity* (New York: Cambridge University Press, 1995), p. 5. Williams calls this *the Plurality Principle* and expresses the challenge determinism poses to free will in this way: "The feared effect of the doctrine in question [determinism] is to reduce in every case the actions open to the agent in the relevant sense to one, and it is this that the Principle denies" (p. 7).

5. Peter van Inwagen, *An Essay on Free Will* (Oxford: Clarendon Press, 1983), p. 8.

6. David Lewis, "Causation," in *Philosophical Papers*, vol. 2 (New York: Oxford University Press, 1986), p. 162. Other formulations of the thesis of determinism include: all physical effects are necessitated by their causes (G. E. M. Anscombe, "Causality and Determination," in *The Collected Philosophical Papers of G.E.M. Anscombe*, vol. 2, Minneapolis: University of Minnesota Press, 1981); and for any given time, a complete description of the state of the world at that time, together with a complete statement of the laws of nature, entails every truth as to what happens at every time (John Martin Fischer, "Incompatibilism," *Philosophical Studies* 43, 1983, p. 135). Some so-called compatibilist authors, for instance A. J. Ayer ("Freedom and Necessity," in *Philosophical Essays*, London: Macmillan, 1954) and R. E. Hobart ("Free Will as Involving Determination and Inconceivable Without It," *Mind* 43, 1934, pp. 1–27), argue that freedom is compatible with the Principle of Universal Causation (UC), according to which every event has a cause. But UC does not entail determinism, for at least these reasons: some causes might be agents; and some causes might not necessitate, but merely produce, their effects.

7. John Martin Fischer (*The Metaphysics of Free Will: An Essay on Control*, Aristotle Society Series, vol. 14, Cambridge, MA: Blackwell, 1994) presents and discusses in great detail different arguments—arguments that he

asserts are powerful—for the belief that determinism is incompatible with the freedom to act otherwise, including especially a "basic version" of the argument, which he claims avoids some of the "dialectical stalemates" associated with other versions and the assumptions of which "resonate with common sense" (p. 110). Nonetheless, Fischer goes on to conclude that, whereas free will requiring the ability to do otherwise is incompatible with causal determinism, it is not needed for moral responsibility, a matter to be taken up in Chapters 5 and 6.

8. Van Inwagen uses a forking-paths diagram to illustrate the situation of an agent with free will in his *Metaphysics* (Boulder: Westview Press, 1993). This device I find extremely useful in making clear the relevant issues. Fischer, as well, returns often in his discussion of the metaphysics of freedom to the image of the future as a "garden of forking paths," as it is expressed by the Argentine fabulist Jorge Luis Borges (Fischer, *Metaphysics of Free Will*).

9. van Inwagen, *Essay on Free Will*, p. 16.

10. Proof: (1.) $B_{S,t} P$. (2.) $B_{S,t} Q$. (3.) $\Box [P \supset (Q \supset (P \text{ and } Q))]$. (4.) $B_{S,t} [P \supset (Q \supset (P \text{ and } Q))]$ (from 3 and rule A). (5.) $B_{S,t} [Q \supset (P \text{ and } Q)]$ (from 1, 4, and rule T). (6.) $B_{S,t} (P \text{ and } Q)$. McKay and Johnson present a structurally identical proof of a rule much like C ("the principle of agglomeration") using a somewhat different operator, van Inwagen's 'Np'. See Thomas McKay and David Johnson, "A Reconsideration of an Argument Against Compatibilism," *Philosophical Topics* 24, 1996, p. 115.

11. van Inwagen, *Essay on Free Will*, p. 93.

12. Ibid., p. 72.

13. Fischer, *Metaphysics of Free Will*, p. 8. Notice the difference in the middle propositions of the power transference inference rules employed by the arguments for incompatibilism we have considered.

14. David Wiggins, "Towards a Reasonable Libertarianism," in Ted Honderich, ed., *Essays on Freedom of Action* (London: Routledge and Kegan Paul, 1973), pp. 31–62.

15. Michael Slote ("Selective Necessity and the Free-Will Problem," *Journal of Philosophy* 79, 1982, pp. 5–24) questions and rejects the principle of the transfer of power necessity. Slote argues that power necessity is analogous to certain other sorts of necessity—for instance, epistemic and deontic—that themselves fail to hold through logical entailment and thus, by extension, the incompatibilist's modal principle is suspect. I have elected not to discuss this intriguing paper of Slote's not because it lacks interest and merit, but because it is already discussed with such insight and attention to detail in Fischer, *Metaphysics of Free Will*. Fischer provides ingenious extended argumentation against Slote's explanation of the "selectivity" of power necessity (see especially pp. 40–45).

16. McKay and Johnson, "A Reconsideration," pp. 113–122.

17. van Inwagen, *Essay on Free Will*, pp. 233–234, note 3.

18. Tomis Kapitan, "Modal Principles in the Metaphysics of Free Will,"
Philosophical Perspectives 10, 1996, pp. 419–445.

19. van Inwagen, *Essay on Free Will*, pp. 78–93.

20. Kapitan anticipates this reaction and says in response that "here we reach a 'dialectical stalemate' . . . or a case of 'burden-tennis.'" Nonetheless, immediately following, Kapitan assumes his position to be *the given*, with the burden of proof resting on the other side: "Without additional moves in these directions [showing the concept of ability with a physical possibility condition to be the one relevant to responsibility and practical thought] then the example stands and the closure principles for power necessity fail in the case of strict ability" ("Modal Principles," pp. 427–428). But, as discussed above, practical thought does require physical possibility for the ability to bring about.

21. David Lewis, "Are We Free to Break the Laws?" *Theoria* 47, part 3, 1981, pp. 113–121.

22. Lewis, "Causation," pp. 165–166.

23. David Lewis, "Events," in *Philosophical Papers*, vol. 2 (New York: Oxford University Press, 1986), pp. 241–268.

24. Kadri Vihvelin, "Freedom, Causation, and Counterfactuals," *Philosophical Studies* 64, 1991, p. 170.

25. For further discussion of issues pertinent to the Lewis and Vihvelin replies to van Inwagen's argument, see Laura Waddell Ekstrom, "Freedom, Causation, and the Consequence Argument," *Synthese* 115, 1998, pp. 333–354.

26. For the development of objections to the counterfactual theory of causation, see Jaegwon Kim, "Causes and Counterfactuals," *Journal of Philosophy* 70, 1973, pp. 570–572; and Paul Horwich, *Asymmetries in Time* (Cambridge, MA: MIT Press, 1987), pp. 167–176.

27. David Lewis, "Are We Free to Break the Laws?" *Theoria* 47, part 3, 1981, p. 120.

28. John Martin Fischer, "A New Compatibilism," *Philosophical Topics* 24, 1996, pp. 49–66.

29. David Lewis defends indexical possibilism in "Anselm and Actuality," *Nous* 4, 1970, 175–188, and in his *On the Plurality of Worlds* (Oxford: Blackwell, 1986).

30. Fischer defends this point in "A New Compatibilism," pp. 60–64.

CHAPTER THREE

Compatibilist Arguments and Free Will Accounts

To briefly take stock: The first chapter made explicit some intuitions underlying the conviction that questions concerning free will are both subtle and significant. The subsequent chapter set out and critically examined several arguments for the conclusion that the minimal supposition of human free will must be false if the thesis of causal determinism is true. Thus far, then, we have put compatibilism in the defensive position only and not in the offensive one. Indeed, this is, from my point of view, appropriate: The arguments for incompatibilism spell out the reasoning behind the pervasive incompatibilist intuitions among ordinary persons exposed to the issue, and I judge those arguments to be overwhelmingly strong. I argued in the previous chapter that the various available compatibilist *responses* to the positive incompatibilist arguments are unsuccessful. But what positive arguments are there for the position of compatibilism? I take up the task of examining such arguments in the present chapter.

The compatibilist position does have a number of attractions. First among them is that it would be useful to be able to uphold our ability to act freely, along with the meaningfulness of our interpersonal relationships and our sense of dignity as persons, *no matter what* physicists ultimately report concerning the nature of the physical world. If we can act freely *even if* causal determinism is true, then a demonstration of the truth of the determinist doctrine cannot undercut significant values and powers of ours. This would surely be a desirable position for us to be in: If compatibilism were true, then we could rest secure, immune from the refutation by scientific discovery of a treasured image of ourselves.

Furthermore, even more so in the past than of late, there has been reason to think that the doctrine of causal determinism *is* true; yet, it is compelling to believe that we have free will, and hence there is motivation to make the analysis of our power to act freely consistent with the doctrine of scientific determinism. Finally, it has seemed abhorrent to many modern enlightened persons to posit an ability of persons that places us outside the realm of causes and effects and makes our behavior scientifically inexplicable—hence the attraction of the compatibilist thesis.

In fact, however, on the view of free action I defend in the subsequent chapter, while incompatibilism is true, our acting freely does *not* require the falsity of the Principle of Universal Causation (the thesis that every event has a cause). Further, on that indeterminist model, our free action is not, in principle, scientifically inexplicable. So some compatibilists may find that their motivating concerns can be accommodated within an incompatibilist framework. Before investigating this possibility, though, let us look at the positive arguments that have been advanced for the thesis that our having free will is, in fact, *compatible with* the truth of the doctrine of causal determinism.

Positive Arguments for Compatibilism

Let me first briefly describe and explain reasons for dismissing two particular arguments for compatibilism, before moving on to set out three more serious contenders. One sometimes hears (rather than reads in print) modern-day compatibilists defend their position in this way: I do not have any positive argument in favor of the truth of compatibilism. But I do not need one. Compatibilism is the default position—it is the position of "the person on the street." The person on the street simply does not take the thesis of causal determinism to be an exculpating factor. The ordinary person, that is, does not think that attributions of responsibility depend upon how physics turns out.

But this reasoning is faulty on a number of counts. At issue is the compatibility or incompatibility of *free will* and determinism, rather than responsibility and determinism. The proponent of the compatibilist line of reasoning above stands in need of an argument for the claim that the notion of acting freely collapses into the notion of acting such that one is responsible for what one does. But these are arguably distinct notions. (The matter of responsibility is yet to be discussed and will be taken up in the final chapters of this book.) Furthermore, the claim to what ordinary persons think is suspect. Completely unreflective intuitions of persons not cognizant of the doctrine of causal determinism *can only be* insensitive to that doctrine. And there is evidence that the judgments of ordinary persons indeed *are* responsive to the consideration of determinism.[1]

Moreover, the incompatibilist has, it seems to me, an even better claim to being the "default" position than does the compatibilist. For, in the absence of an argument to the contrary, it is straightforwardly clear to most all of us as we adopt the practical deliberative point of view toward our own future that the following is true: I am free in what I do at the next moment only if I am not necessitated to do just what I do by the past and the natural laws—only if the way the world is leaves room for me to act in this particular way and leaves room for me to act otherwise.

The compatibilist, then, needs a positive argument in favor of the compatibility thesis. There remains one argument holding sway with many contemporary compatibilists that I will also set aside. That is an argument often called "the *Mind* Argument" (named for the journal in which several different proponents of the line of reasoning published variations on it). In brief, the argument is this: Compatibilism must be true, since all incompatibilist accounts of the nature of free will are incoherent. In other words, since free will cannot be made consistent with the denial of determinism—indeterminism—where this indeterminism is supposed as relevant to human activity, free will must be compatible with determinism.

Call this, if you like, a positive compatibilist argument. It is a positive argument in that it seeks to show the contrary of one's own position to involve an absurdity. The argument, I will grant, succeeds in shifting a certain burden to the incompatibilist who believes that the minimal free will thesis is true. It shifts to such an incompatibilist the burden of attempting to show that some notion of free will on the assumption of indeterminism is coherent. But the *Mind* Argument does not succeed in demonstrating the *truth* of compatibilism. This is because, if the attempt to make coherent some indeterminist model of free action in fact turns out to fail, then *either* we pretheoretically carry about some vague but ultimately incoherent conception of ourselves as free agents *or* there is some serious flaw, after all, in each of the leading arguments for incompatibilism that this book has considered. But since an examination of the incompatibilist arguments has identified no such flaw, and since I have not yet turned to the matter of the incompatibilist's project of constructing a positive model of the nature of free action, a discussion of all of the issues relevant to the compatibilist *Mind* Argument cannot at this juncture be conclusive.

I note that the proponent of the *Mind* Argument serves up to the incompatibilist a particular challenge, and I devote the entire subsequent chapter to taking up precisely that challenge. I will not, however, treat the *Mind* Argument as one of the central, important compatibilist arguments because the failure of the argument to decisively demonstrate compatibilism is already—no matter how the incompatibilist theory-construction efforts turn out—a given. Free will might be inconsistent with event-causal indeterminism in the production of action while at the same time being inconsistent with the thesis of causal determinism. Hence the *Mind* Argument does not prove that compatibilism is true.

This leaves only three positive arguments for compatibilism I know of that have any force. The positive arguments for compatibilism I will consider here are these: First, compatibilism for many has been motivated by a certain kind of analysis of the ability to do otherwise: a *conditional analysis*. I will discuss this analysis in some detail. Second is a compatibilist argument based upon the notion of control and upon the contention that neither the past nor the natural laws can be a *controller*. I discuss in particular Daniel Dennett's proposal of this argument. Third, Keith Lehrer has argued for the compatibilist conclusion by reference to certain facts about the confirmation of hypotheses by empirical evidence.

The Conditional Analysis of Ability

At the start of the previous chapter, I noted the enormously widespread philosophical agreement on the claim that one must at least sometimes be able to do otherwise in order to possess free will. One influential type of positive argument for compatibilism might be put as follows: Free will requires the ability to do otherwise. The correct analysis of the ability to do otherwise shows it to be consistent with the thesis of causal determinism. Therefore, free will is compatible with determinism.

Expressed in this way, of course, the compatibilist argument is invalid. For the consistency with determinism of a necessary condition of free will fails to show the thesis of the compatibility of free will and determinism, since free will may be inconsisent with the thesis of causal determinism in virtue of some other condition on the possession of free will. But recall that I named the *minimal supposition of human free will* the thesis that for some human persons the necessary condition—the ability to do otherwise with respect to at least some actions—is met. Thus, if the compatibilist is right that the correct analysis of the ability to do otherwise shows it to be consistent with the deterministic hypothesis, then the minimal supposition of human free will *is* compatible with determinism. In order to show the consistency of free will and determinism, the compatibilist may put the argument differently: Having the ability to do otherwise at a time suffices for having free will at that time. But the right analysis of the ability to do otherwise at a time shows it to be consistent with the hypothesis of causal determinism. Therefore, free will is compatible with determinism.

The compatibilist then provides support for the second premise of this argument by proposing a *conditional analysis* of the ability to do otherwise. Call such compatibilists *conditionalists*. One sort of conditionalism proposes that the ability to do otherwise is to be analyzed as consisting in the fact that the agent *could* have done otherwise *if* she had chosen to do otherwise (or desired or intended or willed or tried to do otherwise, depending upon the particular proposal or perhaps upon the agent's situation). This sort of proposal, however, is widely taken even among compatibilists themselves to have been decisively proved faulty, largely following the work of J. L. Austin in his famous paper "Ifs and Cans."[2]

Consider the argument that the *could . . . if . . .* proposal cannot be correct, since it makes an agent's possession of an ability contingent upon his choosing (or desiring or intending or willing or trying) to exercise it. But certainly, it is ordinarily thought, persons possess abilities even when they are not at the moment desiring (or choosing or trying, etc.) to use them. For instance, I might have the ability to perform a certain dance movement, a *ronde de jambe*, at a moment when I am sitting still concentrating vigorously on a philosophical argument such that the furthest thing from my mind is getting up to do a *ronde de jambe*. My having the ability at all at some time is apparently not dependent upon my wanting at the time to exercise it. Likewise, agents' abilities in general are, it seems, not dependent for their mere existence upon those agents' turning their attention toward them (in the form of trying or willing or choosing to perform acts that exercise the abilities).

But here we have to be careful. At issue is the ability to do something in particular in the circumstances, and not the mere possession of a skill. The incompatibilist has argued that, although it may often seem as if one is able to act otherwise than one does, if determinism is in fact true, then actually one is never able to do otherwise than to act as one does. Thus the incompatibilist agrees that one could have done otherwise *if* some circumstance of the past (or some fact about the natural laws) had been different. But given the circumstances and the laws as they were, on the deterministic hypothesis, one could not have done anything other than what one did.

The real problem with the *could . . . if . . .* conditionalist proposal is that the notion to be analyzed is part of the proposed analysis. It is unilluminating to propose that what it means to say is that an agent *could have done otherwise* is that he *could have done otherwise* if he had desired (or chosen or tried, etc.). There is some connection between an agent's ability to act and his desire (or intention or choice or volition, etc.): Without the right precursor or explanation, the agent's behavior is not an act at all, and thus if the agent cannot desire (or intend or try, etc.) to *a* at a time, then he does not have the ability to *a* at that time. But what it means to be able or not able to desire or to act (either as one does or otherwise) has not been explicated by the conditionalist proposal under consideration.

Thus the right-minded conditionalist claims that what it means to ascribe to an agent an ability to do some act *a* is that the agent *would* do *a* if she chose (or desired or intended or willed or tried or had good reasons) to do *a*. And hence what it means to say that an agent could have, at a certain time, done otherwise than *a* is that the agent *would have*, at that time, done otherwise than *a* if she had chosen (or desired or intended or willed or tried or had good reasons) at a previous time to do otherwise than *a* at the later time.

This proposal is plausible, the conditionalist argues, because it captures the idea that an agent is *unable* to do otherwise than what she in fact does at a time just in cases in which she is either compelled to do what she does (by an internal force such as a psychological addiction or physiological limitation or paralysis) or coerced into doing what she does (by the manipulation of an external force or agent such as a demonic spirit or, say, a political despot with a cattle prod). In other words, an agent is unable to perform an act other than *a* just in case, *if* she chose to do other than *a*, she *would* not (because of the presence of the compulsion or coercive force). And conversely, to say that an agent is at a time both able to do *a* and able to do not-*a* is to claim that, at the time, there is an absence of internal and external impediments to doing *a*, as well as to doing other than *a*. And this thought is captured by the claim that the agent is able to do otherwise than *a* just in case she would do it if she chose (or intended or desired or tried).

What we care about, according to the compatibilist, is that our actions depend on our choice (or desire or intention or reasons or tryings). And an obstacle that is worth caring about is an obstacle that falsifies the claim that one would perform the action if one chose (or intended or wanted or tried) to do it.

Consider my inability to leap tall buildings in a single bound. Even if I desired (or willed or tried and so on) to do this, I would not. Now the anticonditionalist wants to say this: If I desired to leap tall buildings, I would not—*because* I cannot. My inability explains the truth of the conditional but does not amount to it. In other words, an inability to *a* does not *consist* in the falsity of the proposition that one would *a* if one chose to *a*. The conditionalist, however, maintains this: If I desired to leap tall buildings in a single bound, I would not; *in other words*, I cannot. To assert that I cannot leap tall buildings in a single bound is just to assert that I would not if I desired (or chose or tried) to do so.

If conditionalism is true, then the ability to do otherwise is consistent with determinism. For it might very well be true that one *would* do otherwise *if* one chose to, when it is *determined* by the past and the laws that one will not do otherwise. Hence the first compatibilist argument is this: The *would ... if ...* conditional analysis of the ability to do otherwise is correct; the possession of this ability is sufficient for having free will; therefore, compatibilism is true.

Dennett on Control

Consider an additional argument for compatibilism. The incompatibilist argues by reference to the fixity of the past and the laws of nature that, on the hypothesis of determinism, an agent cannot sufficiently control her own present action. Why can she not control her action? Because what she does is controlled by the past and the laws. But to argue in this way, claims the compatibilist, is to *personify* the past and the natural laws. However, the past and the natural laws neither individually nor together constitute *an agent* with the power to interfere with or to manipulate one's life. It is *not as if* the past and the laws are, for instance, an evil neuroscientist controlling one's thoughts by way of a secret implanted device or, alternately, a divine authoritarian whose puppets we are. The past is only a sequence of events that have taken place, and the laws simply describe the way the physical universe works; neither has any *means* for exercising control over an individual.

Daniel Dennett supports this line of argument with the following analysis of the notion of control: "A *controls* B if and only if the relation between A and B is such that A can *drive* B into whichever of B's normal range of states A *wants* B to be in."[3] A's ability to drive B into some state requires an awareness on the part of A of the range of states into which B can be driven, as well as, Dennett proposes, some feedback from B to A that A can exploit in order to manipulate B's state as desired.

Plainly enough, neither past events (or states of affairs) nor the laws of nature can control anything, on this analysis, given that both lack *wants*. Furthermore, neither past events themselves nor natural laws have any awareness of anything. Moreover, there is no feedback from the present to the past that the past might exploit as a means of control.

Hence the second compatibilist argument, in brief, is this: Since in order for something to be a controller, it must be an agent, and neither the past nor the natural laws are an agent, it follows that the past and the laws cannot be a freedom-obviating external controller on one's actions. Thus determinism is not a threat to free agency.

One may act freely (provided there is no *other* external controller of one's action) even in a deterministic universe.

I turn to examining a third compatibilist argument.

Lehrer on Empirical Evidence

Keith Lehrer proposes the following ingenious sort of argument for the truth of compatibilism: Call the hypothesis that a certain agent could have acted otherwise H_1. Now in the usual case we have a great deal of evidence in favor of this hypothesis. Suppose that the agent in fact made a right turn with his car at a certain intersection and that our claim that he could have done otherwise amounts to the claim that he could have made a left turn instead. (You may notice that the driver could also have pulled the car off the road or gone straight; but for ease of discussion, let us suppose that his doing otherwise amounts in this case only to his having made a left turn, when in fact he turned the car to the right.)

Surely we are justified in asserting that the agent could have done otherwise on the basis of the following evidence: We have observed the man making a left turn with his car many times in the past. In fact, we have seen him previously make a left turn at the very intersection in question. The car appears to be in good working order, exhibiting no tendency to drift or pull to the right. The driver reports that, at the time of his making the right turn, the steering wheel was rotating freely in each direction and that he deliberately guided it to the right (although he *had* guided it to the left just minutes prior in order to make a left turn on a previous street). This evidence makes highly probable H_1.

But notice that this same body of evidence does not make highly probable the hypothesis of indeterminism (the denial of determinism). Call the hypothesis of indeterminism H_2. Our observations of the driver's actions and his car both at the time of the turn and in the past do not lend support to a thesis about the nature of the physical universe. On the face of it, our evidence for H_1 is irrelevant to judging the truth of H_2; at least, that evidence does not (as it does H_1) render highly probable H_2. Consider the following theorem of the calculus of probabilities:

If H_1 is highly probable on some body of evidence e and H_2 is not highly probable on e, then H_1 does not entail H_2.

It follows from this theorem, along with the specifications of the body of evidence and H_1 and H_2 above, that the ability to do otherwise does not entail indeterminism. Hence, if having the ability to do otherwise at a time is sufficient for having free will at that time, then free will does not entail indeterminism; in other words, free will is consistent with determinism, and compatibilism is true.

Incompatibilist Replies

The compatibilist, then, has three forceful arguments in support of his position. If the conditional analysis of ability is independently plausible, and if the possession of this ability at a time is sufficient for having free will at that time, then compatibilism is true. Furthermore, if the past and the laws of nature on the deterministic hypothesis pose no threat to free agency from the consideration of control, then compatibilism is true. And if we have empirical proof for the minimal free will thesis that is not itself proof for physical indeterminism, then compatibilism is arguably true. The following sections present an incompatibilist line of reply to each of these positive compatibilist arguments.

Problems for the Conditional Analysis

Consider first serious difficulties for the *would . . . if . . .* conditional analysis of ability. Critiques in the philosophical literature have taken two forms: one that the conditional account is not *sufficient* for the ability to do otherwise; the other that it is not *necessary*. In the first regard, Roderick Chisholm (1964b) has argued that the proposed conditional, 'would have done otherwise, if he had chosen to', might be true at the same time as it is false that the agent could have done otherwise. This would be the case if the agent was unable to have *chosen* otherwise (though she would have chosen otherwise if she could have): if, for instance, an obsessive-compulsive disorder prevented her from choosing not to scrub the floor rather than to scrub it. So, in the case in which the agent vigorously scrubs the floor, it is true that she would have done otherwise if she had chosen to. But, in the circumstances, she cannot do otherwise, since, as a result of her disorder, she cannot *choose* not to scrub the floor. The same point will apply to the other versions of the *would . . . if*

... analysis. While it is true that the obsessive-compulsive sufferer would have done otherwise if she had desired (or intended or preferred, etc.), she cannot do otherwise than scrub the floor, since she cannot desire (or intend or prefer, etc.) not to scrub it.

One might try to remedy this problem with the conditional analysis by proposing that one could have done otherwise just in case one would have done otherwise if one had chosen (or desired or intended or tried, etc.) *and* one *could have* chosen (or desired or intended or tried, etc.) to do otherwise. But then the italicized "could have" in the previous sentence must be, on conditionalism, given a conditional analysis, so that the proposal becomes this: One could have done otherwise just in case one would have done otherwise if one had chosen (or desired or intended or tried, etc.) *and* one would have chosen otherwise if one had chosen to choose otherwise. But then the same sort of problem cases require the amendment "and one *could have* chosen to choose otherwise." And, of course, this claim to ability is also to be analyzed conditionally, on conditionalism, generating an implausible and endless regress of choices to choose (or desires to desire or intentions to intend, etc.) for the ability to do otherwise.

One might allege that a regress is stopped for a "would have chosen otherwise if S had wanted otherwise" analysis of S's ability to have chosen otherwise, since S's wanting otherwise is not an action itself demanding a further conditional analysis (Davidson 1973). But this move proves unsatisfactory, as a variation on a case from Lehrer[4] demonstrates. Roy buys his wife a dozen white roses. To say that he could have purchased the red ones instead means, according to the conditionalist, just that he would have gotten the red ones if he had chosen to. But Roy has a pathological aversion to blood and so to anything the color of blood. Thus the analysis of his ability to have purchased the red roses, in addition to the "would have if he had chosen to" condition, must include the condition that he could have chosen otherwise.

Now suppose that this latter condition is analyzed in this way: Roy would have chosen otherwise if he had wanted to choose otherwise. But this claim might well be true while at the same time it is impossible for Roy to have wanted otherwise. His pathological aversion is so intense as to affect pervasively his desires; not only can he not choose to purchase something red as a gift for his wife, but he cannot even *want* to choose to purchase something red for her. Thus it remains the case that, while requirements proposed by the conditionalist are satisfied, it is false that the agent could have done otherwise. Hence the conditionalist must add that the agent *could have* wanted otherwise—and if this condition itself is not given a conditional analysis on the grounds that it does not describe an action, then nonetheless it must be given some sort of analysis, and what sort of analysis will the conditionalist give it? It remains the burden of the compatibilist to provide an analysis of the *could have wanted otherwise* condition, to show that it is the right analysis, and to show that it is consistent with the truth of causal determinism.

Therefore, whereas it is initially intuitively appealing to suppose that what it really means to say of an agent that he could have done otherwise at a time is that he would have done otherwise at that time had he previously chosen (or desired or tried, etc.) to do so, conditionalism fails to provide a sufficient account.

It does not provide a necessary condition for the ability to do otherwise, either. Austin has famously argued that the conditionalist's proposed conditional might be false at the same time as it is *true* that one could have done otherwise:

> Consider the case where I miss a very short putt and kick myself because I could have holed it. It is not that I should have holed it if I had tried; I did try, and missed. It is not that I should have holed it if conditions had been different; that might of course be so, but I am talking about conditions as they precisely were, and asserting that I could have holed it. There is the rub.[5]

Austin's point is that the assertion that a person could have done otherwise does not *mean* that the person would have done otherwise if some condition or other had been different (for instance, if she had willed or chosen or tried differently). At least sometimes, the assertion means that she could have done otherwise *given conditions precisely as they were*.

What does it mean to say of Austin that he could have holed the ball? It means, roughly, that he had the skills necessary for holing it and that he had the opportunity for exercising them—nothing prevented him from doing so. But there was some indeterminism between his trying and his holing the ball. As it turned out, given his attempt, he missed. But he might have, in the same conditions and with the same attempt, succeeded instead. One can think of a number of examples of the same sort. Take, for example, the weightlifter who drops his load, announcing in disgust that he could have lifted it. It is not that he would have lifted it successfully if he had wanted to or if he had tried; he *did* want to, and he *did* try. Moreover, his claim to the ability is supported by his having lifted the same amount of weight many times before. Similarly, consider the expert archer who misses the target but plausibly could have hit it— and not only if some condition or other had been different.

But if in some cases an agent's ability to have done otherwise does not amount to the truth of the *would . . . if . . .* claim, then conditionalism fails. Since, as Austin shows, this is precisely the case, conditionalism is unsuccessful.

The True Control Problem

Consider next the second compatibilist argument above: the argument based upon the lack of *control* over our actions on the part of the past and the natural laws. One might, of course, challenge the claim that X's having control over Y requires X's possession of both awareness and desire. The thermostat, one might say, controls the temperature in the house without its having any mental states at all. Likewise, one might describe the shift stick as controlling the gears of the car. It may be countered that both of these examples are of mechanical devices by the use of which *agents* can control some outcome. What is really the case is that I, for instance, control the temperature inside of the house by way of setting the thermostat in a particular manner. And, similarly, the driver of the car controls what gear it is in by means of the shift stick.

But whether A's controlling B depends upon A's having awareness and desire is, in fact, irrelevant to the matter at hand. At issue in the debate over free will is the possibility of agent control, and agents have, anyway, capacities for awareness and desire. What is it for some event or state of affairs to be under the control of an agent? I proposed in the previous chapter an analysis of the notion of its being 'up to agent S at t whether or not it is the case that P'. Another way to express this notion is as its being *under the control of S* at t whether or not it is the case that P. This relation holds between S and P at t just in case the following is true: $A_{S,t} P$ and $A_{S,t} (\neg P)$. Then it is not up to S at t whether or not it is the case that P just in case either $\neg A_{S,t} P$ or $\neg A_{S,t} (\neg P)$. This proposal for explicating agent control is consistent with Dennett's analysis of A's control over B *if* A's ability "to drive B into *whichever* of B's normal range of states A wants B to be in" (emphasis changed) includes A's being able at a time to make it the case that B is in state Z *and* A's being able at that time to make it the case that B is in a state other than Z.

But if so, then Dennett's analysis itself helps to show why the truth of determinism rules out agent control over future events or states of affairs. For an agent cannot at a time be able to make it the case that P and at that same time able to make it the case that $\neg P$ if only *one of* either P or $\neg P$ is physically possible at the time. According to the deterministic thesis, there is at every moment exactly one physically possible future.

I am arguing that granting the Dennett analysis of control does not force one to admit the truth of compatibilism. For free will and determinism may be incompatible for reasons other than the consideration that, on determinism, the past and the laws are *controllers* of current actions. What exactly is the alleged threat that determinism poses to free agency? The incompatibilist's concern is that the truth of determinism does not allow for our actions to be attributable to any genuine selves because our actions, given determinism, are attributable to past events and states of affairs. On the assumption of determinism, what we do now is the necessary unfolding of our genetic makeup and of how our parents (and others in our formative environments) impacted us, which in turn was the necessary unfolding of *their* genetic constitution and how *their* parents (and others in their formative environments) behaved toward them, which was the necessary unfolding of factors in the previous generation, and so on backward into history before we ourselves were born. The incompatibilist's (at least my own) central concern is that the truth of determinism does not leave room for genuine authorship of action; it does not leave any causal openness into which an agent can assert himself to initiate a change of course.

Of course the incompatibilist does not make the mistake of taking the past or the natural laws in themselves to be agential. But events in the past, some of them the actions of other persons and some of them the actions of (previous stages of) oneself, given the laws and the assumption of determinism, do *drive* the events of the present, including our present actions. They drive them in the sense that they push them into being what they are: The past events causally necessitate precisely those (and no other) present events. The past events' occurrence, given determinism, is *sufficient for* the occurrence of the particular present events that occur. And this leaves no "elbow room" for free agency, for full agential control. Hence the compatibilist argument based upon an analysis of control such as Dennett's fails to show that determinism is consistent with free will.

Contra Lehrer

Here is a rebuttal to Lehrer provided by van Inwagen. Many hypotheses about the nature of the world are consistent with our observations of it but inconsistent with our ever being able to do otherwise than we do. Consider, for instance, the following hypothesis.

> (M): When any human being is born, the Martians implant in his brain a tiny device—one that is undetectable by any observational technique we have at our disposal, though it is not *in principle* undetectable—which contains a "program" for that person's entire life: whenever that person must make a decision, the device causes him to decide one way or the other [without his having any phenomenological evidence of this causation] according to the requirements of a table of instructions that were incorporated into the structure of the device before that person was conceived. [6]

It is true that we have evidence in favor of the minimal free will thesis. With regard to a specific agent, the claim that he was able to have done otherwise than he did at a time is supported in a great many cases by our having seen the agent do otherwise in quite similar circumstances in the past. But our evidence rendering highly probable the hypothesis that an agent could have acted otherwise at a time (including, for instance, our observations of his having acted otherwise in very similar circumstances in the past) does *not* render highly probable the denial of (M). Thus, by Lehrer's argument, the hypothesis that the agent could have acted otherwise at a time is compatible with the truth of (M). But this is an obviously false conclusion. Hence, Lehrer's empirical argument for compatibilism is flawed.

Of course, one might counter that the body of evidence rendering highly probable the hypothesis that the agent in a particular case could have done otherwise does, in fact, render highly probable the denial of (M)—for (M) is *obviously* inconsistent with any agent's having free will, so evidence in favor of some agent's having free will is *thereby* evidence for the falsity of (M). Indeed, Lehrer indicates that this is the line of reply he favors.[7] However, as Lehrer himself notices, one's assessment of the strength of this reply is dependent upon how obvious it seems to one that the thesis of causal determinism is inconsistent with free will. For if it is *as* obvious to one that determinism rules out an agent's ever being able to do otherwise as it is that the hypothesis (M) rules out an agent's ever being able to do otherwise, then, by Lehrer's line of reply, the body of evidence rendering highly probable the hypothesis that an agent could have done otherwise *does* thereby render highly probable the denial of determinism; and therefore the original argument for compatibilism based on appeal to empirical evidence is undercut. Hence this line of reply is, in my view, unpersuasive, and the point against the compatibilist argument stands.

Compatibilist Conceptions of Freedom

Thus far in our treatment of the problem of free will we have examined no proposals concerning what specifically constitutes the nature of a free act. Hence what I propose to do now is to examine some compatibilist proposals in this regard. The point is this: Although I have identified no successful positive argument for compatibilism, nonetheless, various philosophers have developed accounts of what it *is* to act freely that are consistent with the deterministic hypothesis. On each of these different conceptions of free action, one may act freely even in a deterministic universe. Hence if one of these accounts answers powerfully to our intuitions, then free action is, as it turns out, consistent with the thesis of causal determinism and does not, contrary to the widely purveyed view in philosophical tradition, require the ability to do otherwise. I turn to examining several of these proposals.

Unilevel Views

At the outset of this book, I characterized the question of the existence of free will in this way: Does the way the world is (including its past, present circumstances, and natural laws) allow for us to act freely in a deep sense, such that our actions are truly attributable to ourselves rather than to something external to us, such as social conditioning or genetic and neurophysiological programming or brainwashing or some other external coercive force? Compatibilist free will theorists rightly focus on the task of delineating what is internal and what is external to the self and moreover stress that it is the *lack* of external coercion of action or motive that fundamentally characterizes free action. From the fact that an act is causally derivative from the past, even in a causally deterministic way, it does not follow, the compatibilist maintains, that the act is the result of an external or coercive force. An act is free, in other words, if it is derivative from the self and is not controlled by anyone or anything external to the self.

One way of drawing the limits of the self is by desire. It is, indeed, a natural root idea in characterizing free action that one acts freely in acting as one wants. Call this the "basic account." Consider a person who is able to get what he desires. For instance, suppose that Harley wants to ride his cycle for days on the open road, feeling the sun and wind on his face, and that he has the means and the time for accomplishing his wish. Harley apparently has all of the freedom that anyone could want. Physical restraints, commitments, and obligations to others "tie one down"; they restrict one's freedom by obstructing one's spontaneous pursuit of the objects of one's whims and passions. In acting on desire, an agent seems to express his self—he shows to the world who he is by carrying out in action his wishes. Thus the basic account has initial intuitive appeal.

But there are problems with the view of freedom as the absence of obstacles to the fulfillment of desire. For one, philosophers have pointed out that, in acting as one wants, one might frustrate one's more ultimate ends and so, in an important sense, bind rather than liberate oneself. Desires themselves can be enslaving, and the care-free pursuit of the satisfaction of each of one's passions is not the right model of a fully free human life.

The central difficulty for the basic account is that even *wants* can be heteronomous. This difficulty divides into two problems. First is an *external manipulation problem*. One can want to do something only because of certain features of the environment or because one's wants are imposed. Harley's desire for a ride on the open road, for instance, may have been induced in the unsuspecting indoor-loving Harley under hypnosis. Since desires can be implanted or coercively imposed in various ways (by means of guilt, social conditioning, brainwashing, implantation by an evil demon or neuroscientist), not every action on the basis of desire is free. Additionally, the basic account faces what may be called an *internal conflict problem:* a problem of conflict within the agent. Here the problem cases are those in which certain desires are acted upon (in some cases because the desires are so strong as to be irresistible) while at the same time from an internal viewpoint they are disdained. Even if a desire is not imposed on the agent by an external source, still it may be one that the agent wishes he did not have or in some way repudiates, so that in acting on that desire, the agent frustrates rather than expresses his self. The repetitive acts of self-injection on the part of a heroin addict who hates her addiction are an example. Thus whereas, as a first approximation, free action amounts to action done on the basis of desire, this account is in need of revision.

Desires and Values

One way of addressing these problems is to distinguish between a person's appetitive aspect and his rational one, understood in a Platonic sense. What a person desires (that is, what he desires *not* as the result of reflection on what is worthy of desiring) is seen as a mere passion, whereas what he values or judges best is viewed as what he *really* wants. In his brilliantly written paper "Free Agency," Gary Watson points out the possibility of a split between these aspects of a person's psychology—between, as he puts it, the *motivational* and the *valuational* systems of an agent. It is in this distinction, Watson proposes, that the key to characterizing unfree action lies: Unfree actions occur when these two systems do not completely coincide.

An agent acts freely, then, in acting on values, which Watson describes as "those principles and ends which he—in a cool and non-self-deceptive moment—articulates as definitive of the good, fulfilling, and defensible life."[8]

Call the proposal that one acts freely in acting upon one's values the "modified basic account." It is clear how the modified account is intended to solve the internal conflict problem for the basic account described above. Not all desires reflect what an agent really wants, and so not all action on desire is self-expressive, or free. The unfree nature of the actions on the part of the addict who hates her addiction may be accounted for in this way: She desires, but does not value, the injection of the heroin. One's normative judgments, on the modified account, define the limits of one's true self: "One cannot dissociate oneself from all normative judgements without forfeiting all standpoints and therewith one's identity as an agent," Watson writes.[9] Thus in acting against her principles, the unhappy (internally conflicted) addict demonstrates her enslavement rather than her freedom.

I find deeply insightful the conception of the agent according to which one's judgments concerning what is worthwhile to pursue are central to who one is. And it is the coupling of this view of an agent's central identity with the understanding of free acts as self-revealing or self-expressive acts that yields the view that acting freely requires acting on one's valuational system. But the modified view cannot stand as it is. One problem is that the conception of the central self on which it rests is too narrow. In "Free Agency," Watson variously describes the agent's values as "what he most wants" (as the outcome of reflection on what is good and worthy) and as his "all-things-considered judgements," relying most heavily on the latter description. But these are surely distinct states—the former a form of desire, the latter a form of belief—both of which deserve inclusion in the account of the self. (One might call the former, as I do in the subsequent chapter, a *preference* and the latter an *acceptance*.)

It is the description of values as all-things-considered judgments that Watson subsequently picks up as the basis for his later repudiation of what I've called the modified view. The picture defended in "Free Agency," he later concludes, is "too rationalistic," since not all desires or states of affairs that one might *value* in a particular

context are ones that one would judge to be good and rationally defensible from a general evaluational standpoint. For instance, one
might choose to do a thrilling act on some occasion (throw caution
to the wind and buy $1,000 worth of lottery tickets, say) rather than
some contrary act one judges to be best; and, Watson alleges, in
committing the thrilling act, one acts freely, since "one's will is fully
behind what one does."[10] The move from delimiting the self by
mere desire to delimiting it by *value* (sufficiently defined) does, in
my view, make some progress over the basic account. However,
Watson's later assessment is correct in this respect: The conception
of the agent according to which he is to be identified with and only
with the general normative principles he would defend in a calm and
non-self-deceptive moment is not sufficiently expansive.

A further problem for the modified account is that it does not
solve the external manipulation problem. One's judgments concerning what is best and defensible may be coercively imposed. Even if
one requires a source in reflective deliberation for the conception of
a *value,* still the problem remains that one's reflective deliberation
might proceed as it does because that is the only way it *can* possibly
proceed, due to hypnosis or brainwashing, or due to the past and
the laws, or due to the control of an external divine or human agent.

Hierarchical Approaches

An alternate approach to dealing with problems for the account of
free action as action on desire is one made famous by Harry Frankfurt and refined and defended by a number of compatibilist philosophers.[11] The foundational insight of the approach is this: Not only
do we persons have capacities for desire and belief, but further we
have the capacity to reflect upon our desires and beliefs themselves,
forming higher-level evaluative and desiring states about those first-
level states. In his widely influential paper "Freedom of the Will and
the Concept of a Person," Frankfurt (1971) proposes that what
makes a desire to perform some act internal to the agent is that
agent's having a second-order desire to have that very desire. Hence a
desire that is not endorsed at the second level is an impediment, and
one acts freely when one acts on a desire that one desires to have.

Such approaches to characterizing free action are called "hierarchical" because they make appeal to a hierarchy of desires, including

both desires to pursue some course of action or another and desires that have as their intentional objects other desires. So, for instance, one might desire to stay up late to watch the end of a movie, but one might desire to desire to get right to sleep, perhaps because one has an important interview in the morning. In Frankfurt's terminology, a second-order volition is a second-order desire that some particular first-level desire be one's will (by which Frankfurt means one's effective desire—the desire that leads or would lead the person to act when or if she acts). So, to take our example, if one succeeds in acquiring the desire to get right to sleep and, while desiring to desire this and while desiring that this desire constitute one's will, one acts on the desire (by turning off the television and going to sleep), then one acts freely because one's will is *one's own*. Frankfurt and other proponents of hierarchical accounts, then, identify the true self with higher-order volitions.

To notice the capacity of persons for forming higher-order mental states is subtle and important. But two particularly difficult problems have been raised for hierarchical accounts of free action. I'll consider each in turn.

The Regress Problem. One is a problem of regress. In fact, hierarchical accounts endorsing some counterfactual condition face *two* separate regress problems. Consider, for instance, Frankfurt's account of freedom of the will (distinct from his account of acting freely), which requires that the agent *could have* made some other first-level desire his will. Whereas Frankfurt himself claims his account to be neutral with respect to the compatibilism and incompatibilism debate, for the compatibilist, the ability to do otherwise required by the Frankfurt freedom-of-the-will account is understood conditionally rather than categorically. So to say that the agent could have made some other first-level desire his will is just to say that the agent *would* have made some other first-level desire his will *if* he had wanted to. One regress problem derives from the compatibilist's reliance on a conditional account of this ability-to-do-otherwise requirement. The regress can be expressed in this way: One's will (effective desire) is freely had just in case it is one's will because one has a second-order volition for it to be one's will and one could have willed otherwise—one would have succeeded in making some other first-level desire one's will, instead, if one had wanted, at the second level, for it to be so. But since the conditional can be true while it is false that one could have willed otherwise, it must be added that one could have wanted, at the second level, to will otherwise. However, in order to know whether or not one could have had a different second-order volition, we must know whether or not it is true that one would have had a different second-order volition if one had wanted, at the third level, for it to be so. But the second-order volition's being freely had requires that the third-level volition in its favor be freely had, which requires that the fourth-level volition be freely had, and so on.

The second and more-discussed regress problem affects both hierarchical accounts with a counterfactual condition and those without one, such as Frankfurt's account of acting freely. To appreciate this regress, consider Frankfurt's description of a willing addict: a person who wants to take the drug and who endorses this desire at the second level (so that he wants to want to take the drug). Even though he could not have done otherwise and could not have had a different will, because of his addiction, it is Frankfurt's intuition that the willing addict acts freely in taking the drug because he is not conflicted over his action: The desire on which he acts is "his own"—that is, favored to be his will at the second level.

But then the account of what makes a desire appropriately action-guiding is apparently just that the desire is itself desired to be action-guiding at the next higher level. So in response to the pertinent question of what makes a particular second-order volition itself authoritative in establishing what is a genuine reason for acting, the hierarchical theorist must posit an endorsing third-level volition. And this volition itself confers authority for directing action on its object only if it itself is favored at the fourth level, and so on.

The problem is not just that one *might* be driven to higher and higher levels of reflection by self-doubt and indecision, but that one positively *must* be so driven in order for one's will to count as one's own. For in the absence of some other account of what makes some desire a *genuine reason* for me to act, the vicious regress of higher and higher levels of desires granting authority for guiding my action stands.

The Identification Problem. A second difficulty for hierarchical accounts is to provide a convincing answer to the question of why higher-level desires, formed for any reason whatsoever, should count as any more the agent's own than the first-level desires. This is the identification problem. In claiming that the willing addict, for instance, acts freely in taking the drug because his will is "his own," we presuppose that an agent's "identifying with" some first-level desire amounts to his having a second-level volition for it and thus that his identity—his real self—is constituted by his second-order volitions. But why suppose that this is an accurate characterization of what the agent *really wants* or of his *real self*? Frankfurt is explicit about the fact that second-order desires do not necessarily represent a person's moral standards or ideals:

> It may not be from the point of view of morality that the person evaluates his first-order desires. Moreover, a person may be capricious and irresponsible in forming his second-order volitions and give no serious consideration to what is at stake. . . . There is no essential restriction on the kind of basis, if any, upon which [second-order volitions] are formed.[12]

Thus second-level desires are just other desires that may be formed on any basis or on no basis at all. And therefore it is mysterious why a desire to desire to *a* makes a desire to *a* internal to the self, whereas a desire to *b* lacking a corresponding second-level desire counts as external. As Watson points out, higher-order desires are just desires, and "nothing about their level gives them any special authority with respect to externality. If they have that authority they are given it by something else."[13]

Nothing in Frankfurt's account successfully rules out second-order volitions' being externally imposed. Indeed, since an entire hierarchical structure of desires might be imposed on the agent by an outside force or agent, not only does the hierarchical approach have difficulty solving what we earlier called the internal conflict problem, but furthermore it needs an answer to the external manipulation problem.

New Directions

Subsequent to his 1971 paper, Frankfurt abandoned the attempt to characterize an agent's identification with particular motivations or courses of action wholly in terms of hierarchies of desires. In his later "Identification and Externality" (1977) and "Identification and Wholeheartedness" (1987a) papers, Frankfurt puts hope in the notion of *decision*, commenting that "decisions, unlike desires or attitudes, do not seem to be susceptible both to internality and to externality"[14] and proposing that sequences of desires of increasingly higher orders are terminated by decision "made without reservation."[15] Subsequent to this, however, based upon noticing even the phenomena of decisions with which a person fails to identify, Frankfurt again changes course and settles in a 1991 address on the view that "identification is constituted neatly by an endorsing higher-order desire with which the person is satisfied."[16] One's being "satisfied" with a desire does not require an endorsing higher-level desire (avoiding the regress problem) but consists, instead, in "simply *having no interest in* making changes."[17]

One might rightly worry about the sufficiency of Frankfurt's latest notion of psychic satisfaction for accounting fully for agential identification with motivation and action. Michael Bratman has recently argued that, in addition, some sort of decision is required, which he proposes is a decision to treat a certain desire as reason-giving in practical deliberation and planning. Further, Bratman argues, in order for one to identify with one's desire, not only must one *decide* to treat it as reason-giving, but also one must actually *treat* it as reason-giving or at least be fully prepared to treat it as reason-giving were an appropriate occasion to arise.[18] Bratman does not take his proposal to be an account of free action, but rather of the notion of identification with desire. Nonetheless, the account does indicate one of the new directions available to compatibilist free will theorists in departing from the basic, modified, and hierarchical accounts we have considered.[19] It remains open to the incompatibilist to respond that our reflectiveness—no matter how complex—is insufficient for grounding freedom, for with respect to any instance of our *psychic satisfaction* or our *decision*, it must be asked whether it could have been otherwise.

We have identified no wholly successful compatibilist account of the nature of free action. I conclude that no such account is sufficiently unproblematic and robust to convince us either to overturn our judgments of the soundness of the incompatibilist arguments of the previous chapter or to give up the intuitively powerful requirement for the possession of free will of the (nonconditionally analyzed but instead categorical) ability to do otherwise.

Notes

1. Clarence Darrow argued that people who committed crimes were not responsible because determinism is true, and that conclusion seemed intuitive to jurors, which shows that the intuition regarding responsibility depends upon what is assumed metaphysically. "Sufficient statistics have been gathered," Darrow wrote, "to warrant the belief that every case of crime could be accounted for on purely scientific grounds if all the facts bearing on the case were known: defective nervous systems, lack of education or technical training, poor heredity, poor early environment, emotional imbalance." His arguments proved effective for many defendants. Quoted in Irving Stone, *Clarence Darrow for the Defense* (Garden City, NY: Doubleday and Company, 1941), p. 92.

2. J. L. Austin, "Ifs and Cans," in *Philosophical Papers* (Oxford: Oxford University Press, 1961).

3. Daniel Dennett, *Elbow Room: The Varieties of Free Will Worth Wanting* (Cambridge, MA: MIT Press, 1984), p. 52.

4. Keith Lehrer, "Cans Without Ifs," *Analysis* 29, 1968, pp. 29–32.

5. Austin, "Ifs and Cans," p. 218.

6. van Inwagen, *Essay on Free Will*, p. 109.

7. Keith Lehrer, personal correspondence with the author, dated October 15, 1998.

8. Gary Watson, "Free Agency," *Journal of Philosophy* 72, 1975; reprinted in Gary Watson, ed., *Free Will* (Oxford: Oxford University Press), 1982, p. 105.

9. Ibid., p. 106.

10. Gary Watson, "Free Action and Free Will," *Mind* 46, 1987, p. 150.

11. Harry Frankfurt, "Freedom of the Will and the Concept of a Person," *Journal of Philosophy* 68, 1971, pp. 5–20. See also Richard Jeffrey, "Preferences Among Preferences," *Journal of Philosophy* 71, 1974, pp. 377–391; Keith Lehrer, "Preferences, Conditionals and Freedom," in Peter van Inwagen, ed., *Time and Cause* (Dordrecht, Holland: D. Reidel, 1980). Insightful discussions of the hierarchical approach include Irving Thalberg, "Hierarchical Analyses of Unfree Action," *Canadian Journal of Philosophy* 8, 1978, pp. 211–226; and David Shatz, "Free Will and the Structure of Motivation," *Midwest Studies in Philosophy* 10, 1986, pp. 451–482.

12. Frankfurt, "Freedom of the Will," in Watson, *Free Will*, p. 89, note 6.

13. Watson, "Free Action and Free Will," p. 149.

14. Harry Frankfurt, "Identification and Externality," in Amelie Rorty, ed., *The Identities of Persons* (Berkeley: University of California Press, 1977); reprinted in Harry Frankfurt, *The Importance of What We Care About* (Cambridge: Cambridge University Press, 1987), p. 68 and note 68.

15. Harry Frankfurt, "Identification and Wholeheartedness," in Ferdinand Schoeman, ed., *Responsibility, Character, and the Emotions: New Essays in Moral Psychology* (Cambridge: Cambridge University Press, 1987); reprinted in Frankfurt, *What We Care About*, p. 170.

16. Harry Frankfurt, "The Faintest Passion," *Proceedings and Addresses of the American Philosophical Association* 66, 1992, p. 14.

17. Ibid.

18. Michael Bratman, "Identification, Decision, and Treating as a Reason," *Philosophical Topics* 24, 1996, p. 12.

19. For some alternate ways of dealing with both the regress and the identification problems, see Laura Waddell Ekstrom, "A Coherence Theory of Autonomy," *Philosophy and Phenomenological Research* 53, 1993, pp. 599–616 (in which I respond to the regress of reasons for acting in the hierarchical account of free action as epistemological coherentists have responded to the epistemic regress of reasons for belief); Eleonore Stump, "Sanctification, Hardening of the Heart, and Frankfurt's Concept of Free Will," *Journal of Philosophy* 85, 1988, pp. 395–412; and Keith Lehrer, *Self-Trust: A Study of Reason, Knowledge, and Autonomy* (Oxford: Clarendon Press, 1997), chap. 4.

CHAPTER FOUR

Varieties of Libertarianism

Bolstered by the sophisticated work of the past two decades designed to demonstrate the incompatibility of free will and determinism—including arguments by van Inwagen, Fischer, Ginet, and others, discussed in Chapter 2—many incompatibilists now rest confident in their incompatibilist position. But that confidence has a way of turning to unease when incompatibilists are asked to articulate their own accounts of the nature of free action and free will. In what way precisely is the assumption of indeterminism friendly to the cause of freedom? Insofar as indeterminacy is associated with chaos and randomness, the truth of the thesis of indeterminism would seem not only to be unrequired for the right account of freedom, but further to be positively antithetical to it. For an act done of one's own free will is an act under one's own control *in excelsis*, yet an act undetermined by a chain of previous events, and hence subject to some indeterminacy, seems an act produced from randomness and not under control.

Arguments for incompatibilism such as van Inwagen's First Argument rest upon the requirement for freedom that an agent be able at the time of acting to do otherwise than she does, where this ability is understood in a categorical, and not a conditional, sense.[1] Given the actual reigning laws and conditions, the free agent is taken to be able to perform more than one action, and her possession of this ability means not only that she has the appropriate faculties for performing a multiple number of actions, but further that she can in the circumstances exercise them. The incompatibilist argument is grounded upon, in other words, an understanding of freedom according to which it must be undetermined by natural laws and events of the past what the free agent will do next.

But holding fixed *everything* about the past up until the moment of action, including even the agent's preference or judgment about what to do next, and maintaining that, crucial to the agent's freedom is her ability to do otherwise than what she, at an immediately prior moment, prefers or judges best to do, presents an extremely puzzling picture of free agency. Is this *where* the incompatibilist proposes to locate the requisite indeterminism—between the agent's preference for acting and her subsequent action? If not, then where else instead?

This chapter takes up these and other fundamental problems for setting out a precise account of the nature of free action encapsulated in the intuitions driving the incompatibilist argument. I first elaborate the central difficulties for presenting an incompatibilist free will theory, giving sense to critics' judgments that some sort of compatibilist analysis of free will *must* be right, since all incompatibilist accounts are doomed to failure through incoherency. Our first question, then, is whether or not an indeterminist model of free agency *can* be made coherent. I believe the answer to this question is affirmative and that many of the prominent critical worries about incompatibilist free will accounts can be assuaged. If so, then, second, what is the best *sort* of indeterminist account that can be offered, the one with the fewest problems and the one best answering to the deep-seated and pervasive conception of ourselves as agents with incompatibilist freedom?

The present chapter thus addresses head-on the perplexing but crucial task of giving a positive incompatibilist theory of the nature of free agency. The chapter sets out various sorts of incompatibilist accounts of freedom, some of which have, in my judgment, more strength and plausibility than others. This discussion leads to the development of a new indeterminist model of free action. I defend this model of free action as superior to competing accounts.

Some philosophers have taken commitment to incompatibilism to imply commitment to a theory of free will invoking a notion of the causation of an event by an *agent* as substance, where this is taken to be fundamentally irreducible to the causation of that event by other events. For instance, in speaking of "the fundamental watershed, in philosophical anthropology, between those who think of human beings as free" in an incompatibilist sense and "adherents of determinism," Alvin Plantinga writes that "what is really at stake in this discussion is the notion of agent causation: the notion of a person as an ultimate source of action."[2] We will look at accounts of freedom appealing to an *agent as cause* as a primitive notion. But incompatibilists have other options for constructing a free will theory. In fact, despite recent attempts to revive the sort of libertarian theory appealing to agent-causation and arguments to the effect that any hope for providing a defensible incompatibilist account of freedom lies in this direction,[3] I want nonetheless to explore here a fuller variety of indeterminist options and ultimately to endorse an account *not* reliant upon the existence of an irreducible form of nonoccurent- or agent-causation.

A large part of the work of this chapter may thus be seen by some as an in-house matter for incompatibilists: that of determining which sort of incompatibilist conception of freedom ought to be endorsed. Since, however, I take the truth of incompatibilism to be demonstrated by successful argument, in my view, this task holds significance for anyone interested in free will, for the matter is, ultimately, the discernment of the *right* or best account of free will. Even those unconvinced of the truth of incompatibilism nonetheless might take an interest in seeing whether or not a successful incompatibilist account of freedom can be worked out. As a benefit to the recalcitrant compatibilist, our discussion here will provide a number of libertarian accounts of freedom for critique.

Libertarianism and Indeterminism

Typically the term 'libertarian' has been used to refer to those incompatibilists who maintain that persons in fact possess free will and hence that the thesis of determinism must be false, whereas an incompatibilist, speaking more generally, might remain neutral concerning the question of freedom's actual instantiation (or even take a negative stance, as does what is sometimes called the 'hard determinist'). But in describing various accounts of free will as libertarian, I do not mean to imply that a defender of such an account necessarily takes free will to be actually possessed by anyone. In using the term, I mean only to group together different accounts of the nature of free will by their common starting point—namely, the contention that a theoretical requirement for free will is that determinism be false. I will describe theories of free will sharing this assumption as 'indeterminist', 'incompatibilist', and 'libertarian', using the terms here interchangeably.

Libertarian theories have been famously charged with being "obscure," "incoherent," and, on some versions, guilty of "panicky metaphysics."[4] According to Arthur Schopenhauer, for instance, the libertarian makes every free action "an inexplicable miracle, an effect without a cause."[5] Libertarians themselves sometimes admit to a certain degree of theoretical impenetrability. Richard Taylor, in speaking of his own version of libertarian theory, comments that "one can hardly affirm such a theory of agency with complete comfort and wholly without embarrassment, for the conception of men and their powers which is involved in it is strange indeed, if not positively mysterious."[6] Especially in light of such admissions, one can understand the suspicion cast in the direction of incompatibilist free will theorists.

But mere bad press from critics (and even some proponents) is not the fundamental problem for libertarian theory. Rather, certain ways of dealing with what are the fundamental problems give rise to accounts that are vulnerable to such charges. Alternate ways of dealing with the central difficulties, however, are not so vulnerable. That is to say, while objections such as the above of incoherency and "panicked" theorizing are perhaps accurately lodged against certain libertarian accounts of the past, I believe that they can be rebuffed by a number of different sorts of contemporary indeterminist account. Let me lead into those accounts by first explaining what I see to be the fundamental problems for incompatibilist free will theory.

The First Problem: Indeterminism Where?

The construction of an intelligible incompatibilist theory of freedom must begin with the libertarian assumption: If we ever act and choose freely, then it is the case that, given the past and the laws of nature, at some moment t (or at some moments $t1, t2, t3, \ldots$), there is *more than one physically possible future*.

But to assert as a metaphysical precondition of free will that, at some moment(s), given the actual laws and past, multiple physically possible futures exist, does not yet locate agents at the crucial junctures. In other words, the denial of determinism does not *itself* provide an interpretation of the alternative-possibilities condition of freedom, since the denial does not itself say anything directly about agents. In order to present a complete account of freedom, the incompatibilist needs to explain in what ways determinism must be false, to say when and where the indeterminism that allows for agents' production of free actions and free choices is *located*. Where precisely are the *gaps* that must exist in nature in the chain of deterministic causal links between events in order to allow for human free will? The mere truth of indeterminism does not ensure that persons can act and choose freely.

This problem for all libertarian theories may be elaborated as follows. Indeterminism is a negative thesis: It claims what is not the case. Specifically, indeterminism is the denial of the thesis of determinism. Indeterminism says that it is not the case that, given the actual past and the actual laws of nature, there is at every moment exactly one possible future. Alternately (and, I take it, equivalently), indeterminism holds that *not* every event is causally necessitated by prior events. Libertarians in common endorse this negative thesis. (Some incompatibilists concerning free will and determinism are, then, compatibilists concerning free will and indeterminism.)

But here is the problem: There are various ways in which it can fail to be the case that every event is causally necessitated by prior events. That is, there are various propositions about the actual world that, if true, would entail the truth of indeterminism. Since this is so, commitment to the compatibility of indeterminism and free will (indeed, further, the requirement of the former for the latter) is where unanimity ends among incompatibilist believers in free will concerning the metaphysical preconditions of free will.[7] Libertarians divide over the matter of precisely in what way the falsity of determinism allows for the agential possession of free will.

Libertarians, then, share the problem of providing a positive thesis concerning the metaphysical conditions enabling free will. Without a solution to the *where's the indeterminism?* problem, libertarian accounts of the nature of free will cannot get off the ground. This problem is the central, most significant difficulty for the endeavor of presenting a plausible incompatibilist account of the nature of free action: locating the requisite indeterminism in the causal history of the act, together with explaining why this precise location is appropriate and important.

The Second Problem:
Distinguishing Free Acts from Mere Accidents

A further problem for libertarians is readily apparent: If what the free agent does at a given moment is not determined by the natural laws and the past, including even the agent's immediately previous preference concerning what to do, then what *is* it determined by? Anything at all? If nothing, then what makes the act any different from a fluke or an accident? Incompatibilists intend in speaking of agential freedom to refer to something other than haphazard events that occur *willy-nilly*, do they not?

Of course, they do. The challenge, once having located the causal indeterminism required for the account, is to explain how it is that the event constituting the agent's action counts as sufficiently his own, sufficiently under his control, to be rightly called freely done by him. Some theorists refer to this as the *problem of control*. The problem gains force from the common philosophical assumption that a certain event is under control insofar as its causally antecedent events determine it to occur. If causal determination by prior events does, in fact, exhaust the scope of the notion of control, then incompatibilists indeed have a very serious problem: Any event that is undetermined by previous events is out of control and hence, it would appear, merely accidental. Incompatibilists, then, must examine the notion of control and explain how, on their own particular accounts, the free agent's act is grounded in his agency and is not a haphazard or accidental happening.

Competing Incompatibilist Accounts:
T-1, A-C, and T-3 Theories

Some ways of dealing with the above two problems generate libertarian theories of free agency that, in my view, are more susceptible to concerns of implausibility and "panicked" metaphysical speculation than are other sorts of indeterminist accounts. Accounts appealing to such factors as power centers that somehow transcend the empirical realm, noumenal selves, or the "Will" as uncaused homunculus within the agent are, in my view, examples.[8] In structuring our discussion of the various viable options for theory construction available to the libertarian, I will trace answers to the *where's the indeterminism?* question, critically examining each alternative especially with an eye toward the problem of control.

I will begin with what I take to be the least plausible libertarian view concerning indeterminism's enablement of free agency. Certainly the libertarian should not claim that indeterminism located immediately prior to an agent's overt bodily movement suffices for free action. An indeterminately caused twitch or sneeze fits this description, even one indeterminately produced by a remote control device activating wiring connected to a person's neurological system. A free act is, of course, in the first place *an action*. The free will theorist's challenge is to identify the conditions that must be added to the analysis of an action to yield *free* action, and the libertarian's particular challenge is to pin down the proper location for the indeterminism she thinks is required to convert action into action that is free.

So we need a characterization of action. The most obvious observation is that an action is a particular sort of event (or perhaps a process, a series of events)⁹, in either case describable as the bringing about of something *by someone*. But ease of agreement, naturally, turns among philosophers immediately to controversy. Some theorists have held that all acts are preceded by a distinctive mental act called *volition*. Other theories of action do not appeal to the notion of volition, but instead, in distinguishing acts from other events, make use of the fact that acts are intentionally done. According to Donald Davidson's well-known suggestion (1980), there are unintended acts, but the events constituting those acts count as acts at all only in virtue of being intentionally done *under some description*.

What is it to act intentionally? According to some theorists (Anscombe 1963; Goldman 1970; Davidson 1980; Audi 1973; Churchland 1970), to act intentionally is to act on desires and beliefs, such that the act stands in the appropriate relation to those desires and beliefs. (Goldman, like Davidson in his early work, maintains that the appropriate relation is causal; Anscombe disagrees.) Some proponents of a desire-belief model of intentional action (for instance, Audi) also endorse a desire-belief model of *intention*. On a desire-belief model, an intention to act is to be identified with some desire-belief complex.

Many current theorists reject the desire-belief model of intention.¹⁰ Michael Bratman (1987) is a prominent critic of the model, basing his case against it largely on the existence of future-directed intentions. These are, he thinks, the "building blocks" of plans, where plans play a crucial role in coordination and ongoing practical reasoning. Intending to act, Bratman argues, is a distinctive mental attitude, not reducible to a combination of desire and belief. Bratman and others have noticed that intending to do something implies *commitment* to the action beyond merely desiring it. So, for instance, my wanting to go to the American Philosophical Association meeting and my believing that if I take a certain flight, then I'll get there, is not equivalent to my *intending* to go to the meeting. The latter implies commitment to going, having a plan to go, whereas the former does not.

A variety of matters in the theory of action are complex and remain contested. And a complication for taxonomizing different sorts of libertarian theory is that proponents of particular accounts of free action often rely upon differing accounts of the nature of action *simpliciter*. In the following characterizations of different types of libertarian theories, I have deliberately left some ambiguity concerning whether it is the action itself, a crucial component of the action, or a particular precursor to the action that is the subject of the crucial event-causal indeterminism—precisely in order to account for this fact. The characterizations are intended to be sufficiently general to group together the three basic sorts of particular libertarian accounts, according to the three different ways in which an act could fail to be the causally deterministic outcome of a chain of deterministically linked events.[11]

Libertarian theories, then, may be classified into the following three sorts.

Theory Type 1 (T-1 Theories): An agent is free with respect to a particular action only if that action is event-causally undetermined in the sense that the action (or a crucial component of, or precursor to, it) is *uncaused*.

Theory Type 2 (A-C Theories): An agent is free with respect to a particular action only if that action is event-causally undetermined in the sense that the action (or a crucial component of, or precursor to, it) is causally determined not by another event, but rather by *the agent* himself or herself. (I call these "A-C" theories for *"agent-causation"*—hyphenated to designate the proposed causal relation between an *agent as substance* and an event, as distinct from our everyday talk of agents causing events, which is ordinarily thought to be reducible to purely event-causal terms.)

Theory Type 3 (T-3 Theories): An agent is free with respect to a particular action only if that action is event-causally undetermined in the sense that the action (or a crucial component of, or precursor to, it) is caused but not determined by a previous event of which the agent is the subject.

For a critic to show that all libertarian free will theories are dismissable in virtue of incoherence, he would have to demonstrate that each particular version of each of these three theory types suffers from unclarity, mystery, or conceptual incoherence that cannot be remedied. I do not know of anyone who has done this, and thus, although it remains a conceptual possibility that this could be shown, I will proceed on the assumption that it remains an open possibility that some particular libertarian theory is coherent and defensible. Below I will explicate and critically discuss particular instances of each of these different types of indeterminist free will theory. And, ultimately, I will propose an account that is a version of the third sort of theory. But first let me describe my reasons for declining to endorse an account of either of the first two sorts.

Free Acts as Uncaused Acts

One often reads in introductory philosophy textbooks that the libertarian position maintains that free acts are uncaused. But, goes the dilemma, we know from our everyday observations of the world that every event is caused, and, furthermore, it is a presupposition of all scientific enterprise that every event is caused. An action is an event; therefore, if libertarians are right about the nature of freedom, then there must be no free actions. Thus, given the libertarian position, our perception of human freedom is, in fact, illusory.

This oft-repeated dilemma too narrowly characterizes libertarianism. For as an incompatibilist, one need not maintain that the way in which the truth of indeterminism allows for free action is in virtue of some events being totally without cause. Some libertarians do, however, take an uncaused event or process to be crucial to the analysis of free action.

Carl Ginet, for instance, is a prominent contemporary defender of an account of this sort. On Ginet's account of free action, at the core of every complex bodily free action is a simple mental act, a *volition*, that is itself uncaused.[12] The mental event of volition, as a simple act, has no internal causal structure. It counts as an action, according to Ginet, in virtue of its having a certain phenomenal quality, characterized by its *seeming* to the agent as if it were caused directly by him, although in fact it was not.[13]

One philosopher has recently defended a libertarian view similar to Ginet's, accounting for freedom by positing a lack of causation at some crucial point. On Stewart Goetz's view, choices are essentially uncaused mental actions.[14] Goetz claims that although choices are uncaused, they are not random, since it is a conceptual truth that agents make them for a reason or purpose. Choices thus have explanations in terms of reasons, where these explanations are viewed as teleological rather than causal. An agent's choice, though uncaused, makes sense in light of the conceived ends for the production of which the choice is made. According to Goetz, the explanatory connection between an action and the reason for which the act is performed is "primitive and unanalyzable." (On this point Goetz parts company with Ginet, who maintains that this connection can be explicated in terms of an intention to act.[15]) On Goetz's view, in choosing, described as exercising a mental power, persons act freely. Libertarian freedom consists in the power to commit uncaused yet purposeful mental actions of choice.

At one time, I thought that any libertarian account making appeal to an *uncaused* event as crucial to the analysis of free action was immediately dismissable.[16] My reasoning was that any event with no causes whatsoever is mysterious and completely arbitrary and that surely a free act (and one for which the agent is potentially morally responsible) must not have at its core any event that is mysterious and completely arbitrary, but must instead be understandable by reference to, as well as directly attributable to, the self doing the acting. Of course, others have shared this thought. Wrote one critic long before my reflection on the subject, concerning a theory of the sort under discussion:

in proportion as an act of volition starts of itself without cause it is exactly, so far as the freedom of the individual is concerned, as if it had been thrown into his mind from without—"suggested to him by a freakish demon."[17]

Now, I still think that ultimately this first sort of libertarian account ought to be set aside in favor of another type. But I no longer think the matter is so clear-cut. T-1 theories make appeal in accounting for free action to an *uncaused* event or process. A-C (agent-causal) accounts, as we will see below, make appeal to an *agent-caused* event or process. The question Goetz asks is: Does it help—is it a theoretical improvement—to appeal, as do A-C theorists, to an *uncaused* agent-causing of a choice (or intention or volition)? It is a potent question. Why not omit the positing of a special sort of causation, causation by an agent as substance, itself in any instance uncaused by previous events, and simply see the act of choice (or the act of volition) as itself uncaused?

Goetz argues that it is a conceptual truth that a choice is uncaused, since a choice is essentially active rather than passive. One contemporary proponent of an agent-causal account, Timothy O'Connor, argues, by contrast, that the agent-causing of (on his particular account) the coming-to-be-of-an-intention-to-act-here-and-now is, as a conceptual truth, uncaused, since the agent-causation consists in a causal *relation* (not an event), and a causal relation is not the sort of thing itself having or requiring a cause. This internal libertarian debate demands some careful attention. Hence, contrary to the immediate thought, neither view merits hasty dismissal.

I nonetheless am convinced that T-1 libertarian theories face a decisive difficulty. Regarding the critical comment quoted above, a mental event compelled by a "freakish demon" would not be uncaused, and so, Ginet would insist, cannot count as the volition crucial to the account of free action. But the problem is that a mental event's having an *actish phenomenal quality* is not sufficient to ground the source of the act in the self. An event with such a phenomenal quality *might* be produced by a demon. And in the case of a genuinely uncaused volition, if the agent as a substance does not causally produce the volition, and neither does any previous event causally produce it, then the simple mental event of volition is not causally produced by anything at all and hence only *seems* to be, but is not in fact, under the agent's control. As David Velleman observes, on Ginet's account, the agential source of all actions is "tainted with illusion."[18]

As for the alternative version of this theory type, under the control of *what* is the uncaused choice that is appealed to in these theories? Goetz will presumably say that, since a choice is in essence the exercising of a power by an agent, that exercise is immediately under the agent's control (and is, further, explicable by reference to the agent's purposes). But it seems to me a conceptual possibility that I might exercise my power to choose and yet that exercise might be controlled by another person (even a freakish demon), in that the other compels me to choose as I do.

Ultimately, I am unconvinced of Goetz's contention that all choices are essentially uncaused. It seems clear that in some circumstances choices are causally necessitated—for instance, by desire, as in the case of genuine addiction—and that an agent chooses *freely* only in situations in which the choice is not causally necessitated. Goetz would, of course, decline to call the "choice" to pick up a drink, if compelled by an addictive desire to drink, a genuine choice. But might not an agent make an act of will without making an act of will *freely*? A choice or act of will might have its source in me sufficiently to count as *my* act of will without being totally without cause.

In the end, libertarian T-1 theories founder on what we earlier called the problem of control. What ought to be fully under the agent's control in cases of free action is what action he does. But a totally uncaused event is an event that derives from nothing, that has its source in nothing. An event that comes from nothing is mysterious in terms of its origin; it is shocking and, without any causal antecedents whatsoever, random. Surely, free actions should not be mysterious, appearing from nowhere. Hence a choice made for reasons, yet completely causally unconnected to either an agent or events of the past, is out of control. Likewise, a complex bodily action having at its center an uncaused mental act of volition is ultimately underivable from anything and hence is out of control.

Agent-Causal Accounts

Libertarians are united by their commitment to the truth of the thesis of indeterminism as a precondition of agential freedom. One way in which it could fail to be the case that every event is causally necessitated by prior events is its being the case that some events are caused, not by prior *events,* but by an *agent.* Hence some incompatibilists have held that, required for providing a plausible account of the nature of free action is the admission of a fundamentally different sort of causal relata in the world than the more commonly acknowledged events and states of affairs. The agent-causal relation consists in the obtaining of a causal connection between a person as agent and a certain event that, depending upon the particular agent-causal theory, is taken to be a decision, or the (free) act itself, or the formation of an intention to act here and now. On an agent-causal account, a person acts freely just in case his act or the crucial precursor to his bodily movement (in the case of overt actions) is not causally determined by previous events but is, rather, causally determined directly by the agent as a persisting entity.

An agent-causation theory of freedom was famously defended by the eighteenth-century Scottish philosopher Thomas Reid and has been adopted and explicated in various ways, as well, by the contemporary philosophers C. A. Campbell, Roderick Chisholm, Richard Taylor, Timothy O'Connor, and Randolph Clarke, among others (although both Chisholm and Taylor later repudiated their agent-causal views).[19] The fundamental tenet of each of these accounts is the same—that some events are brought about not by other events but instead by a *thing* or *substance*, where the causal relation between the substance and the event is an irreducible notion. Let us look further at the articulations of some particular agent-causal accounts.

Reid takes 'the will' to be our faculty of willing actions or of determining what to do, and he observes that the distinction between free and unfree acts applies only to actions preceded by an agent willing that she do them.[20] In determining what one does, one exercises what Reid terms one's 'active power', which is the ability of the mind to produce a certain effect. An act is free on Reid's view if and only if the agent was the (undetermined) cause of the act of willing that caused the act, such that the agent could have willed not to do it just as much as he could have willed to do it. According to Reid, no external cause produced the act of will that resulted in a free act; *the agent* caused the act of will. For a person to be the agent-cause of an act of will is for a person to exert his power to bring about that act of will.

This causation by an agent Chisholm dubbed *immanent* (as opposed to *transeunt*—event or state-of-affairs—causation). Chisholm himself is led to endorse an agent-causal account by his conviction that the ascription of personal responsibility is incompatible with both an event-causally deterministic view of action and an event-causally indeterministic view of action. The latter is the case, Chisholm thinks, since an undetermined event is not caused at all and hence is "fortuitous or capricious."[21] (Notice that this comment reveals reliance upon a controversial, necessitarian view of causation. I will examine an alternative unenvisioned by Chisholm in this line of reasoning below.) Tracing event-causation back to the agent, Chisholm maintains, we will reach an ultimate brain event that was made to happen by the agent, and not by other events. Of course, the agent cannot change or do anything to cause the event in question, because then an event—namely, the event of the agent's willing to do it, or his change—would have been the cause of the act, and not the agent himself. This leads Chisholm to conclude that every agent must be a "prime mover unmoved."[22]

The reference to "prime movers unmoved," and to agent-causation more generally, has been subjected to a fair amount of philosophical heckling. The supposition of our having the ability to be unmoved movers has seemed to some to be a first-rate example of an unlikely posit made in theoretical desperation rather than a genuinely useful construct well supported by evidence. Surely we do have experience of people doing things, *bringing about* events and states of affairs: I might cause a pen to move across my desk by flicking it; you might cause your eyes to widen. But in speaking of ourselves as being the cause of these events, just as when we say that the dog spilled the water, what we really mean is that certain events caused other events: The event of my flicking my finger caused the pen to move; the event of the dog's bumping the dish with sufficient force caused the water to spill. Speaking of an object or an agent as the cause of some event is just shorthand for the more specific event-causal explanation upon which the agent causal explanation supervenes.[23]

But agent-causation libertarians do not see it this way, at least not for all cases of causation. If we ever act freely, then it must be the case, agent-causalists contend, that we, as agents, sometimes stand in nonreducible relation to events. This is the only good way to account for incompatibilist intuitions about free agency—to posit the special agent-causal relation. Critics contend that the notion merely "labels" what libertarians need, without doing anything to "illuminate" the nature of free will.[24]

One recent theorist who has worked to further illuminate and revive the notion of agent-causation is, as mentioned, Timothy O'Connor. O'Connor explicates his version of the agent-causal theory of free will by locating it within a realist understanding of causation in general, in terms of irreducible causal powers associated with an object's occurrent properties. His account builds, in particular, on the version of the nonreductive theory of causation developed by R. Harre and E. H. Madden in their *Causal Powers: A Theory of Natural Necessity*.[25] According to this "powerful particular" account, an object, when put in the appropriate circumstances, manifests its inherent causal powers (which are grounded in the object's underlying structural and dynamic properties) in observable effects. In cases involving nonagential objects, circumstances work to either *allow* the exercise of a power, by removing a barrier in the case of an activity-ready mechanism, or to *stimulate* the exercise of a power by triggering a latent mechanism. The underlying structural and dynamic properties of nonagential objects, together with appropriate circumstances, then necessitate or make probable certain effects.

The agent-causation of an event is then understood as a species of the primitive notion of causal production. O'Connor proposes that intelligent, purposive agents have a *choice-enabling property* (or set of properties) grounding a different sort of causal power: not one that, in appropriate circumstances, automatically gives rise to certain characteristic effects, but rather one that, in suitable circumstances, makes possible the direct, purposive bringing about of an internal event (an immediately executive state of intention to act in a particular way) by the agent who bears the property. Thus O'Connor maintains that there are two basic sorts of causal properties and, accordingly, two fundamental sorts of causation: One of these is agent-causation.

Merits of the Agent-Causal Approach.   Agent-causal accounts provide theoretical backing to the intuitively powerful idea that, when we act freely, what we do is ultimately "up to us," that we ourselves, as agents, are the originators, or source points, of our acts. Free acts, intuitively, derive directly from the self; they are acts over which the self has full authority. Agent-causal theories take this idea seriously, capturing it in direct fashion, and this is their greatest strength. The agent-causal theorist also accounts for what is wanted when we value freedom: We want our actions to be undetermined by anything external to ourselves. Moreover, A-C theories have the virtue of providing an easy answer to the problem of control: Decisions (or intention formations or acts, depending on the version of the theory) are clearly and fully under the agent's control in virtue of the agent's standing in a direct, causally determining relationship to them.

These virtues account for the attractiveness for many libertarians of the agent-causal approach. Agent-causal theories, furthermore, despite the charges of some critics, are not totally incomprehensible or wildly incoherent. Their plausibility, of course, depends both upon their theoretical power and upon the strength of the justification for the belief in a special agent-causal power. The latter, on some leading accounts of epistemic justification, is relative to what else one accepts. So for a person who, for instance, is a causal realist and also a theist, the agent-causal account may have particularly strong epistemic status. This is because the theistic God, as traditionally conceived, is the primary example of agency, the First Cause of the universe, a prime mover unmoved. Having what Reid and Locke refer to as an "active power," God directly causes events, without undergoing any change. For someone, then, who believes that persons are created "in the image of," or in some ways importantly like, God, it is not implausible to believe that intelligent, purposive human agents, like the Primary Agent, have properties grounding an "active power"—the ability to be the undetermined cause of events—although, whereas God's ability is unlimited and perfect, our ability is limited in scope and strength.

Problems for Agent-Causal Accounts. But there are serious difficulties for A-C libertarian theories. Many philosophers have posed the following problem.[26] Take the case of a putatively free act (in virtue of having at its core an agent-caused event), say, my making a promise to myself not to eat so much chocolate. Now I, the agent, existed prior to the occurrence of this act, and I continue to exist after I have already made the promise to myself. But if I exist both prior to the act's occurring and after it is done, without the act's occurring at any of those other times, then what makes the difference at the time it does occur? What makes it happen then? According to the theory, I made the act happen when it did. But my mere existence cannot be sufficient for the act's occurrence, since I exist at many times without the act's occurring.

Consider this problem further. When I freely make a promise to myself, on the agent-causal account, *I directly* make the promise (an event), or the intention to make the promise (an enduring state), occur or come to exist. But how can *I*, as a persisting entity, *make something happen* (or come to exist)? Normally, when something happens, something else happened previous to it to cause it to occur. (For instance, before the dog's water spilled out of his dish, the dog bumped the dish, causing the water to spill.) But *I* do not happen; I simply exist. And I exist both before and after the event in question. So what caused the promise to stop eating so much chocolate to occur when it did? You did, answers the agent-causalist. But what explains the promise's occurring *when* it did, and not at some other time instead?

We have run together two problems. First is a concern about the coherency of the notion of agent-causation itself. Our worry in the first place is with the proposition that an agent can stand in a causal relationship with an occurrence. How can an agent cause an event without its being the case that some change in the agent—some occurrence, such as a decision or an effort—*initiates* that event? Is the idea that an immaterial substance may serve as a causal *relatum*, standing as determining cause (never as determined effect) in relation to a physical event, and, if so, how can this idea be understood? The accounts of Campbell, Reid, Chisholm, and Taylor do not explicate the nature of agent-causation particularly well, each leaving unanswered the question of what specifically constitutes the agent. This contributes to the conviction of critics of agent-causation accounts that such views are "mysterious." On this point, agent-causalists must provide further explication both of the nature of an agent, including principally the properties allegedly underlying its "active power," and of the freedom-enabling agent-causal relation.

Second, there are concerns over the resources of the agent-causal theory for answering questions about the timing of an agent-caused event. Perhaps one will say that the act occurs *when* it does because I exert some effort to make it happen then. But, of course, the question then arises of what makes the exertion event occur when it does. The A-C theorist cannot reply that an agent must have exerted his power to bring it about at that time, for then an agent would have to cause an infinite number of exertions in order to produce any act of will. To this question, then, the agent-causalist might answer that the agent him- or herself makes the exertion event occur when it does: There is a direct causal relation between the agent and the exertion of effort. But, again, the agent cannot change or *do* anything to make the exertion event occur—or else an event, and not the agent him- or herself, will be what stands in causal relation to the effect. And so the question remains as to what makes the causal relation obtain when it does, and not at any other time instead.[27]

Some have argued against A-C accounts by alleging that they are not an improvement over T-1 accounts, since A-C accounts appeal to an *uncaused* agent-causing. If T-1 accounts leave something *uncontrolled* in appealing to an uncaused event, then so do A-C accounts—namely, the agent's causing the target event. And if T-1 accounts do not leave something uncontrolled, then the appeal to agent-causation is useless, since free acts have explanations in terms of reasons.

This objection I do not find particularly compelling. I do think that T-1 accounts founder on the problem of control. But I find persuasive the reasoning on behalf of the A-C theory that an agent-causal relation is intrinsically an exercise of control—it has internal causal structure (unlike a simple mental act of volition). Since agents are not causally simple states or events, agent-causation, if there is any such thing, cannot be caused.[28]

However, three particular difficulties for agent-causal theories remain sufficiently perplexing to drive an interest in finding a different sort of libertarian alternative. The prospects for resolving these difficulties look distressingly dim. The problems are these: (1.) How will the agent-causalist explain how *two different forms* of causation could systematically interact in a single human being?[29] (2.) The A-C account lacks resources, as discussed above, for explaining why the agent-caused event occurs *when* it does, since nothing about the agent, no change he undergoes, can explain its happening then. (3.) It is not clear that we have sufficient reason to believe that agents in fact *have* the requisite properties for subsisting the sort of causal power that agent-causalists envision: to directly cause at will, on

O'Connor's account, for instance, the coming to be of immediately executive intentions. With regard to the third concern, I acknowledge that, as mentioned, believing so might have some support from a theistic outlook. But I deny what O'Connor asserts—that all of us in general have *evidence* of our possessing the power to be agent-causes in the form of observations of it in our acting freely.[30]

For these reasons, rather than endorsing an agent-causal account, it seems to me that libertarians should look for a third type of alternative. Perhaps the appeal to a primitive notion of *agent-causation* is unnecessary. Chisholm once remarked (against scoffers at the notion of an agent as a primitive cause) that philosophers do not have the right to make such jokes until they have a proposed analysis of such statements as "Jones killed his uncle" into purely event-causal statements, an analysis that captures the participation of the agent. Without such an analysis, he claims, "the joke is entirely on you."[31] David Velleman's reply to this remark is, I think, particularly apt. Velleman declares, "The proper goal for the philosophy of action is to *earn* the right to make jokes about primitive agent-causation, by explaining how an agent's causal role supervenes on the causal network of events and states."[32] While this comment is directed toward the philosophy of action in general, I see it as expressing precisely the right goal for libertarian free will theory.

In the remainder of this chapter, I would therefore like to see how far we can get in constructing an indeterminist model of free will *without* making appeal to agent-causation as an irreducible notion. The goal is to produce a model that explains how our ordinary description of an agent's causing an event is in fact reducible to event-causal terms.[33]

Event-Causation Views

I have thus far discussed a view according to which the requisite event-causal indeterminism in the history of an agent's free act obtains in virtue of the act's being totally uncaused (T-1 theories), as well as a competing account (the A-C account) on which the event-causal indeterminism obtains in virtue of an event's being caused by an agent as a persisting entity. Both of these theories of free will, I have urged, suffer from problems sufficiently significant to warrant the search for a different sort of indeterminist account. A third and alternate way in which there might be event-causal indeterminism in the history of an agent's free act is in virtue of the action's (or some crucial component of, or precursor to, it) being caused—but not determined—by a previous event.

Not all causation is determination, as Elizabeth Anscombe has pointed out.[34] Her argument for the claim that it is wrong to associate the notion of *cause* with necessity is based on two fundamental considerations. First, we can recognize and speak of causes in the absence of known, relevant, exceptionless generalizations or necessities. For instance, the question of whether or not there is an elaborate set of specifiable conditions under which one invariably contracts a certain disease does not have to be settled before we can understand what is meant by speaking of contact with someone contaminated with the disease as the cause of one's getting it. Likewise, it is conceptually coherent that a child's falling and scraping his knee may cause him to cry without its being the case that he had to cry or that he always cries upon falling. Second, Anscombe insists that the core, common feature of all causality consists in the derivativeness of an effect from its cause. But the laws of nature do not show us that the effect derives from, or has its source in, the cause. If *A* comes from *B*, then this does not imply that every *A*-like thing comes from some *B*-like thing, or that *A* had to come from *B*. These conclusions may be true, but if they are, then they are additional facts. So causation is not identical to necessitation.

If Anscombe is right about this, and it seems to me that she is, then there are necessitating causes and nonnecessitating causes.[35] A *necessitating cause C,* of a given kind of effect *E,* is one such that it is not possible (on the occasion) that *C* should occur and should not cause *E,* given that there is nothing that prevents *E* from occurring. A *nonnecessitating cause* is one that can fail to produce its effect, even without the intervention of anything to frustrate it. Anscombe's example of a nonnecessitating cause is a collection of radioactive material that activates a Geiger counter connected to a bomb. Via the Geiger counter, the material causes the bomb to explode. It was not determined, but merely happened, that the radioactive material emitted particles in such a way as to activate the Geiger counter sufficiently to set off the bomb.

Many philosophers have come to admit cases of indeterministic causation. David Lewis, for instance, declares the following:

I certainly do not think that causation requires determinism.
. . . Events that happen by chance may nevertheless be caused. Indeed,
it seems likely that most actual causation is of just this sort. Whether
that is so or not, plenty of people do think that our world is chancy;
and chancy enough so that most things that happen had some chance,
immediately beforehand, of not happening. These people are seldom
observed to deny commonplace causal statements. . . . We had better
provide for causation under indeterminism, causation of events for
which prior conditions were not lawfully sufficient.[36]

Indeterministic accounts of causation commonly share a certain
motivating idea: that a cause increases the probability of the effect.
Lewis's theory, in particular, differs from some other probabilistic
accounts in two respects. First, it applies to causation by one particular event of another event, rather than conduciveness of one *kind*
of event to another kind (so that its probabilities are single-case
chances). And second, his analysis is in terms of counterfactual conditionals about probability rather than in terms of conditional probabilities. (Lewis is concerned by a certain difficulty raised for the attempt to use inequality of conditional probabilities to express that
event C raises the probability of event E—namely, that the inequality may hold due to the fact that C and E are both effects of a common cause. Some philosophers maintain that this problem can be
handled by specifying suitable background conditions.)

I will not pursue here the details of the variety of theories of
probabilistic causation but will only note that several such accounts
are available (e.g., Ellery Eels 1991; I. J. Good 1961–1962, 1980;
Christopher Hitchcock 1993; David Lewis 1973; Hans Reichenbach
1946, 1957; Wesley Salmon 1998; Patrick Suppes 1970). The notion
of probabilistic causation is widely acknowledged in the philosophy
of science. Now suppose that mental states and events can be nonnecessitating or indeterministic causes of other mental states and
events. T-3 theorists exploit this possibility in an attempt to make
room for free will within a naturalistic framework and without requiring the existence of a second sort of (substance) causation (in
opposition to A-C theorists). As I have said, I think this is the right
way to go. An early developer of an account of this sort is Robert
Kane, whose *Free Will and Values* (1985) presents an indeterminist
account later refined and further defended in his rich and intriguing

book *The Significance of Free Will* (1996b).[37] An additional account of a T-3 sort is that proposed on behalf of the libertarian (but not adopted) by Robert Nozick in his *Philosophical Explanations*.[38]

Let us work through some possibilities for the design of a T-3 theory. Suppose that we take an account of the nature of action appealing to the existence of intentions as distinct mental states, such as the following familiar account, commonly attributed to Donald Davidson's later work.[39] On this causal theory of action, a certain complex of an agent's desires and beliefs causes an intention to act in a particular way, and the intention consequently causes corresponding bodily movements in execution of the intention. The motivating desires and beliefs are the agent's reasons for acting—they justify the act, in that the agent desires a certain end and believes that acting in a particular way will help him to achieve that end. The reasons are also causes, and, provided that the causal processes between the desire-belief complex and the intention, and between the intention and the bodily movements, proceed in a nondeviant or "normal" sort of way, the agent's movements mark the achievement of an *action*.[40]

Beginning with acceptance of basically this standard sort of account of action, where in the process described by it might the T-3 libertarian theorist want to place the required event-causal indeterminism?

Appeal to an Indeterministic Intention-Behavior Connection. One possibility is the spot immediately prior to the overt bodily movement. On the adopted theory of action, this location for the indeterminism would be between the agent's formed intention concerning how to act here and now and the subsequent behavior. This view is expressed in theories I will designate as type 3a.

Theory Type 3a (T-3a Theories): An agent is free with respect to a particular action only if that action is event-causally undetermined in the sense that the action is indeterministically caused by way of a normal causal process by the agent's intention to perform it here and now.

A libertarian can certainly countenance indeterminism in the location specified by T-3a. But the account does not, in my view, specify the right place to *require* it. For the account does not accord with our considered ordinary understanding of our power to act freely. It is not as if our conception of our free agency is this: We reflect on what to do, decide what to do, form an intention for acting (where all of this is the purely causally deterministic outcome of the past, given the natural laws), and then, subsequent to our intention formation, there is a bit of causal openness, so that the future is accurately depicted by forking paths representing the fact that we *may* act in accord with the intention but we may not.

If an agent's proximal intention only indeterministically, and not deterministically, results in his act, then there is a chance, given the agent's intention and the reigning conditions and natural laws, that the act will not follow. But then a model requiring such indeterminism simply provides the agent with a *liability* and not the positive asset commonly thought to be secured in the possession of agential freedom. Imagine: On the basis of your desires and beliefs, you form a certain intention for acting here and now. But since the causal link between your intention and your overt act is an indeterministic one, you must wait and see whether your act will or will not follow your intention to perform it.

An account on which causal indeterminism is required between one's intention and one's behavior is defeated by the charge that it makes one's act too chancy, too much out of one's control, to be free. An account of free action should not require that an act merely *happen* to follow the agent's intention to perform it and never regularly follow it as a causally deterministic outcome of that intention. If there is a viable location for the T-3 libertarian's required indeterminism, then it is further back in the causal process leading to the act.[41]

Free Acts as Acts Caused by Freely Formed Intention.   The way to fix this problem is to firm up the relation between the free agent's intention and her act. Thus the indeterminism allowing for free action is not to be located immediately prior to the act itself, but instead somewhere prior to the pertinent intention (e.g., the intention to perform that act here and now). Thus we arrive at the following:

> *Theory Type 3b (T-3b Theories):* An action is free only if it results by way of a normal causal process from a pertinent intention (e.g., an intention to perform that act here and now), where the intention itself has event-causal indeterminism in its immediate causal history.

Uniting plausible libertarian conceptions of freedom, then, is commitment to the claim that a free act results from a freely formed intention to perform that act, where an intention is freely formed only if it is event-causally undetermined. One central problem now is to explain how an event-causally undetermined intention can be under an agent's control and not random. The other fundamental problem is to specify the best account of the intention's event-causal indetermination.

The pertinent intention (e.g., the intention to perform a certain action here and now) might be event-causally undetermined in any one of three different ways. First, the intention might be event-causally undetermined in virtue of its being uncaused. To further delimit account T-3b in this way would make it into a T-1 theory, which we have set aside. Second, the intention might be event-causally undetermined in virtue of its being caused, but not determined, by a prior deliberative event of the agent's (such as a preference to act in the way specified in the content of the intention). Third, the intention might be event-causally undetermined in virtue of being caused by the agent. Where this third option is given a nonreductionist reading, to take it is to endorse an A-C libertarian account. But the third option might also be given a *reductionist* reading. I think, in fact, that the third option is best but that it need not be understood in a way that makes appeal to a primitive notion of agent-causation. Instead, the notion of an intention's being caused by an agent can be reduced to event-causal terms.

But consider the second option. One way in which an intention could be event-causally undetermined is by being caused by a deliberative event or events in an indeterministic way. The intention may be caused by a prior consideration of the agent's—a deliberative event involving the agent—but not determined or necessitated by that event. Consider the following account:

> *Theory Type 3c (T-3c Theories):* An action is free only if it results by a normal causal process from a pertinent intention (e.g., an intention to perform it here and now) that is caused but not determined by an immediately prior deliberative event of which the agent is the subject.

Suppose, as is plausible, that the deliberative event immediately prior to the formation of the intention is either a judgment or a preference concerning what to do. Then the free agent, on this view, after deliberating, forms a judgment (or preference) concerning the best course of action in the circumstances. Since this judgment (or preference) does not lead necessarily to the formation of a corresponding intention for action, the corresponding intention may or may not follow. Thus when the agent concludes, what I prefer (or judge best) to do is *a,* this only raises the probability that an intention to *a* will be formed and does not (on this proposal) causally determine the occurrence of the intention. On this proposal, then, free will amounts to the ability to deliberatively form preferences or judgments concerning the best course of action (where these states themselves are the causally deterministic outcome of the past and laws) without being able to be sure that one will intend appropriately given the preference or judgment.

But is it *freedom-enhancing* to require that one's preference (or judgment) concerning what to do must not causally determine an intention to act as one prefers (or judges best) but must instead lead in a causally *indeterministic* way to the intention? The problem with the T-3c view may be put this way: An intention that *may or may not* follow the agent's judgment (or preference) to act as specified in the intention seems to be insufficiently under the control of the agent. Suppose that you make a decision concerning how to act, forming a judgment concerning what to do. But on the proposed account, you must wait to see whether the corresponding intention to act will or will not be formed. An act with such a causal history—one that happened to follow upon what the agent judged best but might not have—seems a lucky accident. If this were what constituted free action, it is hard to see why anyone would want the ability to act freely, where the ability to act freely would be the ability to form best judgments or preferences for acting, without being able to be certain whether or not one will consequently intend to do what one decisively prefers (or judges best).

In short, this account has the same problem as account T-3a—simply a level up. In other words, the intention seems too unconnected to the preference for the resulting act to be under the agent's control. There ought to be, in the usual case, a firm deterministic causal relationship between the agent's preference concerning what to do and her intention for acting (as well as between her intention and the act), or at least the libertarian should not require that the causal connections at these points be indeterministic ones. So on the most plausible incompatibilist model of free action, it is not the presence of alternative possibilities after a decision has been made concerning what one prefers (or judges best) to do that are crucial for freedom. Rather, the crucial alternative possibilities are located further back in the causal history of the act. On my view, as I will explain, these alternative possibilities are found between the agent's considerations about what to decide and her decisively formed preference for acting itself.[42]

Undefeated Authorization of Preference

In previous work, I defined the notion of *'preference'* as an evaluatively formed desire (formed by a process of critical reflection with respect to one's conception of the good) for a certain first-level desire to be effective in action.[43] The context of this stipulative definition was a discussion of Harry Frankfurt's account of free will in terms of a hierarchy of higher-level desires, or desires about desires. I remain convinced that we sometimes form preferences about what desires to have and to act upon. But Gary Watson[44] is right in pointing out against Frankfurt that, in usual cases, the objects of practical deliberation are particular courses of action themselves, rather than desires to have certain other desires or the state of affairs of some desire's being effective in action. Hence I wish here to broaden the notion of preference: We might form preferences for having or acting on certain desires; but more ordinarily, I suppose, we simply form preferences for acting in certain ways. I will think of a *preference*, then, as a specially processed desire—a desire (for instance, for performing some act) formed by a process of critical evaluation with respect to one's conception of the good.

The term 'decision' is variably and sometimes ambiguously used in free will literature. In developing the view to be proposed, I will use the term 'decision' to refer to a process: the sequence of events describable as the consideration of various factors by the agent's deliberative faculty, leading up to the formation of a state of mind settling the agent's uncertainty.[45] I view the momentary mental act ending the decision process as part of the process, the end event of the process. The decision process might be settled either by the formation of an intention to act or by the formation of a preference. That is to say, if the decision concerns simply what to commit oneself to

doing, then the outcome of the decision process—its settlement
state—is an intention to act (now or in the future). If the decision in
question concerns what to desire (so that in deciding one asks oneself, What do I *want* to do or to desire?) and if, in the process of
making the decision, the agent considers centrally her acceptances
concerning what is good and as the outcome of that consideration
reflectively endorses a certain desire or course of action, then the
outcome of the decision—its settlement state—is a preference.[46] The
event of preference formation thus settles the agent's indecision concerning what she wants to do. When we say of an agent S that "S's
decision is made," I will take this to mean that S has ceased deliberating over a given matter by forming a particular preference (or intention, depending upon the type of decision) for action.[47]

Action upon desire is not necessarily free. I might desire and intend to do X because I am addicted to doing X. Then, although I desire to do X, when I do X, I do not act freely but, rather, addictively.
In Frankfurt's terms, although I want to X, I do not want to want to
X. Then in doing X, I frustrate rather than express my *self* (which
Frankfurt would explicate in terms of higher-order desires, but
which is better characterized, I believe, in terms of preferences and
acceptances, as I will explain). In acting addictively, I frustrate the
goals and values (otherwise expressible as the preferences and acceptances) intimate to—that is, in part constitutive of—me.

The introduction of the notion of preference is intended to solve
this problem (the *internal problem*) with the basic account of free
action as action on desire. Since a 'preference' represents what an
agent wants as the outcome of her reflection on what is good (and
not what she wants simply as an instinctive drive or as an addictive
desire), when an agent acts on a decisively formed preference, bar-
ring external manipulation of the reflective process, she is involved
in the action—she is its source. In other words, action on preference
is authored by the agent.

One might, then, propose that action causally derivative from an
agent's uncoerced preference is freely performed. But here is a problem with taking *action on uncoerced preference* as free. Consider an
agent making an important decision, such as whether or not to quit
his full-time job in order to make a go at it as a musician. Suppose
that he decides to quit his job and undertake the new endeavor, and
this outcome of the decision appears to have been "up to him." But

further suppose that, as the agent reasoned about the situation, weighing various factors, consulting other people, considering what he accepts and prefers, he was causally necessitated to reason in just the way he did. His deliberative or evaluative faculty was the source of the preference he formed, but, in fact, he was causally determined by factors such as his genetic makeup, environment, past experiences, and physiological constitution to evaluate potential courses of action in just the way in which he did evaluate them. (If someone had known all of the past events and the laws of nature, she could have accurately predicted exactly what he would decide.) In fact, though his preferences are his in that they were formed as a result of his own reflection on what he takes to be true and good, they are not, we might say, *ultimately* his, since the past, the current conditions, and the laws of nature conspire to make him prefer just what he does. This is because causal necessitation implies a unique, determinate outcome, an outcome that could not have been otherwise. In such a case, the agent could accept and prefer nothing other than what he did at the time, given the conditions and natural laws as they were.

Normally, we think of what an agent accepts and prefers as elements of his mental life that are up to him, under his full authority. But the arguments for incompatibilism are designed to show that, if those states are the deterministic outcome of previous events together with the laws of nature, then those states are not in fact under the agent's own full authority after all.

Consider the notion of *undefeated authorization* of preference. A preference with undefeated authorization is one fully attributable to the self. Its claim to being authentic to the agent is not *defeated* by the claim that it is merely the causally deterministic outcome—the sole physically possible outcome at the time—of the past and the laws. An act that one performs as the normal causal outcome of a preference with *undefeated authorization* then is strongly self-determined in a way that is sufficient for that act to be free. Undefeated authorization is defined as follows:

> *Undefeated Authorization:* S is authorized in preferring A in a way that is undefeated if and only if S's evaluative faculty was neither coerced nor causally determined by anything to form

the preference for *A*, but rather the preference for *A* was indeterminately caused by *S*'s considerations.

Freedom of action may then be defined in terms of preferences with undefeated authorization. Many of us conceive of ourselves as an agent possessing a certain kind of power: the power to form and reform one's own character. This power, we suppose, is often an uncoerced and undetermined determinant of our actions. It is the correctness of this very conception, I suggest, that allows (or would allow) one to act freely. An agent enjoys freedom of action in performing an act at a particular time, on this proposal, if and only if it is true that the agent's act results by a normal causal process from a preference for the act whose authorization is undefeated.[48]

To say that an action is free just in case it results, by a nondeviant causal process, from an *event-causally undetermined* and uncoerced decisively formed preference is to say that the agent could have, prior to forming the preference, decided in a number of ways. The outcome of her decision to prefer to act in a particular manner was neither coerced nor necessitated; there was a range of options for preference formation within the agent's power at the time. During the decision process, we experience thoughts, desires, insights, preferences, and the like. On the view being proposed, the libertarian maintains that a preference-forming decision process can lead ultimately to a free action only if the outcome of that process (the event of preference formation) is caused, but not determined, by other deliberative events—by the occurrence to the agent of particular thoughts.

Merits of the Proposed Approach

The proposed view has the merit of not making whether or not a free act follows an agent's decisively formed preference to perform it a matter of chance. Notice that the preference-forming decisions at the center of the account need not immediately precede the act in time: One might form a preference for committing a certain act at a particular time in the future, leading to the formation of a future-directed intention that, together with the belief that the time has become appropriate, generates an immediately executive intention, which, in turn, if all goes well and the agent does not change his mind, leads normally to the act. Alternately, one might deliberately form a preference to act in a certain way in the future, not at a particular time, but whenever certain circumstances arise, such that one then has a *standing* preference from which free acts can arise without immediately following a deliberative process. For instance, the first time I chose a caregiver for my child, I may have had to put in a great deal of consideration (concerning such matters as my values, my child's needs, and the qualifications of various candidates) before forming a preference concerning whom to hire. But subsequently, when the need arises again, I may simply phone the regular baby-sitter and do so freely, without needing to elaborately reevaluate the matter, but instead acting from a *standing* preference to use the person in question when he or she is available. In counting my view as a T-3 account, then, I am taking the preference leading to the act, whether standing or just formed, to be sufficiently *crucial* to count as a crucial precursor to the act.

The proposed view claims not that preferences with undefeated authorization are uncaused, but that they are undetermined—they could have been otherwise. The indeterminism involved in free agency is thus held by this view to be located between the factors that influence an agent's decision concerning what preference to form and the decisively formed preference itself. The action resulting from the preference is free only if the formation of the preference for acting is caused, but not determined, by events involving the individual's evaluative faculty or intellect. What is involved is indeterministic but probabilistic causation—the inputs to deliberation do not determine a particular decision outcome, but they make more probable the formation of certain preferences.

Suppose, for the purpose of illustration, that Kim is deciding whether or not Jason is the one to marry. The possible outcomes to her deliberation process are: the preference to marry Jason, the preference to marry someone else instead now or in the future, and the preference to never get married at all. Various considerations occur to her, including: the thought that Jason is intelligent and funny; a desire for security; a preference for lifelong companionship with someone who shares her values; a desire for freedom; the arguments of some feminists she has read that marriage is an outdated patriarchal institution; a slight attraction toward Steve; an overwhelming attraction toward Jason; the suggestion of her father that she marry someone financially secure; the acceptance that Jason is not at present financially secure; the suggestion of her mother that she not marry at all; a preference for having children one day soon; and her own conviction that children are best off being born to married parents. Each of these deliberative inputs points rationally toward one or another of the differing conclusive preferences; and each raises the probability of one of the three potential deliberative outcomes.

Suppose Kim decides to marry Jason. If she acts freely in marrying him, then her preference for marrying him must have been neither coerced nor causally necessitated by the past. That is, during the decision process, she was able to have formed any of the three potential outcome preferences. Given the inputs to her deliberation and the natural laws, in other words, it was physically possible for any of the alternate preferences to result.

Note that the compatibilist cannot require strictly sufficient conditions for an event in order for that event to be nonrandom. To do so is question begging, for what the libertarian affirms is precisely that there is a third option between determined and random. The third option, according to this view, is that the decision is explicable by reference to the deliberative events that caused the decision to be what it was. Why did the free agent decide in that way? Because of reasons x, y, z, and so on. Why did those reasons lead him to decide as he did? The determinist would answer: Because of a deterministic causal law linking such reasons to such a decision. But the proposed account answers: Because the agent exercised his evaluative faculty in a particular way. Why? For reasons that inclined but did not necessitate a particular outcome to his deliberation process. These causal statements report necessary, but not strictly sufficient, conditions for the decisively formed preference. In order to be explicable, the decisively formed preference need not be necessitated. But in order to be free, the decisively formed preference must not be necessitated. It may be tempting to suppose that a preference cannot be explained if it might have been otherwise, given all of the considerations of the agent and holding fixed the natural laws. But this supposition is only what Christopher Hitchcock calls a "demon of determinism." Not all explanation is deterministic.[49]

Certainly there are a number of factors that influence us as we deliberate. These include the media, friendly advice, the attitudes of one's colleagues, one's own acceptances and preferences, the wishes of one's parents, subconscious needs and desires, dreams, the political climate, concern for the environment, the interests of one's children or siblings, regard for what is true and right, and so on. What we desire when focusing on freedom is that none of these factors necessitate particular outcomes of our decisions. We welcome the influence of any such factors if we are reasonable, but what we abhor, when concentrating on the value of freedom, is the causal determination of our deliberative process by any of these influences. We do not want the deliberative process to be driven down a single path by previous factors. Freedom is opposed to constraint, and *having* to form a preference to act in any particular way—no matter how appealing that way may be, or how objectively right it is, or how much one's parent approves of it—is constraining.

So the view under consideration has intuitive plausibility. Furthermore, this sort of libertarian theory has the benefit of not positing mysterious agents in the form of "unmoved movers." It is a naturalistic libertarian view, not in that it requires the truth of naturalism, but in that it is *consistent* with a naturalistic conception of the world. The proposed account appeals only to causal relations between events (or states of affairs). There are no entities posited that we must believe in when we think of ourselves as having libertarian freedom, such as immaterial souls, and we need not ourselves, as substances, stand somehow in causal relations to events.

Initial Objection

But wait a minute, the reader might object. True enough, the proposed T-3 libertarian view does not share the problems had by an A-C account, and its naturalistic orientation is a benefit. But does not the proposed account face a certain difficulty, that is, providing a satisfactory answer to the problem of control? We considered earlier the view (T-3a) that an agent is free with respect to a particular action only if that action is event-causally undetermined in the sense that the action is indeterministically caused by the agent's intention. But the reason for rejecting this view is that, to require that the link between an agent's intention to act and the act itself not be necessary, but only probabilistic, is to make the act accidental, not in the agent's control. A problem for the present view is that it suffers from a similar weakness. Just as indeterminism between the agent's preference and her intention, or between her intention and her action, seemed to leave the action out of the agent's control, so too indeterminism between the factors that influence the agent's formation of preference and her decisively formed preference itself seems to leave that preference, and hence the resulting act, out of the agent's control.

Surely an agent does reflect on a variety of considerations prior to making a choice, including reasons for deciding in one way and reasons for deciding in a different way. Given the influences upon the agent, including these considerations, we are asked by the proposed view to imagine that which decision outcome results from these deliberations is undetermined. Given the deliberations, a certain potential decision outcome may or may not follow. But does this not make the particular way in which the indecision is resolved *arbitrary*? A decisively formed preference that may or may not follow upon the particular considerations that strike an agent during the deliberation process seems to be a preference that is not under the agent's authority. If there is some random element between the considerations serving as input to the decision and the decision outcome itself (so that the decisively formed preference has no strictly sufficient conditions), then the preference and the act to which it leads are uncontrolled by the agent.

The Proposal Further Elaborated

This is a natural concern and a fair one. However, the specification of the theory is not completed. In particular, I have not yet fully filled in a conception of the agent. Suppose we take an agent to be constituted by a character, together with the power to fashion and refashion that character. A character, or *character system*, is an aggregate of preferences and acceptances. Then an agent is an evaluating and choosing faculty (by which she creates preferences and acceptances), along with the character system, made up of those preferences and acceptances.

In previous work, I defended this notion of the self, or agent.[50] Surely, I urged, the faculty for shaping the character—for evaluating desires, beliefs, and courses of action with respect to standards—ought fairly uncontroversially to be taken as a constituent of the self. We clearly have some faculty for deciding what becomes a component of our character, what remains a component of our character, and what gets discarded as no longer an element of our character (although whether or not the operation of this faculty is causally necessitated by prior factors remains less clear). And this conception of the *character* is plausible, I think, for several reasons. For one, unlike hierarchical conceptions of the self as structured solely by desire, the proposed conception of the self incorporates some beliefs. Our convictions concerning the truth are central to who we are. But, appropriately, not just any beliefs and desires count as parts of the character. Opinions that one holds unreflectively and passions that overtake one are too common, as well as too blindly had, to be part of the character. For a character is the complex of attributes or features that mark and *distinguish* the individual. Elements of the character—preferences and acceptances—are the outputs of the individual's own evaluative activity.[51]

I may thus now alternately state the proposed T-3 libertarian theory: An act is free just in case it results by way of a normal causal process from a pertinent intention (e.g., an intention to perform the act here and now) that is agent caused. The agent causation of an intention is, in my view, an ontologically and conceptually *reducible* notion. Take an agent to consist of evaluated reasons (preferences and acceptances, as a group constituting the character), together with an evaluating and choosing faculty (in other words, a power to fashion and refashion character). Then an intention is agent caused just in case it results by a normal causal process from a preference for acting as specified in the content of the intention, where the preference itself is the output of an uncoerced exercise of the agent's evaluative faculty, the inputs into which (various considerations) cause but do not determine the decisive formation of the preference.

Why did the occurrence of considerations r_1, r_2, and r_3 raise the probability of decision outcomes preference$_1$, preference$_2$, and preference$_3$ occurring to 0.51, 0.90, and 0.75, respectively? The reply "Because r_1, r_2, and r_3 are good reasons for the decision outcomes preference$_1$, preference$_2$, and preference$_3$, respectively, and r_2 is the best" can be given no substance without reference to a *perspective* from which the reasons are judged to be positively relevant to the particular decision outcomes and a *point of view* from which the reasons are estimated to be good or worthwhile, with r_2 judged to be the best. This point of view is built into the proposed account: The agent's evaluative faculty is the source of the evaluation of reasons and of the subsequently produced decision outcomes. Thus I endorse an indeterminist account of the following sort:

Theory Type 3d (T-3d Theories): An action is free only if it results, by a normal causal process, from a pertinent intention (e.g., an intention to perform that act here and now) that is *caused by the agent,* where this latter term *('caused by the agent')* is reducible to event-causal terms.

Consider again the problem of control. In response, although the notion of control does require elucidation in some causal terms, it does not require deterministic explanation. In the case of deliberation preceding a free act, which decision-settling event it will be that occurs is not determined until it occurs. The formation of preference x or preference y or preference z may happen at t_{-1}. At t, suppose that preference x is formed. Its formation has a causal (and rational) explanation in terms of the agent's considerations.

Furthermore, the *act* resulting from the preference, in the case of free action, is controlled by the agent in being causally determined by the agent, since the agent on my view, is to be identified with a set of preferences and acceptances, together with the power to fashion and refashion the character. The decision concerning what preference to form—which in part, given this analysis of the agent, is a decision about what sort of person to become—is caused, but not fully determined, by the past. One may object that this means that it is partly or wholly out of one's control what sort of person to become, and that this is problematic. However, the location for the indeterminism specified by the proposed account is precisely where we *want* the indeterminism to be in a free will model. What is especially objectionable about determinism is the thought that our character is fully determined by the past, that we could not have become different sorts of individuals, given the causal determination of our traits by the events of the past and the natural laws.

Thus, although an agent may be unable *at t* to do otherwise than *a,* she is free in performing *a* at *t* only if she is genuinely self-determined with respect to *a*—that is, only if she performs *a* for reasons *and* those reasons are genuinely her own, in that she was not coercively caused to have them and in that the reasons were not causally determined to be her preferences by previous deliberative events.

In sum, the central merits of the proposed libertarian view of free action as action on undefeated authorized preference I take to be these: (1.) The account appropriately captures intuitions concerning what we *want* in valuing freedom: It proposes some causal openness in the construction of the self, so that who we are is not the necessary unfolding of the past and the natural laws. Yet, what preferences we form is explicable, both causally and rationally. (2.) The account is a phenomenologically accurate one: It seems that the ending point of deliberation is the outcome of our considerations yet that during deliberation there are genuinely available alternatives, multiple branching paths before us. (3.) The view is consistent with a wholly naturalistic metaphysics. We need not believe in immaterial souls in order to believe in free will, and we need not believe in an uncaused substance-event causal relation. The view of free action as action on undefeated authorized preference leaves free acts within the realm of what is scientifically explicable, and there is no need on this account to deny the antecedently plausible principle that every event has a cause.

In short, given the power of the arguments for incompatibilism, *some* indeterminist model of free action must have a hold on us, and the proposed account, I have argued, is the best of the available options.[52] When I act freely, the preference leading to the act is generated by the evaluative faculty that in part constitutes me, and the preference is not coerced by an external source. Hence, on the proposed view, when the appropriately formed preference leads to my act, *what I do is "up to me," since I, quite literally, causally determine it.*

Challenges to the Proposed
Indeterminist Model of Free Agency

I will now raise and respond to several objections to the proposed indeterminist account.

1. What about cases of action that seems not preceded by critical evaluative deliberation, such as a person's automatically getting up to get a drink of water when thirsty? Normally, a person does not have to think about the situation or reflectively evaluate his desire to get a drink of water. Yet his act seems freely done, so long as it was not coerced by another person or outside force. So is not the proposed account incorrect in requiring the act to be done from a deliberatively formed preference, a desire evaluated with respect to one's conception of the good?

The preference required for a free act, on my view, does not have to be formed immediately prior to the act. There may be a previously (deliberatively and indeterministically formed) *standing* preference, such as to drink when thirsty, that leads in a given case to the act, allowing the act to be free. In such a case of free action, the standing preference, "activated" or brought into play by the belief that one is now thirsty, leads in a causally normal way to the formation of an intention to drink here and now, and the intention in turn leads in a causally normal way to the act. Furthermore, the deliberation required for preference formation need not be protracted or psychologically torturous. The person in question presumably accepts that it is good to drink when thirsty. In getting up to get the drink of water, the person may well have formed a preference to do so, quickly and without much effort.

The objector may be concerned with cases of weakness of will. Suppose that the man in the example prefers *not* to drink water when thirsty. (Maybe he has certain views about water contamination. Or perhaps he is not supposed to drink for twelve hours prior to a medical test.) So he gets up and in a moment of weakness drinks the water, despite a preference to do the contrary. Why think that he does not act freely in such a case, when he *acts* but not from a preference to so act? A problem for my view, so goes the objection, is that not all desires that are formed by reasoning oblivious to considerations concerning the good are addictive or compulsive desires. And so action on nonaddictive *and* nonpreferential desire ought to count as free. *Thrilling* acts, for instance, one might allege, are unpreferred but free.

In reply, in cases of weakness of will, the act is intentionally done but does not express or reveal the self. A desire wholly isolated from any of the agent's considerations concerning what is good is mysterious in the sense that it is inexplicable by reference to the agent's critical reasoning. One's critical reasoning is, by the nature of it, done with reference to what one takes to be true and good. One's own conceptions of what is accurate and what is worthy of pursuit form the core of critical deliberation. This is not to say that a sociopath engages in no critical reflection. A person's own conceptions of what is accurate and worthy of pursuit may, of course, be at odds with what a majority of others see as good and true and with truth and goodness in some other way objectively defined.

So, my response to the objection is this: Show me an action allegedly done from desire and not preference that seems as if it ought to count as free. I reply that the action arguably was done from preference, since a preference is not a moral principle or a puritanical judgment; it is a *want* evaluatively formed concerning particular circumstances and need not represent what one would want on every similar occasion. Hence one might well prefer to engage in the thrilling act on some occasion, just as one might prefer to sometimes indulge in the decadent dessert even when one's *general* conception of the good includes living a healthy life. (One might, surely, consistently accept that it is good sometimes to let the pleasure of taste outweigh considerations of nutrition.)

On the other hand, *if* for the instance raised by the objector there is no plausible case to be made for the action's derivation from preference, then I challenge the freedom of the act. I challenge its freedom for this reason: An unevaluated desire is accurately described as an instinct or a mere impulse or a passion that has overtaken the individual, and so an action done on the basis of it has no source in the self.

2. Maintaining that the deliberation leading to the formation of preference need not be protracted helps to account for cases such as the previous case of a person getting a drink of water when thirsty, as well as the case of, say, a person in improvising a dance, both of which seem to show that a person can act freely without acting on lengthy and involved deliberation. But then how will we pick free acts out from unfree ones? How do we tell whether or not an act counts as free?

This is an epistemological problem of discerning when the conditions of the account are met. But my project is to provide a metaphysical account of the nature of a free act, not to address the epistemological question. Why should the epistemological issue be a constraint on the construction of a theory of our concept of free action? Perhaps one will reply that the epistemological problem is an appropriate theory test because we generally think we can tell the difference between a free and an unfree act without much difficulty. But if my account gives conditions that make it extremely difficult to tell when those conditions are met and when they are not, then the account must be mistaken because our applications of the concept of free action simply are not sensitive to those factors. In response, I believe that our applications of the concept of free action *ought* to be sensitive to the factors of causal determinism and reflective deliberation and that, in fact, they are, after some reflection on our self-conception and exposure to incompatibilist arguments.

3. Do we not hold persons morally responsible for acts done on desires that fail to count as preferences (i.e., desires that are not formed by a process of evaluation with respect to what is good)? When a person acts from an unreflective impulse and does something morally right or wrong, do we not appropriately hold him morally responsible for it, simply when he did it intentionally?

What we do, in fact, in holding persons morally responsible might differ from what we ought to do. Additionally, there are various specifications of the function of moral responsibility ascriptions. These will be discussed in the following chapter. Holding a person responsible for acting on an unevaluated impulse may have justification given a certain view of the point of holding persons responsible, but may be unjustified on other views of the function of moral responsibility ascriptions.

Acts done from an unevaluated immediate impulse of fear, self-preservation, or rage are examples of intentional acts for which, on a certain conception of moral responsibility, we ought not hold persons morally responsible. Juries have found persuasive the excuse that a husband was "out of his mind" with rage when finding his wife in bed with another man and rashly attacking her lover, and arguably rightly so, if we take the pronouncement to concern what the man deeply deserves on the basis of a self-revealing act; a mild-mannered and gentle man may act in such a circumstance on an overwhelming impulse wholly out of character. Other examples include action on an unreflective desire for self-preservation in an act of self-defense or a parent's violent act from rage upon walking in on the abuse of a child. In cases of automatic and unreflective action, agents are arguably not the fit subjects of credit or discredit for their acts.

4. Suppose you are right that we should hold persons morally responsible in acting only if they have acted from preference. But why think that the preference must be uncoerced?

Suppose that my boss has given me a large sum of money to deliver to the bank, and on my way, a mugger puts a gun to my head. Suppose that, in this case, I *do* have the time and presence of mind to reflectively evaluate potential desires and courses of action and that, consequently, I form a preference to hand over the money. Whereas my boss may be angry about losing his money, he should not view *me* as deserving of his wrath, even though, as a result of preference, I handed the money over to someone other than the bank teller. I did not hand over the money freely, because the preference to hand it over was formed coercively.[53]

Consider another case. Suppose that a neurosurgeon has, unbeknownst to me, installed in my brain a device by which he can, at will, manipulate my brain in such a way as to cause me to form certain preferences. Suppose that the mechanism by which he causes me to deliberate and ultimately to form just the preferences I do form has some randomizing device in it, so that when he pushes a certain button, say, indicating that I form preference C, in fact I might or might not form preference C, since his pushing that particular button is a nonnecessitating cause of the preference C. Whereas the preference is indeterministically caused, surely action on preference C is not free, as the preference leading to the act is coercively imposed.

5. Take the case of an act done from an uncoerced preference. Now why should we think that it is required for a person's freedom in acting that the preference have an indeterministic causal explanation? The indeterminism seems to undercut, rather than to add to, the person's freedom in, and credit for, performing the act.

Any incompatibilist model of freedom is going to have to locate the event-causal indeterminism somewhere in the history of the free act, and the specified place—between the considerations and the decisive formation of preference—seems to me the most reasonable place to locate it. One might, instead, locate the indeterminism *prior to* some of the considerations that occur to the agent during the deliberative process, so that what is undetermined is which (and perhaps at what points during the process) particular considerations

come into the agent's mind.[54] But if this were the only place specified for required indeterminism, then an act might be the purely
causally deterministic outcome of the considerations that happen to
occur to the agent and yet, on the proposal, count as free. Such an
account is too weak to ground agent freedom and deep responsibility, since, given the occurrence of the particular considerations in
any case, one particular act follows of physical necessity, as the
completely deterministic unfolding of previous events.

Consider an agent whose act is, in such a sense, "libertarian free."
Now a duplicate agent in exactly similar circumstances governed by
the same natural laws and subject to the same occurrence of considerations at the same points in the deliberative process will form exactly the same judgment concerning the best thing to do and will act
accordingly. But then, given the consideration pattern that occurs
(but might not have), there is no "wiggle room" for the agent in
forming an evaluative judgment—it simply falls out, of necessity,
from the consideration pattern. Hence such an account does not
leave sufficient room for free agency.

Where causal indeterminism is best located, instead, is after the
considerations (which in the usual case have been determined to
occur by previous events, such as how much rest one has had, what
one has recently eaten, with whom one has recently spoken, what
one has read) yet prior to the decisive formation of preference, such
that given the exact consideration pattern, the agent may decide to
prefer *a* and may decide to prefer otherwise. The considerations
themselves are indeterministic causes of the preference.

Again, every libertarian model of free action has to locate the indeterminism somewhere in the history of the act. Where else would
one put it? One might, out of dissatisfaction with the proposed
model, opt to be a compatibilist. But then one must face the fact that
the arguments for incompatibilism considered in Chapter 2 are
powerful and that no response to them is, as I have argued, particularly persuasive. Thus some incompatibilist model of free action is
needed. Furthermore, the intuitions underlying our deep-rooted
notion of human dignity, our commonsensical conception of the future as we engage in practical deliberation, and commonly held
judgments concerning deserved attributions of moral responsibility
are incompatibilist in nature. It is central to our self-image as practi-

cal deliberators that there are forks in the path in front of us representing causally open future alternatives. Where are the junctures that are important to us for acting freely?

The proposed model, I have urged, appropriately locates them. Moreover, I have argued that the other available models of incompatibilist free action are problematic. I have aimed to avoid an appeal to the agent as a primitive sort of cause, for reasons discussed above.

6. *On the proposed account, it seems that what is partially not "up to me" is who I am, what sort of person I become. But this is odd as an account of free agency grounding human dignity and moral responsibility.*

But it is up to me in a significant sense or to a significant degree who I am, because it is *my* deliberative faculty doing the reasoning in light of considerations and forming the preferences and acceptances. Also, on *any* indeterminist model, there is something that is not 'up to me', if by this phrase one means something that is causally undetermined by previous events. Control cannot be equated to event-causal determinism without begging the question against all sorts of libertarian theory. Also, *the act* done, on the proposed account of free action, is completely up to the agent. In fact, it is caused by the agent, since the agent is taken to be the evaluative faculty together with the preferences and acceptances. So one's free act is fully under one's control in being causally determined by one's self.

7. *How does the proposed account meet the two initial problems posed in the previous chapter for the basic account of free action as action on desire: the manipulation problem and the internal problem?*

It meets the internal problem by requiring preference for action. Action on a desire that is not a preference is not free. Hence "the unwilling addict," as Frankfurt calls him, does not act freely on my account. Does "the *willing* addict" (that is, an addict who prefers to take the drug) act freely on my account? No, because his preference is causally determined to be what it is by physiological factors responsible for the addiction. His preference, given the addiction, could not have been otherwise. So his evaluative faculty, as he decides what to do, is determined to reason just as it does and thus is causally determined to form precisely the preference formed.

The account of undefeated authorized preference is designed to address the manipulation problem posed by threats, posthypnotic suggestions, and the like. An agent has undefeated authorization for her preference just in case her evaluative faculty is neither coerced nor causally determined by anything to form that particular preference, but rather the preference is indeterministically caused by her considerations. The preference leading to a free act must be uncoerced and caused by an indeterministic deliberative process. The proposed account has need, then, of the same list that the compatibilist needs concerning the act's (or preference's) not being the product of coercion by threat, direct brain stimulation by an evil neuroscientist, posthypnotic suggestion, and so on, in order to rule out foul play in the formation of the preference.

8. *How is it, again, that the free act on your account is controlled by the agent, when there is some indeterminism in the production of the act? Insofar as an act is not causally determined by prior causes, it is out of control, a mere random event. Your model of free agency replaces causal determinism, in the process leading to the act, with randomness. But then your account does not provide a right account of action that is under the control of the agent, or free action. Why should anyone want to be able to act freely as characterized by the proposed account, since that account only gives to an agent the status of being prone to a random process in the generation of action?*

First, the incompatibilist not appealing to agent-causation is distinctive among proponents of free will models in defending a third option other than an event's being causally determined or its being random. To assert that those two alternatives are the only alternatives begs the question against all T-3 views. Every incompatibilist who thinks that the notion of free action is coherent alleges precisely that there is a third alternative between an event's being causally determined by previous events, on the one hand, and an event's being random, on the other.

Furthermore, on the particular incompatibilist account I have proposed, *the act* is causally determined: It is causally determined by the agent. Recall the proposed account of the self as the evaluative faculty together with the character. The free act is *agent caused* on the proposed account, where this notion is reducible to event-causal terms.

The problem of control is, I admit, the most serious difficulty facing the type of view I have defended. But consider the alternatives. We could, in accounting for free action, appeal to agent-causation as a primitive notion, irreducible to causation among events. But I find this approach unsatisfactory, as have many philosophers. The agent-causal theory, indeed, seems merely to *label* rather than to illuminate the problem of free agency. In light of problems for the A-C approach, as Robert Kane has urged (1996b), why not see how far we can get in constructing an indeterminist model of free action *without* relying on primitive agent-causation before giving up and making such an appeal?

Alternatively, we could adopt a T-1 approach, relying on the posit of an uncaused volition or choice. But to adopt a T-1 theory requires that we believe in something—uncaused events—with which we have no familiarity in the physical world. Uncaused events of volition or choice can be explained by reference to the agent's purposes, but they cannot be causally explained; they derive from absolutely nothing. In other words, with regard to any uncaused volition or uncaused choice, we can answer the question, *Why* did it occur? (by citing the agent's goals), but we cannot answer—it is impossible to answer—the question, What *made* it occur? This is unsatisfying. On the T-3 view I have defended, free actions result from preferences, and those preferences are formed noncoercively for reasons that are probabilistic causes of them.

9. How might the proposed indeterministic model of free action be actually realized? What evidence is there for thinking that we in fact have free will in this sense?

Several recent theorists have done interesting exploratory work on the matter of how indeterminism at the quantum level might be magnified if the brain is a chaotic system.[55] Additionally, if we have evidence for thinking that we are morally responsible (in what I will call in the subsequent chapter the 'metaphysical' sense) and if incompatibilist freedom is required for such moral responsibility, then we have reason to think that we have incompatibilist freedom. Further, if we have reason to think that we have dignity, that our most intimate relationships are genuine, and that our commonsensical conception of the future as we practically deliberate is accurate, then we have reason to think that we have incompatibilist freedom.

10. You have proposed that, between the considerations serving as input to the agent's evaluative process and its outcome, there is non-deterministic or probabilistic causation. Suppose that one particular consideration is so powerful that it raises the probability of a certain decision outcome to 0.99999. Then suppose that that outcome in fact occurs and leads appropriately to the agent's act. Why is such an act free, whereas it would not have been free had the probability been equal to 1 that the preference for that act would occur, given the previous considerations?

We sometimes speak of a range of freedom of action, some acts being fully free and others less so. The probabilistic model gives one way of making sense of degrees of freedom. Perhaps the *most* free acts derive from preferences whose probability of occurring was raised by the occurrence of certain previous considerations to values within a range of, say, 0.2–0.8, whereas the act would be less free when resulting from a preference at either end of the spectrum, that is, in cases where the considerations made the probability of the preference's occurrence near 0.9 or 0.1.

Consider the case of a cancer patient's agreeing to a round of chemotherapy treatment by signing a particular document. It seems to me that in such a case the agent retains her freedom in signing the document, provided that she does so as the result of a normal causal process from an evaluatively formed preference for signing it that was neither coercively formed nor causally necessitated. The patient must have been able to form a different preference instead (namely, the preference for refusing the treatment) in order for her act of signing to be freely done.

But although the signing act is free, it seems to me less so than a different act done such that considerations did not make it so highly probable that there would be one particular outcome of the decision process. That is, given the agent's acceptance that if she refuses chemotherapy treatment, she will very likely die, her preference for signing the form has a high probability value. Compare a case in which I am deciding whether to give a certain sum of money to a charitable cause or instead to use it for a family vacation. I accept the great worthiness of the cause and prefer to use my money to benefit others as well as my own family; yet, I am convinced that my family members would enjoy the trip and relax during a vacation, and I prefer that we occasionally spend focused time together. Suppose that the matter is a "toss-up," given all of my prior considerations. Acting in one way or another then manifests my full freedom.

11. You have appealed to something unverifiable in characterizing the agent, namely, his "evaluative and choosing faculty." Why is your account not just as vulnerable as is the A-C account to a charge of mysterious agency?

In characterizing free action, I have appealed to a feature of persons that has been described as an agent's evaluative faculty for forming preferences and acceptances in light of his conception of the true and the good. But the critic may protest that this feature of persons is not empirically observable and, in this sense, is mysterious. However, this charge puts at risk of being dismissed as "mysterious" *any* posited ability or faculty of persons. How do we become aware of the existence of any ability? By observing its exercise or its effects. Normally, of course, we cannot discern simply by looking at a person at any time whether or not he has the ability to solve complex mathematical problems, but we can observe him in the process of exercising the ability and, from this evidence, justifiedly infer the ability's existence. Similarly, though it is true that we cannot directly observe another's evaluative faculty from the external standpoint, we can, from that standpoint, observe his exercise of the power as he fashions and refashions his character—in other words, as he deliberates among alternatives and decides upon forming one preference or acceptance rather than another. We justifiedly infer the existence of the ability from our observation of its exercise. We can and do witness others considering various factors and making up their minds, settling on a decision outcome. Others report verbally about their deliberations and their decisions; their facial expressions change as they deliberate; they hesitate, stop what they are doing, and so on.

12. But the evaluative faculty you have proposed is not just the ability to form one's character; it is further the ability to do so without being determined by anything to decide as one does. It is a particularly unverifiable position to assert that we have the ability to decide in a way that is not necessitated by anything. How could we ever know whether or not this is the case?

To claim that persons retain the power to fashion and refashion their character, without being necessitated by anything to do so in one way rather than another, is not to assert something incomprehensible or utterly opaque. We know from the inside what it is like to deliberate among competing desires or courses of action and to exercise our faculty to decide to form one particular preference rather than another, without being necessitated by any prior factor to decide as we do. It is commonplace, at any rate, to operate on the assumption that we have such an ability, and there are various considerations that justify this assumption on our part.[56]

The account I have presented does not make free action wholly mysterious. It does not place agents entirely outside the causal nexus, and it does not require for the existence of freedom the falsity of the Principle of Universal Causation (the principle that every event has a cause). Further, free actions, on the view, are not random or arbitrary; they are directly under the agent's control in being determined by and only by the agent, and the notion of an agent is explicated rather than left as a primitive. Free actions are explicable in terms of an individual's character.

Consider, again, the internal evidence. We often introspectively observe ourselves or directly experience choosing without being necessitated to choose in any particular manner. We may, of course, be wrong. Our evidence of how it feels to make decisions about what sorts of people to be and about what to do, without being either coerced or determined by the past, may be deceiving. However, in the absence of any good reasons for thinking so, and in the presence of reasons for thinking that our internal observations of the process are accurate, it is legitimate to *account for* this evidence by positing an undetermined evaluative faculty, which is not to be conceived as an immaterial substance, but as an ability to form preferences.

13. A decision to form a particular preference should be reasonable or rational for the agent, rather than arbitrary, in order for the act resulting from that decision to be free. But if the agent's deliberative process comes up with the answer that, all things considered, A is the best choice, then it seems that she ought to be necessitated to choose A. To require for freedom that her choice outcome remain undetermined by the reasons seems to require an odd ability: the ability to decide against the best reasons. But no one wants this ability.

To require for freedom that an agent be able to choose otherwise in the categorical sense *after* the occurrence in her mind of various considerations—that she be able to choose A and that she be able to choose B, given the laws of nature and all of the facts about her and

her past, including the deliberations of her evaluative faculty—
seems to require for freedom the ability to act irrationally. As
Robert Kane expresses the problem, what is difficult to understand
and in need of explanation is "how I could have reasonably chosen
to do otherwise, how I could have reasonably chosen B, *given exactly the same prior deliberation* that led me to choose A, the same
information deployed, the same consequences considered, the same
assessments made, and so on."[57]

Once A has been judged to be the right decision outcome, a
choice of B would appear to be irrational. In cases in which the deliberative faculty reveals one best answer, the proposed account of
freedom, the critic charges, requires something nondesirable: the
ability to choose what is *not* the most rational alternative. To want
the ability to act freely as I have characterized it might then seem to
be, in the words of Susan Wolf:

> not only to want the ability to make choices even when there is no
> basis for choice, but to want the ability to make choices on no basis
> even when there is a basis. But the latter ability would seem to be an
> ability no one could ever have reason to want to exercise.[58]

But on the proposed account, it is not true of choice outcomes
that they have no basis whatsoever; they are, rather, caused indeterministically by prior considerations. Suppose that my decision outcome is preference A. Now, what does it mean to say that I could
have reasonably formed preference B, given exactly the same prior
deliberation that led me, in fact, to choose A? We know what it
means to say that I *could have* chosen otherwise than A: I had the
skill required for forming some choice outcome other than A, and,
given the past and the laws, it was undetermined what choice outcome would follow. In other words, the physical conditions and
laws *left room* for the exercise of my skill. As to the question of how
I could have *reasonably* chosen otherwise, suppose that I had decisively formed preference B (rather than preference A), that preference B was uncoerced, and that preference B was indeterminately
caused by my prior considerations. Then preference B was *reasonable*. That is, if formed, the preference for B would have been
caused and justified by reasons. In fact, so long as the choice out-

come follows on reasons considered by the agent in the deliberative process, it is *reasonable* in some sense: in the sense that it results for a reason, although it is not necessarily the most rational option, given the total set of the agent's reasons.

If the objector claims to prefer at every juncture being determined to decide as he does by the best considerations rather than by just any considerations, then this merely shows something about the objector's values: that he prizes being right over being free. Being pushed into deciding in a certain way by anything—whether one's grandmother, one's genetic blueprint, or overwhelmingly powerful considerations—is antithetical to free agency. Contrary to Wolf's claim about what we want, in deciding what to do and what sort of person to be, we do not want to be determined by anything. Rational and causal influence is one thing; determination of choice is another. Again, freedom is opposed to constraint, and *having* to choose in any particular way, no matter how rational or objectively right that way may be, is constraining.

On the proposed account, then, *prior to* the working of the agent's evaluative faculty, the agent can form a preference for A and can form a preference for B. Both preference A and preference B could, at that point, be rational for the agent if she has reasons supporting each preference. A preference probabilistically caused by considerations of the agent's is not a preference formed "on no basis." The objection might be construed as a request for an explanation of how either of two alternate decisively formed preferences that the agent could potentially form could be rational for that agent, if formed. The answer, then, is that whichever one *is* made is rationally explicable by reference to the agent's evaluative process and its inputs. Suppose she decided to form preference A. Why did she do so? Because of prior considerations that reasonably supported that particular decision outcome. The decisions from which free acts result are those that the agent forms on some basis, yet no basis is causally determining of what she decides.

Notes

1. Thus it is not that the agent could or would do otherwise if certain circumstances had been different, but rather that the agent has open to her at

the moment more than one possibility for acting, given the past and the circumstances exactly as they are.

2. Alvin Plantinga, "Advice to Christian Philosophers," in Michael D. Beaty, ed., *Christian Theism and the Problems of Philosophy* (Notre Dame, IN: University of Notre Dame Press, 1990), pp. 29–31.

3. Timothy O'Connor, "Indeterminism and Free Agency: Three Recent Views," *Philosophy and Phenomenological Research* 53, 1993, pp. 499–526; Timothy O'Connor, "Why Agent Causation?" *Philosophical Topics* 24, 1996, pp. 143–158; Randolph Clarke, "Toward a Credible Agent-Causal Account of Free Will," *Nous* 27, 1993, pp. 191–203.

4. See, for instance, Gary Watson, "Free Action and Free Will," *Mind* 46, 1987, pp. 145–172; and Kadri Vihvelin, "Freedom, Causation, and Counterfactuals," *Philosophical Studies* 64, 1991, pp. 176–177.

5. Arthur Schopenhauer, "Essay on the Freedom of the Will," in *Essay on the Freedom of the Will*, trans. Konstantine Kolenda (Indianapolis, IN: Bobbs-Merrill, 1960); reprinted in Joel Feinberg, ed., *Reason and Responsibility* (Belmont, CA: Wadsworth, 1989), p. 360.

6. Richard Taylor, *Metaphysics* (Englewood Cliffs, NJ: Prentice-Hall, 1974), p. 58.

7. Incompatibilists may further agree on some broad conditions for freedom also acknowledged by compatibilists, such as that free will is possessed only by persons with certain reflective capacities, including the capacity to set ends for oneself and to form values.

8. Robert Kane is a contemporary incompatibilist who also rejects such views as implausible. See Robert Kane, *Free Will and Values* (Albany, NY: SUNY Press, 1985) and Robert Kane, *The Significance of Free Will* (New York: Oxford University Press, 1996).

9. Fred Dretske defines behavior as a process in *Explaining Behavior* (Cambridge, MA: MIT Press, 1988).

10. See, for instance, Michael Bratman, *Intention, Plans, and Practical Reason* (Cambridge, MA: Harvard University Press, 1987); Myles Brand, *Intending and Acting* (Cambridge, MA: MIT Press, 1984); Carlos Moya, *Philosophy of Action* (Oxford: Blackwell, 1991); and Alfred Mele, *Springs of Action: Understanding Intentional Behavior* (New York: Oxford University Press, 1992).

11. O'Connor ("Indeterminism and Free Agency" and "Why Agent Causation?") classifies libertarian theories into three types: *simple indeterminism*, *causal indeterminism*, and *the agency* (or agent-causationist) *theory*. But an example of the first sort (Stewart Goetz, "Libertarian Choice," *Faith and Philosophy* 14, 1997, pp. 195–211) makes appeal to something uncaused that is not a causal simple. And all libertarians who affirm free will believe in "agency," as all alike are committed to *event-causal indeterminism*. I do not have any better names for the theories T-1, A-C, and T-3 set

out below, but I have tried to characterize these three libertarian theory types in a way that is comprehensive and useful.

12. Others taking *volition* to be central to the analysis of action include Hugh McCann ("Volition and Basic Action," *Philosophical Review* 83, 1974, pp. 451–473) and Brian O'Shaughnessy (*The Will*, 2 vols., Cambridge: Cambridge University Press, 1980).

13. Carl Ginet, *On Action* (Cambridge: Cambridge University Press, 1990), pp. 13–32.

14. Goetz, "Libertarian Choice." (Goetz notes that one anonymous referee called his view "eccentric.")

15. Ginet, *On Action*, pp. 145–146. For critical discussion of Ginet's position on this issue, see Goetz, "Libertarian Choice," pp. 205–207.

16. In Laura W. Ekstrom, "Freedom, Coherence, and the Self," Ph.D. dissertation, University of Arizona, 1993, I abruptly dismissed all such views.

17. R. E. Hobart, "Free Will as Involving Determination and Inconceivable Without It," *Mind*, 43, 1934, pp. 1–27.

18. See J. David Velleman, "What Happens When Someone Acts?" *Mind* 101, 1992, pp. 461–481; reprinted in John Martin Fischer and Mark Ravizza, eds., *Perspectives on Moral Responsibility* (Ithaca: Cornell University Press, 1993), p. 194, note 3. For a discussion of this problem for Ginet's account, see O'Connor, "Why Agent Causation?" p. 146.

19. Thomas Reid, *Essays on the Active Powers of the Human Mind*, Introduction by Baruch Brody (Cambridge, MA: MIT Press, 1969); C. A. Campbell, "Has the Self 'Free Will'?" in *On Selfhood and Godhood* (London: George Allen and Unwin, 1957), pp. 158–165, 167–169; Roderick M. Chisholm, "Human Freedom and the Self," The Lindley Lecture, University of Kansas, 1964 (reprinted in Gary Watson, ed., *Free Will*, Oxford: Oxford University Press, 1982, pp. 24–35); Richard Taylor, *Metaphysics*, 4th edition (Englewood Cliffs, NJ: Prentice-Hall, 1992); Clarke, "Toward a Credible Agent-Causal Account," pp. 191–203; O'Connor, "Why Agent-Causation?" and *Persons and Causes: The Metaphysics of Free Will* (Oxford: Oxford University Press, forthcoming). I am grateful to O'Connor for making available to me two chapters of his unpublished manuscript.

20. On Reid's view, only those actions that a person wills or determines to do are truly his actions. See Reid, *Active Powers*.

21. Chisholm, "Human Freedom," p. 27.

22. Ibid., p. 32.

23. Reid, by contrast, takes agent-causation to be the primary, most obvious form of causation, lost sight of and only supposed to be mysterious since Hume biased the philosophical world toward event-causation.

24. See Thomas Hobbes, *The English Works of Thomas Hobbes*, vol. 5, ed. W. Molesworth (London: Scientia Aalen, 1962), pp. 35, 77, 113; Gary Watson, "Introduction," in Watson, *Free Will*, p. 10; and John Bishop, *Nat-*

ural Agency: An Essay on the Causal Theory of Action (Cambridge: Cambridge University Press, 1989), p. 69.

25. R. Harre and E. H. Madden, *Causal Powers: A Theory of Natural Necessity* (Oxford: Blackwell, 1975).

26. See, for instance, C. D. Broad, "Determinism, Indeterminism, and Libertarianism," in Sidney Morgenbesser and J. H. Walsh, eds., *Free Will* (Englewood Cliffs, NJ: Prentice-Hall, 1962) and Ginet, *On Action*.

27. O'Connor replies by rejecting the demand for an explanation of every contrastive fact that obtains in virtue of an event's occurring ("Why Agent Causation?" p. 150). In effect, O'Connor asserts that sometimes the only explanation we have of some event or fact is simply that it just did turn out that way. It remains puzzling to some to countenance agent-causation without an account of what makes the relation obtain when it does and not at other times.

28. O'Connor, *Persons and Causes,* manuscript p. 5.

29. I realize that, as it stands, this question expresses only the suspicion of a problem. However, the burden lies clearly with the agent-causalist to show how his appeal to the special sort of causation fits together with the causation between neurological (and other physical) events.

30. O'Connor, "Why Agent Causation?" pp. 150–151.

31. Roderick Chisholm, "Comments and Replies," *Philosophia* 7, 1978, pp. 597–636, regarding his 1976 *Person and Object: A Metaphysical Study* (quoted in Velleman, "What Happens?"; reprinted in John Martin Fischer and Mark Ravizza, eds., *Perspectives on Moral Responsibility,* Ithaca: Cornell University Press, 1993).

32. Velleman, "What Happens?"; reprinted in Fischer and Ravizza, p. 197.

33. One might question the commitment to reductionism motivating this project. Eleonore Stump has pointed out in incisive comments on the manuscript of this book that certain philosophers of science have recently provided powerful antireductionist arguments. For instance, John Dupre, in his book *The Disorder of Things: Metaphysical Foundations of the Disunity of Science* (Cambridge, MA: Harvard University Press, 1993), argues that entities at many different levels of organization initiate causal chains. If Dupre is right, then to believe that human beings initiate causal chains is not so odd, since we are not the only genuine causal entities, but have a host of company in the natural world. Even if the reductionism I presuppose in launching the project that follows is subject to controversy, let me make clear that it is not unreflectively presupposed. I find working out a model of free action for one convinced of the success of incompatibilist arguments and at the same time skeptical of antireductionist arguments a highly interesting project.

34. G. E. M. Anscombe, "Causality and Determination," in *The Collected Philosophical Papers of G.E.M. Anscombe,* vol. 2 (Minneapolis: University of Minnesota Press, 1981).

35. For an event to have a nonnecessitating cause is not necessarily for it to violate a law of nature. And the truth of this assertion does not require some laws of nature to be indeterministic. For laws of nature to be deterministic is for them, together with the description of the situation, to entail unique results. It may be that some laws of nature are indeterministic. But, alternatively, it may be true that all laws of nature are deterministic, while it is also the case that not every event is covered by or falls under a law. Since the laws of nature may not cover every event that happens, the laws' being deterministic does not tell us whether or not the thesis of determinism is true.

36. David Lewis, Postscript to "Causation," in *Philosophical Papers*, vol. 2 (New York: Oxford University Press, 1986), p. 175.

37. Kane names his view a "free willist" account (see Kane, *Significance of Free Will*). Focusing in particular on his account of moral and prudential choices, Kane proposes that *the effort of will* to resist temptation and instead perform the right act is an indeterminate process, analogous to quantum indeterminacy at the subatomic level. Kane suggests that processes in the brain could amplify indeterminate events at the microlevel and that we experience these processes as efforts of will. The indeterminacy, on Kane's account, is resolved by the agent's choice, which is a causally undetermined event. As an effort of will is taken to be a response to conflicts *within* an agent's motivational system, whichever effort of will it is that is made is explained, but not determined, by the agent's motives (Kane, *Significance of Free Will*, pp. 126–142).

One might wonder about the source of the choice described by Kane as inducing determinacy into the system (analogous to the quantum measurement). It does not come from the indeterministic effort of will process, so is it conceived as agent-caused or as uncaused? Kane replies that the choice is part of what he calls the "self-network," described as a network of neural connections representing the agent's general motivational system. Kane suggests that "The feeling that certain events in the brain, such as those corresponding to our efforts and choices, are things we are doing rather than things that are merely happening has its basis in the superposition of the synchronized wave patterns (or patterns of oscillations of neural firings) of the self-network upon those neural events. The suggestion, in other words, is that the neural events corresponding to our efforts and choices would be overlaid by the wave patterns unifying the self-network—so that the wave patterns and the effort or choice events are coupled, causally influencing and interacting with each other" (*Significance of Free Will*, p. 140).

Distinctive of libertarian free willings, on the account, are that "the contributing patterns of oscillations of the self-network would *involve chaotic indeterminacies*," so that the choice outcome is not causally determined, and, further, "there would be more than one feasible option . . . that the patterns of the self-network might push over the top, thus triggering the choice outcome. Whichever outcome is pushed over the top, however, would be the product of the self-network whose distinctive oscillations would be crucial to its coming about" (*Significance of Free Will,* p. 141).

Kane and I agree on the thesis of incompatibilism, and he is right in emphasizing the need for the development of a positive incompatibilist model of the nature of free action. Furthermore, Kane is right to seek an account not dependent upon the notion of agent-causation as a primitive notion. Thus, although our accounts were independently developed and differ in several details, I am very much in agreement with the general spirit of his account.

38. Robert Nozick, *Philosophical Explanations* (Cambridge, MA: Harvard University Press, 1981), pp. 291–316. For critical discussion of Nozick's, as well as Kane's, account, see O'Connor, "Indeterminism and Free Agency," pp. 499–526.

39. Although, as Velleman notes, the account is likely traceable at least to Thomas Hobbes (see Velleman, "What Happens?").

40. For discussion of the need for "normal" or nondeviant causal chains, see Bishop, *Natural Agency,* and Mele, *Springs of Action.*

41. Alfred Mele, although not a libertarian, agrees with this assessment. He defends the claim that the most viable location for indeterminism in a libertarian account of free action is further back in the causal history of the act. See Alfred Mele, *Autonomous Agents: From Self-Control to Autonomy* (New York: Oxford University Press, 1995), p. 215.

42. So I *do* think, as John Martin Fischer does in arguing from a semicompatibilist viewpoint in *The Metaphysics of Free Will: An Essay on Control* (Aristotle Society Series, vol. 14, Cambridge, MA: Blackwell, 1994), that we should focus on the *actual-mechanism sequence* producing the act, and not on the counterfactual-mechanism sequence. The actual sequence, on my view, needs to have some indeterministic causal links, and they need to be located in the right places; this is, of course, what makes the view incompatibilist.

43. Laura Waddell Ekstrom, "A Coherence Theory of Autonomy," *Philosophy and Phenomenological Research* 53, 1993, p. 603.

44. Gary Watson, "Free Agency," in Watson, *Free Will,* p. 109.

45. Robert Kane describes a decision as the settlement of conditions of doubt or uncertainty about what to do, which forms an intention that will

guide an agent's action now or in the future. This "settlement" is itself an act. Kane, *Significance of Free Will*, p. 23.

46. The formation of the preference counts as an act in virtue of its causal history—in particular in virtue of its being preceded by an intention to decide what to prefer (or the intention to form some preference or another). Likewise, on Mele's view, decisions to *A* are preceded not by intentions to decide to *A*, but rather by intentions to decide what to do (see Alfred Mele, "Agency and Mental Action," *Philosophical Perspectives* 11, 1997, pp. 231–249).

47. This should not be taken to imply that an agent might not realize that she ought to rethink the matter and subsequently begin another decision process, leading to the formation of a type-identical preference (or intention) or a different preference (or intention).

48. Consider the following objection. Take the case of the decisive formation of preference. Is this a free act? In order to be so, it must, on the proposed account, be preceded by (indeterministically and uncoercively formed) preference. But then that act of preference formation, to be free, must derive properly from a preference, and so on. Thus it seems that there is a regress problem with the proposed account. (Alfred Mele suggested this potential problem in his comments on an earlier version of this chapter.)

But, in response, I deny that the act of preference formation must be free in order for the act generated by the preference to be free. For, as my friend David Robb has said, I can make you angry without myself being angry. That is, not every property had by an effect is present in the cause. Thus an act is controlled by an agent in being causally derived from a preference (a preference that is itself formed by and, as I explain below, partially constitutive of him); and just prior to the formation of the preference is the right location for the indeterminism shown necessary by the incompatibilist arguments for acting freely. Preference formation may be an act (in having a certain kind of causal history involving crucially a pertinent intention) without itself needing to be preceded by preference.

49. Christopher Hitchcock writes: "It has become close to orthodoxy in the philosophy of science to believe that indeterministic explanation is possible. There are, no doubt, strong pre-theoretic intuitions linking explanation and determinism. Through a series of powerful arguments (Hempel [1965], Jeffrey [1971], Salmon [1971], [1984], Railton [1978], [1981], Lewis [1986b], Humphreys [1989]), however, we have been trained to repress these intuitions. I wholeheartedly accept the conclusions of these arguments; nonetheless, it would be idle to deny that we still carry these intuitions; we are all occasionally haunted by the demons of determinism. It is even possible to entice these demons to rise by phrasing our questions in

the right way: since the photon *could have* been absorbed, then surely we have not *fully explained* why the photon was transmitted? We must not give in to temptation" ("Contrastive Explanation and the Demons of Determinism," *British Journal for the Philosophy of Science,* forthcoming, typescript p. 2). Hitchcock goes on to argue that, not only is it possible to provide explanations of indeterministic outcomes, but also it is possible to provide *contrastive* explanations of those outcomes. Preferences indeterministically caused by an agent's considerations can be explained and, furthermore, if Hitchcock is right, then explanation may be available for why an agent prefers *A* rather than *B.*

50. Ekstrom, "Coherence Theory of Autonomy," pp. 599–616.

51. The account in Ekstrom, "Coherence Theory of Autonomy," further specifies one's *central* self to consist in the evaluative faculty plus a subset of the preferences and acceptances, namely those that cohere together, and subsequently characterizes autonomous action as action on a cohering or *personally authorized* preference. That account does solve certain problems with hierarchical accounts of self-directed action, such as Frankfurt's account, but at the cost, I am afraid, of making it untenable that autonomous action so conceived is necessary for morally responsible action.

52. In the free will literature, there are two accounts of a sort similar to the one I have proposed (besides those of Kane and Nozick) worthy of mention. Daniel Dennett sketches—without himself endorsing—what he contends is the best model of free agency available to a libertarian ("On Giving Libertarians What They Say They Want," in *Brainstorms,* Montgomery, VT: Bradford Books, 1978, pp. 286–299). Dennett describes a scenario in which an agent must make a decision about what to do—namely, to accept academic job offer A or to accept academic job offer B. According to the model, "It just might be the case that *exactly* which considerations occur to one in such circumstances is to some degree strictly undetermined" (p. 294). In Dennett's example, considerations A through F occur to Jones, and on the basis of them, she decides to take a job at Swarthmore. But had consideration G also occurred to her, she would have taken a job at the University of Chicago instead. As it happened, G did not occur to her, although it might have, given the past and the laws. The proposal is that the indeterminism required for an act to be free is quite far back in the causal history of the act in question: just prior to the events describable as certain considerations occurring to the agent as inputs to the process of deliberation over what to do.

Dennett's proposal—set out only on the way toward making the ultimate point that incompatibilist freedom is not really the sort of freedom we want—is closely related to the model of libertarian autonomy proposed (but, again, not endorsed) by Alfred Mele (see Mele, *Autonomous Agents*). Mele's proposal is this: What should be held by the libertarian to be causally undetermined is "which members of a shifting subset of Jones's relevant nonoccurrent beliefs will become occurrent and function in his deliberation" (Mele, *Autonomous Agents,* p. 214). So, some beliefs will come to mind and some will not, and of those that come to mind, a subset of them are undetermined to occur by the past and the laws—they just *happen* to occur when they do in the deliberation process, but they might not have. Mele takes judgments concerning what to do to be the outcome of practical deliberation. So, *what* an agent decisively judges best in the case of deliberation leading to free action remains causally open until deliberation ends, and *when* deliberation ends remains causally open, since it is causally open whether a certain belief will come to mind and prolong deliberation. Mele claims as virtues of this account of modest libertarianism the following: (1.) compatibilists have no good reason to insist on determinism at this point in the deliberative process as a requirement for freedom; (2.) this sort of internal indeterminism is, for all we know, a reality; (3.) such indeterminism does not diminish the agent's control over his deliberations (*Autonomous Agents,* chap. 12).

The views set out by Dennett and Mele offer another interesting T-3 libertarian alternative. But, in my view, they locate the indeterminism in the wrong place. Specifically, the views are too *weak,* in virtue of the indeterminism location, to secure agential freedom. On these views, free agents are subject to luck in what thoughts come into their minds as they are deliberating about what to do. But once the thoughts occur and the last of them has occurred during deliberation, there is a deterministic causal connection between the particular pattern of beliefs that has happened to occur and the subsequent decision outcome. But this is problematic. For I might be a free agent, on Dennett's or Mele's account, while being a victim, with regard to what I judge best and what I consequently intend and do, of what thoughts happen to occur to me at the time. Granted, there are "forks in the road" of some sort on this picture of free agency (alternate physically possible futures). But it is not up to me, the free agent, which one I take. Which one I take is decided by which considerations happen to come to mind, where this is indeterministically caused by some previous events. On both Dennett's and Mele's views, once a certain pattern of considerations has happened to occur to the agent, a particular action may follow of physical necessity and yet count as free. Since neither of the views includes an account of the nature of the self, they leave unanswered the question of why an act that is the causally necessary outcome of whatever considerations have happened to occur is plausibly claimed to be originated by the agent.

53. The utterance "Do *X* or die" is surely a coercive threat. For accounts of the nature of coercion, see Harry Frankfurt, "Coercion and Moral Responsibility," in Ted Honderich, ed., *Essays on Freedom of Action* (London: Routledge and Kegan Paul, 1973); H. J. McCloskey, "Coercion: Its Nature and Significance," *Southern Journal of Philosophy* 18, 1980, pp. 335–352; Bernard Gert, "Coercion and Freedom," in J. Roland Pennock, ed., *Coercion* (Chicago: Atherton, 1972); and Michael J. Murray and David F. Dudrick, "Are Coerced Acts Free?" *American Philosophical Quarterly* 32, 1995, pp. 109–123.

54. Mele, *Autonomous Agents;* Dennett, "On Giving Libertarians."

55. See, for instance, Kane, *Significance of Free Will*, pp. 128–130; and Jesse Hobbs, "Chaos and Indeterminism," *Canadian Journal of Philosophy* 21, 1991, pp. 141–164.

56. Considerations justifying the assumption include, for instance, its being required for our having dignity, for our taking part in significant relationships, and for our being held morally responsible in a certain sense.

57. Kane, *Free Will and Values*, p. 57. Kane raises this objection and then goes on to answer it.

58. Susan Wolf, *Freedom Within Reason* (New York: Oxford University Press, 1990), p. 55. This is the sort of consideration that leads Wolf to conclude that the determination of one's choice by reason does not compromise the freedom of that choice.

CHAPTER FIVE

The Concept of Moral Responsibility

What distinguishes an act for which a person is morally responsible from an act for which he or she is not? Of course, the act must at least be *morally significant*: It must be an act that could reasonably be described as either morally right or morally wrong (or, perhaps, as morally ambiguous, although clearly of moral consequence). So, for instance, the act of eating a dish of vanilla ice cream rather than a dish of blackberry ice cream is not an act for which a person is either morally responsible or not morally responsible, since the act itself is morally insignificant. (It is morally insignificant unless, that is, one eats the last of the vanilla ice cream as a malicious attempt to deprive one's uncle of his dying wish for that flavor of ice cream, or one eats it under some such circumstances giving moral weight to the act.) Given a morally significant act—breaking a promise, say, or telling a lie or reporting a crime—what is it about a person's performance of the act that makes it appropriate to praise or blame her, or to punish or reward her, for what she did? A common suggestion is that the person must have done the act of her own free will. The problem of specifying the right conditions for acting freely, or of one's own free will, is therefore connected to the topic of moral responsibility.

As should be clear from the foregoing chapters, though, I do not take the problem of free will to reduce to the problem of moral responsibility. Some philosophers, by contrast, treat the issue of free action as precisely the issue of morally responsible action. For instance, Susan Wolf says at the beginning of the book *Freedom Within Reason*, when defining her topic: "We can express the problem of free will in the form of the question. . . . 'What kind of beings must we be if we are ever to be responsible for the results of our wills?'"[1] Throughout the book, Wolf speaks of "free and responsible action," blurring the topics, and she repeatedly tests competing theories of freedom by their intuitive satisfiability as accounts of responsible action. For philosophers such as Wolf, the problem of giving a correct account of the nature of free action apparently just *is* the problem of giving a right account of action for which an agent is morally responsible. And so, of course, for such persons, issues concerning moral responsibility are relevant to discussions of free will, since those issues are the same as the issues concerning freedom.

But one need not subsume all discussion of free will into a discussion of moral responsibility.[2] As discussed at the outset of the book, a number of sources drive us to reflect deeply on the topic of free agency, including concern for personal dignity, interest in maintaining an accurate self-concept, and certain interpersonal relational issues. Some may see all of these concerns as deriving more basically from a concern with persons' moral responsibility. But these sources of interest need not be derivative from the moral responsibility interest. One might quite respectably be concerned with whether or not there *is* such a thing in the actual world as a free action or a free will, or with the question of what it would take for something to count as a free action or a free will, regardless of whether or not, in fact, there are any such things. And one might think that what guides our intuitions concerning the proper use of the terms 'free action' and 'free will' is not solely, or even primarily, a set of convictions regarding moral responsibility, but rather a cluster of concerns relating to personhood, dignity, explanation, causation, and self-direction. To see the problem of free will in this way is to see it as fundamentally a metaphysical problem rather than as primarily or only an ethical one. Robert Nozick succinctly expresses this point of view:

> My interest in the question of free will does not stem from wanting to be able legitimately to punish others, to hold them responsible, or even to be held responsible myself. Without free will, we seem diminished, merely the playthings of external forces. How, then, can we maintain an exalted view of ourselves? Determinism seems to undercut human dignity, it seems to undermine our value. . . . The philo-

sophical discussion focusing upon issues of punishment and responsibility, therefore, strikes one as askew, as concerned with a side issue, although admittedly an important one.[3]

For those of us, then, who see free agency as a specialized topic in metaphysics and the philosophy of mind, the problem of free will does not reduce to the problem of moral responsibility. The problems are, nonetheless, importantly connected, in virtue of the fact that an act's being freely done is widely regarded as a necessary condition—and by some regarded as also a sufficient condition—for a person's being morally responsible for that act. The question of whether freedom is necessary or sufficient (or both) for moral responsibility is itself important and engaging. Thus one might avoid the subsumption of free will talk into moral responsibility talk while acknowledging questions of moral responsibility to be connected to the problem of free will.

I have argued in previous chapters for the conclusion that there are complex metaphysical requirements of an incompatibilist sort for free action. If freedom is necessary for moral responsibility, and if it is true that freedom has requirements that entail incompatibilism, then there are complex incompatibilist metaphysical requirements for morally responsible action, as well. It could turn out, on the contrary, that the sort of freedom involved in important parts of our self-concept—the parts pertaining to our dignity, deliberative powers, and capacities as the originators of actions—is distinct from the sort of freedom necessary for moral responsibility. In principle, surely, these could pull apart. John Martin Fischer, in fact, takes the issues to pull apart. The kind of freedom had by an agent possessing what Fischer calls "regulative control" requires available alternatives; this sort of freedom, Fischer argues, *is* incompatible with causal determinism. Hence Fischer is an incompatibilist concerning determinism and the kind of freedom involving the ability to do or to decide otherwise. But regulative control is distinct, in Fischer's view, from the sort of freedom that is necessary for moral responsibility: "guidance control." Hence moral responsibility, according to Fischer, does not require available alternatives.[4]

The central question with regard to free will and moral responsibility, then, is this: Is acting freely required for being morally responsible for one's act? And, if so, then acting freely *in what sense*?

Is the sort of freedom that undergirds human dignity and that is a part of our natural view of ourselves the same sort of freedom that is required for our being morally responsible for those of our acts that are morally significant?

The task of this chapter is to make a start on answering this question. But before undertaking to answer it, it is important to take a look directly at the issue of what we are doing when we hold people morally responsible for what they do. Discussions of free will and moral responsibility usually rely upon intuitions concerning particular cases, and of course this is a natural place to start. But often philosophers depend upon such intuitions without bringing out explicitly the views regarding the function and nature of moral responsibility behind the intuitive judgments. Asking first what it *is* to hold persons morally responsible for their acts will put us in a better position to assess claims such as Fischer's concerning the sort of freedom required for responsibility. For whether, and in what sense, freedom is required for moral responsibility depends upon the question of the true function of moral responsibility ascriptions. Hence the following section considers varying accounts of what we are doing when we hold ourselves and others morally accountable.

The Function of Moral Responsibility Ascriptions

Suppose that Sam and Nancy, after a period of casual acquaintance and friendship, decide to have an exclusive romantic relationship with each other. They talk about it, decide to "take the plunge" of commitment, and mutually agree to have a relationship characterized by trust and respect. Suppose that they have such a relationship for several years. They are committed, in love, and mutually trusting. But then one day Sam, behind Nancy's back, has a sexual encounter with another woman. When Nancy painfully discovers this fact, she regards Sam as blameworthy for violating their agreement and betraying her trust. Complex psychological and relational issues are likely at play in this scenario, issues that make difficult a complete moral assessment of the situation. Nonetheless, it would surely be agreed by many that Sam has done something wrong in violating a significant interpersonal agreement and, in so doing, mistreating Nancy. We do not have to deride Sam as a "lout" or a "loser" in order to regard him as morally responsible for his infidelity. Certainly, at any rate, we can raise the question as to Sam's moral responsibility for his act, and it is the *nature* of this question that is of particular philosophical interest.

What would it be to say that Sam is morally responsible for his act of infidelity? More generally, what is it that we are doing when we hold persons responsible for what they do? A number of competing views describe the point, or function, of ascribing moral responsibility to individuals for their actions.

The Pragmatic Approach

One view takes holding persons morally responsible to be nothing more than attempts at behavior control. So to see Sam as blameworthy and to tell him that he is blameworthy for what he did is just to attempt to control Sam's future actions: to keep him from misbehaving again. There is no metaphysical fact about the matter of whether or not Sam is morally responsible. He's morally responsible if we say that he is, and we say that he is when we want to try to get him to act in certain ways in the future. According to the philosopher Moritz Schlick, for instance, "The question regarding responsibility is the question: Who, in a given case, is to be punished [or rewarded]?"[5] For Schlick, this question is a practical one: Those to be punished are those whose behavior we want to mold into socially preferable ways or, alternately, those whom we want to use as examples to others in order to mold others' behavior. Thus, in deciding whether or not to punish someone, we consider whether or not doing so is likely to get that person and other members of the society to act in preferable ways in the future. Writes Schlick: "Punishment is an educative measure, and as such is a means to the formation of motives, which are in part to prevent the wrongdoer from repeating the act (reformation) and in part to prevent others from committing a similar act (intimidation). Analogously, in the case of reward we are concerned with an incentive."[6] There is no relevant question about how people *deserve* to be treated in response to their acts, according to this view of the function of moral responsibility ascriptions. Instead, the justification of praise and blame, and of punishment and reward, is social utility.

Certainly there are pragmatic functions of social institutions for punishment and reward. Prison terms for sex offenders protect potential victims, for instance, and tax deductions for charitable contributions encourage generous donation. It would be foolish to deny the usefulness of moral responsibility ascriptions and the accompanying practices of praise and blame, punishment and reward. But it would also be shortsighted to accept the pragmatic theory as accurately characterizing the central function of such ascriptions. Several important objections diminish the force of the purely pragmatic notion of moral responsibility.

For one, whether or not it would be socially useful to punish or reward a person often separates out from the issue of whether or not he, in fact, did the act and did it in a way that makes him deserving of punishment or reward. For instance, it could be plausibly argued that it would be socially useful to punish Timothy McVeigh very severely for the 1995 bombing of the Oklahoma City federal building: Punishing him severely would send a strong message to other potential bombers, notifying them of likely harsh recrimination in response to similar acts, creating a deterrent; and if McVeigh is allowed to live, then punishing him would also mold his future behavior. But this fact alone does not give a full account of that in which Timothy McVeigh's moral responsibility consists. There is the further question of whether or not he actually committed the bombing in a way that makes him deserving of severe punishment. Perhaps McVeigh did not do it. Or perhaps he did it under serious threat. Perhaps in some other way he was forced to do it. The point is that there is evidence relevant to ascertaining his moral responsibility, evidence that does not consist solely in pragmatic considerations. Relevant evidence includes information concerning the truth about what McVeigh did, the truth concerning what Daniel Dennett calls his "total, before-the-eyes-of-God Guilt."[7]

Now Dennett, who, like Schlick, endorses a pragmatic approach to moral responsibility, says regarding this kind of before-the-eyes-of-God Guilt that, in fact, "*that* condition is never to be met in this world."[8] Dennett claims that once we realize "the social utility of the myth of free will," we will "wonder if we are obliged by any further reasons to go along with the institution and, in the private arena of our own hearts, hold ourselves responsible."[9] But we can hold ourselves responsible, Dennett goes on to say; doing so makes sense when we want to mold our own behavior in certain ways for the future. Dennett continues:

How should one respond to the idea that one is guilty? If the concept of guilt one is contemplating applying to oneself is the traditional, absolute concept of guilty-before-the-eyes-of-God, then one has as much reason to dismiss it as one does to dismiss the other dubious absolutist notions that are its kin. . . . No one, not monsters like Hitler or Eichmann, not ordinary sane criminals like Agnew or Vesco, and not you when you last broke a law, or broke a promise, is or could be guilty in that sense. For that sense of guilt has been screwed so tight by philosophical and theological tradition that the condition it purports to name defies description.[10]

Of course, if this passage is supposed to be, by itself, a refutation of the claim that a person could be guilty-before-the-eyes-of-God, it is clearly unsuccessful. The idea that absolute responsibility from a God's-eye point of view is nonexistent is, no doubt, initially appealing to us as persons who have at times committed wrong acts. However, Dennett has not shown this to be the case. Furthermore, the sense of guilt that Dennett claims defies description will be described below, in the context of the third view concerning the nature of moral responsibility. But what is interesting about this passage of Dennett's is that it illustrates both a motivation and a defect of the pragmatic theory. A motivation of the view is skepticism about our ability to discern any fact concerning whether or not a person really is guilty for committing a wrong act and so deserves blame and punishment for it (or, alternately, whether he really did a good act in a way making him deserving of praise and reward for it). There is no need to attempt to ascertain any such fact, on the pragmatic view. Our holding persons responsible establishes their guilt (or innocence), and we hold persons responsible for the purpose of establishing certain patterns of behavior in society. But this motivation is also surely a defect of the view. For no matter how difficult it is to establish the facts concerning a person's guilt or innocence, our practice of searching for the facts indicates our deep commitment to the notion that there are some, as well as our commitment to the truth that it is these facts, and not our fiat, that determine genuine responsibility.[11]

A further problem for the pragmatic account is that it reduces seriously considered, heartfelt judgments of moral responsibility to simple attempts at manipulation. For instance, the view makes Nancy's feelings of outrage at Sam's betrayal and her expressions of blame toward Sam into mere vehicles of interpersonal control. On the pragmatic view, by blaming Sam, Nancy is only trying to get him to act as she would like him to act in the future. Naturally, one would think that if Nancy wants to stay with Sam and continues to hope for their having an exclusive and respectful relationship, then she would like for him to be faithful to her in the future. But surely in holding Sam morally responsible for his act of infidelity, getting him to be subsequently faithful is not *all* that Nancy wants. She is, understandably, outraged at *this* instance of infidelity, and in telling Sam she blames him for what he did to her, she is expressing this fact. The pragmatic view misses something deep and essential to moral responsibility.

Strawson's Expressive Theory

What is missing in a purely pragmatic view of the nature of moral responsibility, according to Peter Strawson, is observation of the fact that interpersonal relations are not only governed by broad-scale social practices and institutions designed for behavior control. They also involve complex and subtle personal attitudes. Strawson points our attention to the fact that, frequently, we experience such attitudes as resentment, gratitude, hurt feelings, hatred, affection, love, and forgiveness when people do things to our benefit or to our detriment. Such attitudes are common to personal relationships, and they involve deep concern with others' attitudes toward us. If we think that someone is being cruel, by being dismissive or arrogant or belittling toward us or toward another person, then it is natural to feel hurt or angry or forgiving. These attitudes Strawson calls "reactive" because we have them in reaction to what we perceive others' attitudes to be toward ourselves and toward other persons.[12] The various reactive attitudes, Strawson observes, are natural to persons, and so in some sense, he argues, they are legitimate and justified.

Imagine what it would be like to completely give up the reactive attitudes. Then the actions of ourselves and other people would be viewed much like the behavior of the wind or rodents or the chance falling tree branch. If a branch should fall from a tree causing a dent in the hood of one's car, one might be annoyed, but one would hardly react toward the branch with the kind of indignation and resentment one might have toward a person who deliberately and with malicious intent bashed one's hood. To have only objective, nonreactive attitudes toward all persons is scarcely something we can envision, and, furthermore, Strawson thinks, it is practically impossible. The reactive attitudes are, indeed, suspended in favor of objective attitudes in special sorts of cases. Those cases include ones exhibiting excusing conditions, which show that the person does not really have the sort of will his actions would normally betray (such as haste, inattention, nervousness), and others in which there are exempting conditions, which show that the person should not be expected to meet the basic demands of decent moral conduct (such as insanity, early childhood, and hypnosis). The fact that the excusing and exempting conditions suspend the reactive attitudes is explained by the lack of efficacy of praising and blaming in those sorts of cases.[13] But cases of this kind are exceptions to the widespread human tendency to react to ourselves and others with such attitudes as love, hatred, moral outrage, resentment, gratitude, and the like. Because we apparently have an unrenounceable commitment to the reactive attitudes and to their accompanying practices of punishment and reward, Strawson concludes that the justifiability of the reactive attitudes and practices is supported.

Strawson's view of the nature of moral responsibility takes the reactive attitudes centrally into account. Praise and blame, punishment and reward, on his view, are not just methods of behavior control, although they do serve this function; they are also and more importantly means of expressing the reactive attitudes. On the expressive theory of moral responsibility, then, when we punish and reward persons, we are not merely trying to mold their behavior, but we are further expressing or giving vent to natural human reactions. The point of saying that Sam is morally responsible for his act of betraying Nancy, on the expressive view, is both to try to mold his and others' future behavior *and* to give expression to Nancy's (and our) attitudes of anger, resentment, and moral indignation at his having violated a significant interpersonal agreement and treated a loved one in a disrespectful way. To be a morally responsible agent, on the expressive theory, is to be prone to being reacted to, by oneself and others, with reactive attitudes. There is no more fundamental belief that gives a justification or rationale for the reactive attitudes or for the practices of praising and blaming. Holding persons responsible is a natural fact about human life. It is not in need of further philosophical justification.

While the expressive theory gets closer than does the pragmatic theory to describing the heart of the nature of moral responsibility, the expressive theory shares, in my view, a certain defect with the pragmatic theory. The defect is that both views make moral responsibility wholly a matter of human contrivance. The pragmatic view states that the point of holding persons responsible is to mold the future behavior of the actor and other members of the society. The expressive theory acknowledges this as one function of moral responsibility ascriptions but adds what its proponents see as the central function, which is to express natural reactive attitudes toward the agent for his or her deed. But both the expressive and the pragmatic accounts make a person's moral responsibility consist in her being *taken to be* responsible by herself or others—in other words, in her being reacted to in particular ways by herself or other members of the society.

That this feature of the accounts is problematic can be seen by considering the fact that persons in a society are notorious for being mistaken about the facts. In Salem, Massachusetts, in the late 1600s, for instance, young women who in some ways did not behave "normally" according to the standards of their society were reacted to with bitterness, moral indignation, and contempt. Labeled "witches," they were held responsible for various misfortunes and maladies suffered by other individuals. On both the pragmatic and the expressive theories of moral responsibility, the "witches" *were* morally responsible for the problems they were accused of perpetrating (since it served a useful social function to punish them and since they were prone to be reacted to by others with reactive attitudes). But surely we recognize that it was not the fault of some young woman who was unfortunately labeled a "witch" that another prominent member of her society contracted, say, the measles.

As Fischer points out against the expressive theory, "There seems to be a difference between being *held* responsible and actually *being* responsible."[14] Certainly, a person can be held responsible by mistake because the evidence makes it appear as if he is guilty, when really he is not. And, likewise, in an alternate sort of case, a person may not be blamed by others because he appears to be innocent, although in fact he is guilty of a moral wrongdoing and has only been lucky having escaped being the subject of negative reactive attitudes on the basis of his misdeed. Similarly, a person might react toward herself with attitudes of guilt and shame, which on the expressive theory would be constitutive of her moral responsibility, when in fact she has done nothing deserving of blame. Hence being *taken to be* morally responsible by oneself or other members of one's society and *being*, in fact, morally responsible are distinct. Strawson's theory obscures the difference between these two issues.

We can put the point in a different way by questioning Strawson's inference from the apparent naturalness of the reactive attitudes to their justifiedness.[15] From the fact that there are certain kinds of widespread feelings and attitudes toward a person for his behavior, it does not follow that those feelings and attitudes are right or that those attitudes *should be* widespread. Imagine, for instance, a society in which individuals with cerebral palsy are reacted to with moral indignation, resentment, and condemnation for their failure to behave in what the community sees as appropriate ways. The fact that there is a widespread and apparently "natural" negative reaction to such persons in their community does not establish or constitute their blameworthiness. The expressive theory does not leave sufficient room for the existing practices of praising and blaming in such a society to be criticized along the lines of rational appropriateness or justification. And this raises questions about the ability of the theory to direct appropriate change.

Rational Accessibility and Desert

The above criticisms of the expressive view suggest that being morally responsible for an act consists not in being the actual recipient of the reactive attitudes of oneself and others in one's society on the basis of one's act, but rather in being the *appropriate* recipient of such attitudes. On a third view of the nature of moral responsibility, to say that a person is morally responsible for her act is to say that she is the fit subject of, or rationally accessible to, the reactive attitudes, as well to the accompanying practices of praise, blame, punishment, and reward on the basis of the act.[16] The question immediately arises as to what constitutes *rational accessibility* to the reactive attitudes and the attendant practices. A compelling suggestion is that it is rational to hold a reactive attitude toward a person just in case the reactive attitude is appropriate, and it is appropriate just in case it is deserved. On this view, then, punishment is seen as retribution that is *deserved* by the wrongdoer, and reward for having done something good is, likewise, grounded in desert.

I will call this the "metaphysical" view of moral responsibility. The point of holding persons responsible, on the metaphysical view, is to state the facts as justice requires. In blaming and praising persons for what they do, we tip back the scales of justice: We give credit where it is earned and blame where it is due. The function of moral responsibility ascriptions is to keep accurate moral accountings, as required by fairness. Rewards are compensations for good acts. Punishments are retributions for wrongs, retributions that offenders deserve on the basis of their acts. The rapist is punished, on this view, not simply because his punishment is an attempt at rehabilitation or deterrence, but primarily because he deserves to be punished for his act of rape. In blaming him, we are not merely expressing a reaction of indignation and disgust at his act, but we are, further and most importantly, stating the truth concerning what justice requires.

According to the metaphysical view, in assessing Sam's moral responsibility for his act of infidelity, we are asking the following question: Is it rational to react to Sam with such attitudes as indignation, moral outrage, anger, and perhaps, ultimately, forgiveness? (Or, rather, is there something about him or the conditions under which his act was done that makes him the inappropriate subject of such attitudes?) The question of what attitudes it is rational to adopt toward Sam depends upon the question of what Sam deserves on the basis of his act. And the idea that there is some type of response deserved by Sam presupposes that there is a fact about whether or not he did something wrong and about whether he did it in a manner worthy of retribution. Thus, in holding Sam morally responsible for his act of infidelity, we imply that a person knowledgeable of all of the relevant facts—such as someone occupying a God's-eye point of view on all of reality—could see the fact that Sam is deserving of blame for it. So in judging Sam to be rationally accessible to the reactive attitudes on the basis of his act, we are claiming that, as best we can tell about the facts (as close as we can come to ascertaining the God's-eye point of view), Sam appears to be *deserving* of blame for his act of infidelity.

One motivation for endorsing the metaphysical approach to moral responsibility is commitment to theism, as various religious traditions' sacred texts support the proposition that human actions are sometimes deserving of blame or praise on the basis of the facts as they are ascertained from a divine perspective. Judaism, Christianity, and Islam maintain that there is one God to whom human beings are accountable for their behavior. The philosopher Thomas Reid endorses this point of view:

> That man is a moral and accountable being, capable of acting right and wrong, and answerable for his conduct to him who made him . . . are principles proclaimed by every man's conscience; principles upon which the systems of morality and natural religion, as well as the system of revelation, are grounded, and which have been generally acknowledged by those who hold contrary opinions on the subject of human liberty. I shall therefore take them for granted.[17]

One might object to the metaphysical view of moral responsibility by expressing the doubt that there is, in fact, anything or anyone to whom human persons can be said to be answerable for their moral conduct except human conventions. Such a thought might lead one to accept either a pragmatic or an expressive approach to moral responsibility. Recall, for instance, Dennett's view of moral responsibility as a matter of intrapersonal and interpersonal manipulation. Dennett takes persons to be mere biological reasoning machines, more complex than other biological organisms, such as spiders and ants, but just as wholly physical and just as subject to deterministic causal laws in their behavior. Our existence has a thoroughly naturalistic evolutionary explanation and not a divine one, Dennett maintains; there is no such thing as "before-the-eyes-of-God Guilt."[18]

For the theist, by contrast, there is more to life than Dennett perceives—more depth, more objective meaning, and more genuine accountability (that is, accountability to God). From a theistic point of view, then, Dennett's picture of human life is pale, impoverished, and, ultimately, incorrect. Hence, given background metaphysical commitments that include assent to the proposition that there is a divine lawgiver to whom persons are accountable for their conduct and who is able accurately to ascertain what each person deserves (by way of complete divine knowledge of the causes and motivations of all acts), the metaphysical account of the nature of moral responsibility is most compelling.

One need not be a theist, however, in order to view the metaphysical approach to moral responsibility as superior to the alternate approaches discussed above. As both Reid and Peter van Inwagen point out, those who claim to reject the thesis that persons are sometimes morally responsible in a metaphysical sense belie their true position when they react with indignation to a personal affront, with gratitude to a kind gesture, and with resentment, blame, pride, guilt, or shame to the actions of themselves and other persons and when they, further, take these attitudes to be appropriately grounded in the facts, rather than misplaced. Asserts van Inwagen: "In my view, the proposition that often we are morally responsible for what we have done is something we all know to be true."[19] Van Inwagen cites psychopaths as possible examples of persons who genuinely reject the idea that they are morally responsible agents, and by this he means morally responsible in the metaphysical sense.[20]

The pragmatic and expressive accounts ought to be rejected by the theist and the nontheist alike, on the grounds that they are simplistic. The accounts problematically reduce the practices of praise and blame, punishment and reward to kinds of moral manipulation and the therapeutic airing of attitudes. The pragmatist would have us believe that we do treat—and that it is fine to treat—persons as we treat performing animals and pets, merely applying methods of behavior conditioning. And the expressive theorist holds that, because our reactive attitudes are natural (no matter how racist or unfair), they are therefore justified. But essential to the nature of various of our reactive attitudes, such as resentment and gratitude, as well as to our understandings of fair punishment and reward, is the notion that they can be appropriate or inappropriate, deserved or undeserved, depending upon certain facts about agents' control over their actions. If we were never concerned with whether or not our gratitude, for instance, was appropriately grounded in agent control, then gratitude would lose its distinctiveness from gladness or merriment or glee that things have happened to turn out as we would like. As Susan Wolf writes, "The metaphysical stance is appropriate . . . because the concepts of free will and responsibility that are already firmly established are intrinsically metaphysical concepts. That is, it is an essential criterion for the application of these concepts that they be subject to the demands of justification by the facts."[21]

Indeed, in describing the distinction between moral responsibility and legal responsibility, Joel Feinberg relies upon the fact-dependence of the notion of moral responsibility. Notice that asking about Sam's *moral* responsibility for his act is distinct from questioning his legal accountability. Infidelity may be legal yet be an act for which Sam is morally blameworthy. Feinberg explains:

> A stubborn feeling persists even after legal responsibility has been decided that there is still a problem—albeit not a legal problem—left over: namely, is the defendant really responsible (as opposed to "responsible in law") for the harm? This conception of a "real" theoretical responsibility as distinct from a practical responsibility "relative" to the purposes and values of a particular legal system is expressed very commonly in the terminology of "morality"—*moral* obligation, *moral* guilt, *moral* responsibility.[22]

I conclude that on both the pragmatic view and the expressive theory, moral responsibility is given only a superficial justification and not a sufficiently rich or grounded one. The decisive point against both of these views is that it is a common and deeply rooted practice, in adopting the complex of attitudes associated with the concept of moral responsibility and in applying the practices of punishment and reward, to appeal to what is fair and deserved in line with the facts.

Accounts of Moral Responsibility

We began by asking whether freedom is required for responsibility and, if so, freedom in what sense. Often in discussions of free will and moral responsibility, the various notions of moral responsibility are not explicitly set out and distinguished. But it is important to do so. For surely one's account of the function of the concept of moral responsibility will alter one's view of the conditions for the right application of the concept. Furthermore, keeping in mind the competing theories examined above may serve to disentangle various lines of thought regarding free will and moral responsibility that speak at cross-purposes. So, for instance, one philosopher may assert that acting freely in the sense specified by his particular incompatibilist theory is required for moral responsibility, where he implicitly endorses a metaphysical view of moral responsibility. And another philosopher may reply that acting freely as specified by the first philosopher's theory is certainly *not* required for moral responsibility, where the second philosopher has a pragmatic theory of the function of moral responsibility ascriptions lurking in the background. Hence what appears to be a disagreement about free action is really a disagreement about the point of moral responsibility ascriptions. The differences between Dennett and van Inwagen are a concrete example; rather than to each other, they speak *past* each other.

One's view as to what centrally is being done in holding persons morally responsible will thus affect one's perspective on the question of the right application of the concept. For a pragmatist about moral responsibility, whatever patterns of moral responsibility ascription best mold persons' behavior are the appropriate patterns. There is no point in holding a person morally responsible for her act when future benefit in terms of behavior manipulation cannot be attained by doing so. Is it required for a person's being morally responsible for her act, according to the pragmatist, that she did the act freely?

I do not see any reasons internal to the theory why it would be required. In fact, we might wonder whether it matters whether the person did the act at all. Suppose that Sam's apparent infidelity to Nancy turns out, after all, to have been an elaborate and unfortunate illusion. Ned, out of desperate passion for Nancy, wanted to break up Sam and Nancy's relationship, so he went to great lengths to set up evidence framing Sam for infidelity. But Sam really did not do it at all. No matter, says the pragmatist—it may still be useful to blame and even punish Sam. Perhaps Sam was thinking about having an illicit affair, and blaming him for having one will be just what is needed to steer him toward fidelity for the future. Perhaps blaming and punishing him will be a disincentive for other persons thinking of betraying their loved ones. So blaming Sam is perfectly justified, even if he did not really do it.

Perhaps I am not being fair to the pragmatist; perhaps he will claim that of course the person must have *done* the act for which he is held morally responsible, and maybe that he must have done it *freely.* But I do not see any resources within the pragmatic theory for upholding this claim. After all, the point of ascribing moral responsibility to persons is, in Schlick's words, to provide "reformation," "intimidation," and "incentive." Punishment and reward, on the view, are behavior modification tools like those used in training dogs and rats. They are species of manipulation. The question of whether it will be useful to punish or reward a person for the purpose of molding his or other persons' behavior seems not at all dependent upon an answer to the question of whether or not the person actually did the act or did it freely.

Then again, the pragmatist may claim to be providing only *one* function of moral responsibility ascriptions, not the sole function. And surely we must admit that praising and blaming, punishment and reward do serve to mold people's behavior. (What student is not at least somewhat moved to work by the prospect of grades?)[23] However, the pragmatic theory is distinguished from alternate views by its presenting behavior modification as the *central* function of moral responsibility ascriptions. Both the expressive and metaphysical accounts can recognize behavior modification as one function of the practices and institutions of praise and blame, punishment and reward. Both deny, though, that it is the central function. If the pragmatist were right about the central function of ascribing moral responsibility, then free action would seem to be unnecessary for it.[24]

What is the relation between freedom and responsibility on an expressive theory? Whether or not and what sort of freedom would be required for moral responsibility on the expressive account depends upon what sorts of considerations are attended to by our natural reactive attitudes. Strawson argues that our reactive attitudes are *not* attentive to the question of whether or not determinism is true. They are, instead, attentive only to the issue of what sort of will or attitude toward ourselves and others that we take others' actions to display. But here, again, Strawson's account runs into problems in virtue of his reliance on what is allegedly "natural." For many of us, it is natural to think that a person is only appropriately praised or blamed according to what he deserves on the basis of action fully under his control, where the truth of determinism rules out the kind of agent control required for desert. Furthermore, regarding those who react to others as they wish regardless of considerations of non-deterministic agent control, we think that their reactive attitudes *ought* to become attentive to precisely such considerations.

We have examined three competing accounts specifying distinct central functions of moral responsibility ascriptions. Since I have set aside the pragmatic and expressive approaches to moral responsibility as deficient in important ways, our inquiry concerning the right conditions for the application of the moral responsibility concept will focus on moral responsibility on the metaphysical account. This is, anyway, the account of moral responsibility either explicitly or implicitly endorsed by a large majority of the prominent contemporary English-speaking philosophers working on the subject of free will and moral responsibility, including Fischer, Ravizza, van Inwagen, Kane, Chisholm, Stump, Wolf, Nagel, Ginet, and Frankfurt. In specifying certain requirements for a person legitimately to be described as morally responsible for an act, these writers propose rival accounts of the same thing: moral responsibility in the metaphysical sense. Hence our inquiry in the remainder of this and the subsequent chapter will focus on the following question: What is the content of the freedom-relevant condition for moral responsibility, understanding moral responsibility as it is described on the metaphysical theory set out above?

Return to the case of Sam. The question of what Sam deserves on the basis of his act of infidelity, we said, presupposes that there is a fact about whether or not he did something wrong and did it in a manner that makes him worthy of retribution. What makes the manner of acting appropriate as a ground for an agent's being worthy of retribution on the basis of the act is the agent's having done the act freely, such that the act was fully under his control. A plausible suggestion as to what makes Sam *deserving* of blame (and perhaps punishment) for his act, in other words, is that he did it completely of his own accord, such that the act was wholly up to him. Another way to put the question on which we now focus, then, is this: Specifically what sort of *control* is required for an agent's being morally responsible (in the metaphysical sense)?

The Incompatibilist Presumption

The most persuasive account of what it takes for an act to have been wholly up to the agent is the agent's having done the act with incompatibilist freedom. I have argued for this position above. Hence the conclusion concerning the freedom-relevant precondition of moral responsibility that I judge to be most reasonable is this: It is the agent's doing the act freely in an incompatibilist sense that grounds her being the fit subject of the reactive attitudes and the accompanying practices of punishment and reward. I begin our inquiry into the sort of freedom required for moral responsibility, then, with a presumption in favor of an incompatibilist account of that freedom. I wish to make this explicit and to explain further. Compatibilist accounts of freedom do not get us enough for genuine responsibility, in short, because everything seems to be a "setup" if the world unfolds deterministically in one particular way from initial conditions.

In particular, from a standpoint that allows for the possibility of divine retribution and reward, compatibilist accounts of freedom appear unsuccessful. Although important theologians have disagreed with this judgment and some may view the line of reasoning in support of it as proceeding too quickly, nonetheless, the following is a common line of reasoning and a compelling one. Part of the concept of the theistic God is that God is wholly loving and perfectly just. But for God to grant persons eternal bliss or eternal damnation based upon their acts and convictions during earthly life is apparently unloving and unfair *if* nothing could ever have gone differently in each life than it did in fact go, given past determinants and the laws of nature. Consider the case of a hypothetical person who ends up damned, eternally separated from God in the afterlife. On the compatibilist analysis of the freedom condition of moral responsibility, this person freely decided and acted as he did during his earthly life, yet there were no forks in the path of his life. Each decision and action was the deterministic unfolding of events that preceded it. His life traversed a single path along which no alternative paths were ever genuinely accessible to him. Given the initial conditions into which he was born and the actual reigning laws of nature, each event in this person's earthly life was the causally necessitated outcome of previous events. His road was a straight and unforked road to hell.

How could this possibly be a fair scenario? The sort of control granted to an agent on any compatibilist account of the freedom-relevant condition of moral responsibility appears woefully insufficient for grounding what an agent deserves. To be *deserving* of punishment or reward (and this is especially vivid when we are considering *eternal* punishment and reward) seems to require that an agent face, with regard to at least some morally significant decisions or actions, genuinely forking paths into the future. Therefore, considerations of fairness from a theistic point of view support an incompatibilist freedom requirement for moral responsibility.[25]

In order to test this conclusion, however, let us examine some important theories according to which the kind of freedom required for responsibility is compatible with determinism. Perhaps one of these analyses will show itself to be enough for giving the content of the freedom condition for metaphysical moral responsibility. Hence I turn to a consideration of different compatibilist accounts of moral responsibility. Each of these accounts, I ultimately argue, is significantly flawed.

Responsibility and Compatibilist Self-Direction

Uniting all compatibilist views is the idea that it is irrelevant to establishing a person's moral responsibility for his act to discover whether or not the state of mind that lead to the act was causally determined by previous events. This is the negative claim. The positive claim characterizing traditional compatibilism can be most simply stated as the view that responsible action is action done by will.[26] On David Hume's view, for instance, a person is responsible for an act he undertakes in normal circumstances not subject to conditions of constraint. A responsible act is not opposed to one that is caused, but rather to one that is constrained.[27] The compatibilist A. J. Ayer subsequently refined the view by spelling out specific conditions in which an act should be seen as done under constraint: when done under compulsion by the threat of another person; or by subservience in a "strong habit of obedience" to another; or by way of a psychological condition that makes one's process of deciding what to do irrelevant to one's behavior.[28] Writes Ayer:

> If I suffered from a compulsion neurosis, so that I got up and walked across the room, whether I wanted to or not, or if I did so because somebody else compelled me, then I should not be acting freely. But if I do it now, I shall be acting freely, just because these conditions do not obtain; and the fact that my action may nevertheless have a cause is, from this point of view, irrelevant. For it is not when my action has

any cause at all, but only when it has a special sort of cause, that it is reckoned not to be free.[29]

Ayer here speaks of freedom, but it is clear from the larger context of the above passage that he is concerned with analyzing the type of freedom required for moral responsibility. In claiming "if I do it now, I shall be acting freely, just because these conditions do not obtain," Ayer assumes something that is the crux of the traditional compatibilist account of responsible action: that his doing it now will be up to him—directed by his will or his self. The idea of self-direction is likewise espoused by the compatibilist Thomas Hobbes: "Liberty is the absence of all the impediments to action that are not contained in the nature and intrinsical quality of the agent."[30]

The first compatibilist view under consideration, then, I will take to be the view that morally responsible action is self-directed action.[31] I will call this the compatibilist Self-Direction View. As a traditional compatibilist view, of course, the compatibilist Self-Direction View takes the requisite self-direction to be attainable even if causal determinism holds. We are morally responsible, roughly, when we do what we resolve to do, and not when we act as we do because of constraint. Various specific versions of the compatibilist Self-Direction View have in common the claim that a person is morally responsible for a (morally significant) act that she intends (or chooses or decides or values or desires) to do (where this varies according to the particular theorist's model of the self), and it is not required that determinism be false.

Two contemporary theories of responsibility that I take to be species of the compatibilist Self-Direction account include the "Real Self View" as characterized (but not ultimately defended) by Susan Wolf and the view of Jonathan Glover, who states in *Responsibility:* "To sum up crudely: for the purposes of blame, a person is his intentions, except where his intentions are unalterable."[32] On the Real Self View, an agent is morally responsible for performing an act if and only if that act is properly attributable to her "real self," or character, where an act is properly attributable to the agent's character just in case the agent is able, at the time of acting, to govern her behavior by her valuational system.[33] An action proceeding from an agent's real self is under the agent's control, in the sense that the act is done for the agent's reasons (because he really

wants to do it or because he values doing it). Since an action resulting from an agent's real self is under the agent's control, the action is
deemed an appropriate candidate for being deeply attributable to
him, and the agent is an appropriate candidate for praise or blame
with regard to the act.

The compatibilist Self-Direction View accounts for many of our
intuitions about the correct attributions of responsibility. The problem with the theory, however, is that attributability to a self or even
a "real" self is not sufficient for responsibility. We frequently question the responsibility of a person in acting because we doubt that
she is responsible for having the self or the values that she does.
That is, it is not hard to think of cases of individuals who have characters or selves but who do not seem to be appropriately held responsible for the actions that result from them. For instance, persons who had extremely deprived or traumatic childhoods are often
thought *not* to be ultimately responsible for having the characters
that they have. The issue of how a person's self was formed seems
crucial to judging responsibility for actions directed by that self.

The case of Robert Harris provides a ready example. Harris was
executed in California in 1992 for the murder of two boys.[34] After
the point-blank shootings, Harris is reported by his brother, Daniel,
to have been in a lighthearted mood: "He smiled and told Daniel
that it would be amusing if the two of them were to pose as police
and inform the parents that their sons had been killed." Later, when
Harris looked at the blood stains and remnants of flesh on his
Luger, he said, "I really blew that guy's brains out," and he again
started to laugh.[35] A fellow death row inmate at San Quentin re-
portedly said of Harris: "The guy's a misery, a total scumbag; we're
going to party when he goes."[36]

If anyone is an appropriate candidate for severe blame and punishment, Harris would initially appear to be one. But now consider
the fact that Harris was raised in an environment of horrific violence and abuse. He was brought into the world when his father
kicked his mother in the abdomen repeatedly until she began hem-
orrhaging. Robert was beaten and tortured from infancy and, by
adolescence, had inhaled, ingested, and injected such chemicals as
airplane glue, gasoline, oven cleaner, paint, typewriter correction
fluid, cocaine, heroin, seconal, methamphetamine, PCP, and LSD.[37]

His mother routinely battered him, requiring Robert to bring her the sticks she would use on his body, and his father had a habit of sending the family members outside to run and hide while he readied his gun to hunt them down like animals, threatening to shoot any he found.[38] Robert's sister described him as a child: "He wanted love so bad he would beg for any kind of physical contact. He'd come up to my mother and just try to rub his little hands on her leg or her arm. . . . She'd just push him away or kick him. One time she bloodied his nose when he was trying to get close to her."[39] While in a youth detention center for car theft as a teenager, his sister said, Harris was raped several times and twice slashed his wrists in suicide attempts.[40] Certainly Robert's is a case in which the physical, emotional, and chemical abuse inflicted in childhood lead us to question his responsibility for the self he had. Given the conditions of his life from infancy on, he seems to be someone who did not have a *chance* to have become a different sort of person than he was.

Problem cases for the traditional compatibilist Self-Direction View of responsibility are those that, like this one, make us worry about the fairness of praising or blaming persons for their actions when we can see a determinate causal explanation for the intentions, values, and desires leading them to act. Although the agents in the problem cases can control their action by what they are, they are not responsible for what they are. And this makes us question whether they are really morally responsible for their actions after all.

Some try to fix this problem for traditional compatibilism by appealing to reflective evaluation, and, indeed, I think this goes some way toward solving the problem, although ultimately not far enough. According to Charles Taylor, for instance, persons make themselves responsible for who they are by a certain kind of complex reflection. He writes: "Human subjects are capable of evaluating what they are, and to the extent that they can shape themselves on this evaluation, are responsible for what they are in a way that other subjects of action and desire (the higher animals for instance) cannot be said to be."[41] Reflective evaluation of the kind important for personhood and responsibility, Taylor stresses, is not the simple weighing of alternatives by strength of desire plus calculation of consequences; rather, the reflective self-evaluator characterizes desires using a vocabulary of worth, as "higher and lower, noble and base, and so on."[42] He continues: "We consider people deep to the extent, *inter alia*, that they are capable of this kind of radical self-reflection."[43]

Taylor uses this notion of reflective self-evaluation to explain the responsibility for self that is, in his view, essential to persons. Extending the account, action for which an agent is morally responsible is action resulting from a self for which the agent is responsible. It is unclear whether Taylor thinks the capacity for reflective self-evaluation must have been *exercised* in the formation of a self from which comes action for which a person can be held responsible, or whether the capacity needs only to be present. He writes:

> Because this self-resolution is something we do, when we do it, we can be called responsible for ourselves; and, because it is within limits always up to us to do it, even when we don't—indeed, the nature of our deepest evaluations constantly raises the question whether we have them right—we can be called responsible in another sense for ourselves whether we undertake this radical evaluation or not.[44]

The latter part of this passage suggests that Taylor takes our possession of the capacity for reflective self-evaluation to be sufficient for responsibility for oneself, although the former part suggests that the exercise of the capacity is necessary. Regardless, the appeal to reflective evaluation does not solve the problem for the compatibilist Self-Direction View, since, given that the account is supposed to be consistent with the truth of causal determinism, a person's reflective evaluation may proceed exactly as it does of causal necessity, as a deterministic result of factors over which she has no control.

Consider the case of a person whose medication for the residual pain of a limb amputation causes a side effect of depression. The medication causes her thinking to proceed in such a way that it generates uncaring and selfish states of mind, where the states are "hers" in being in her mind and endorsed by her reflectively, assented to in higher-level mental states. Her evaluations of situations, desires, and other people are often negative, and the propositions she accepts are self-defeating and hopeless. As a result, she is sometimes backbiting in her derogatory comments about people who understand themselves to be her friends. Although her hurtful actions toward herself and toward others result from her negative character, we are inclined not to blame her wholly for them, since her having the sort of character she does is not her fault: It is not of her own creation to a sufficient extent. Although she engages in reflective evaluation, the evaluation proceeds as it does in a deterministic manner under the influence of her medication. At any rate, to the extent that we believe that her evaluative faculty, and hence her character, is affected by the drug, we are inclined to excuse her from the consequences that would normally follow her harmful acts.[45]

In each of the problem cases I have sketched for the compatibilist Self-Direction View, the agents are in control of what they do in some sense, but their control is only mediate, and not ultimate. Though their behavior results from their character, the content of their character results from some external source, and the external force manipulates who they are in a way that they are powerless to choose or to resist. The control they have over their actions is therefore superficial.

Considering the extent to which various external forces shape human character leads us to consider the possibility that *all* of us have a character determined to be what it is by factors not under our control. We prefer that certain foods be cooked in particular ways because our parents prepared them that way when we were children. We are inclined to pursue or to avoid various athletic endeavors because of our genetically determined physiological features and talents. If we think of ourselves as beings whose preferences and beliefs are determined by heredity and environment, then the control we have over who we are appears minimal or nonexistent. And the control we have over our behavior consequently appears, like the depressive's and that of the victim of severe childhood trauma, superficial. Responsibility seems to require that one's action be determined by one's self, and that one's self not be determined to be just the self it is by previous factors. Responsibility requires an openness—forking paths—in possibilities for the construction of the self.

Hence the idea that responsibility requires alternative possibilities is appealing and natural. We have not reached the conclusion based on the above considerations that alternate actions have to be available to a person at the moment of acting; only that causal necessitation of an agent's decisionmaking faculty as she forms her choices, intentions, values, or preferences rules out moral responsibility.

The Reason View

Wolf's diagnosis of what is wrong with the compatibilist Self-Direction View is not that it needs the addition of the falsity of determinism in order to allow for indeterministically generated selves, but rather that it needs the addition of a requirement of sanity (in a particular sense). The compatibilist Self-Direction View goes wrong in considering persons responsible who behave badly from distorted or evil selves. But such persons should be held responsible, Wolf thinks, only if they had, when acting, the ability to have acted from an understanding of what is right, instead. Without their having that ability, Wolf seems to think, blaming wrongdoers is unfair: They acted as they saw fit, but they could not have appreciated what would have been a better thing to do even if they had tried.

Hence on what Wolf calls the "Reason View," necessary and sufficient for free and responsible action is "the ability to act in accordance with the True and the Good."[46] A person's status as a responsible agent, on the view, rests on her ability to form, criticize, and reform her values on the basis of an appreciation of what is really true and good. The Reason View generates an "asymmetry thesis," according to which, when one does the right thing for the right reasons, one need not have had the ability to do otherwise at the time, in order to be praiseworthy. This is so since, in the case of a good-acting agent who acts for right reasons, the agent, at the time of acting, must have *had* the ability to act in accord with the True and the Good because she *exercised* it. So the assessment of good-acting agents is rather simple for the Reason View proponent.[47] Yet, when one does the wrong thing, one is blameworthy only if one did have the ability to do otherwise at the time one performed one's act, since every wrongdoer must have had the ability to have acted, instead, in accord with the True and the Good.

Cases highlighted by Wolf in defending the Reason View include a swimmer who rescues a drowning child, though she was unable to do otherwise than rescue the child, and a gift giver who claims she "couldn't resist" buying her friend the gift.[48] Regardless of lack of options, Wolf urges, in virtue of the response to right reasons, each of these agents acts freely and responsibly (in rescuing and in purchasing, respectively). Hence, it is argued, our intuitions support the asymmetry thesis. When one's friend buys one a gift and claims that she "couldn't resist," her comment is not construed as an excuse; the fact that she could not have done otherwise does not make her any less praiseworthy for buying the gift. By contrast, central to our concern when assessing the blameworthiness of bad-acting agents is an assessment of whether or not the agent had knowledge of the relevant norms and so was able to have done the right thing: If so, then the agent is blameworthy, but if not, then she is excused.

The argument for the sufficiency of the ability to act in accord with the True and the Good for responsibility based upon such examples is not particularly persuasive. For if such phrases as "I couldn't resist" upon purchasing a gift do not exempt one from praise, this is likely due to the fact that such phrases are ordinarily taken as exaggerations in the name of humility. When one's friend presents one with a gift, claiming that she "couldn't resist," one thinks that one's friend is simply being polite: She really could resist, and if she *could not,* then there is something wrong with her, something that destroys her responsibility for buying the gift.

Surely there is some initial plausibility in the idea that, to take a different case, honest Abe is praiseworthy in telling the truth even if he cannot tell a lie. We are to think of Abe not as bound at gunpoint or as under the influence of a truth serum, but as so convinced of the merit of the reasons in favor of telling the truth that lying is unthinkable, even psychologically impossible, for him. That he cannot lie apparently does not absolve him of responsibility for telling the truth, but rather seems to undergird our conviction that he is especially praiseworthy.

However, it is possible that such intuitive judgments are colored by hidden factors that, when brought to light, alter the judgments. In particular, the judgment that an agent who does the right thing from an appreciation of right reasons is praiseworthy for his act may presuppose the idea that the agent's good character is ultimately of his own making, such that, at some points in time, when making decisions that led to his forming the character he has, he really *could* have, in a categorical sense, done otherwise. In considering an agent such as Abe, who has become so good that he is at some point no longer likely to do what is wrong, and in judging his act to be one for which he is morally responsible, we assume, I believe, that at some point in the past, the agent faced genuine options and performed free actions to which his ability to do the right act for right reasons can be traced. Telling the truth is a good act, but it is an act for which Abe intuitively deserves praise only if we assume that he is now of such a constitution that he is unlikely to lie because of the past free acts—in an incompatibilist sense—that have shaped his character. He must have faced forks in the road at times with regard to decisions of how to act and what sort of person to become, or else he bears no responsibility for being the sort of person he is. If Abe really *cannot* refrain from telling the truth and could not at any point in his life have ever been a dishonest person, then, just like the gift giver, there is something wrong with him, something that destroys his responsible agency.

Let me explain further the problem I see for the Reason View. The problem is that being pushed along a single path (representing the physical possibilities for one's life), *even if* that path is the path of the True and the Good, is inconsistent with having the sort of control over one's action that is required for responsible action. This problem is brought out by the following case, which I take to be a successful counterexample to the Reason View.

Suppose that Anne's neighbors have suffered a tremendous loss: the death of their son. Since Anne herself has also tragically lost a child, she in some measure understands the depth of her neighbors' pain. Hoping to comfort her neighbors in their grief, Anne invites them over for dinner. Anne does the right thing (helping the neighbors) for the right reasons (she understands their pain and wants to help alleviate it).

But further suppose that Anne, as a teenager, became a member of a cult. One of the cult's tactics for growth was to inculcate in its members the desire to befriend and help their neighbors when those neighbors have need of assistance. The ultimate purpose of such beneficence, from the point of view of the cult's leaders, is for the neighbors subsequently to be converted. But the members of the cult have no knowledge either of the source of their desires to help neighbors or of the purpose toward which their acting on those desires is ultimately to be put by others.

As a result of past group hypnosis, the desire to befriend and aid her neighbors still exists in Anne. The hypnosis has been so successful that Anne could not, in the instance in which she invites her grieving neighbors over for dinner, think in any way other than as believing that, of course, she ought to invite them. She asks them to dinner because she wants to and because she values helping others, but the evaluative faculty by way of which she forms her desires and values is compelled to evaluate and decide as it does because of her past hypnosis. Furthermore, were it not for the hypnotic influence, Anne would not be the sort of person who reached out to others in their times of grief. Prior to her teenage involvement in the cult, Anne was not herself that kind of person; she was private and preferred to keep to herself. Anne acts, in this instance, in accordance with the True and the Good. But it hardly seems that Anne acts freely and is praiseworthy for entertaining her neighbors, since she could not have done otherwise, could not have decided otherwise than to invite them, and could not even have evaluated the relevant considerations in any other way than exactly as she did because of her past hypnosis. Thus, contrary to Wolf's view, the ability to act in accordance with the True and the Good is not sufficient for freedom and responsibility.

A likely objection is that, in this case, Anne does not really do the right thing for the right reasons. While it should be agreed that Anne does the right thing in reaching out to her grieving neighbors, it may be objected that she does not really do so *for the right reasons*. Anne befriends her neighbors because she has been conditioned to do so, according to the objection, and not because she freely decides that it is the right thing to do. However, Anne does do the right thing for the right reasons; she simply could not have found compelling the reasons to do otherwise. If the analysis of 'doing *x* for the right reasons' requires the possibility that the agent who does *x* be motivated by right reasons *and* the possibility that the agent be otherwise motivated, then the Reason View requires the absence of causal necessitation, and hence the ability to act in accordance with the True and the Good is not sufficient for responsibility.

The objection assumes that Anne did not invite the neighbors for the right reasons because she could not have been otherwise motivated and so could not have done otherwise than invite the neighbors. But the Reason View is committed to the irrelevance of the ability to do otherwise in the case of good-acting agents. The Reason View requires only that an agent be capable of being moved by Reason, or by the right reasons, at the time she acts. It dismisses inquiry into *why* the agent is so moved, when she is, as irrelevant to

assessments of freedom. But why should we praise a person for acting on her ability to do what is right if she is incapable of doing
what is wrong and, furthermore, if she has the ability to do what is
right, at the time, not as a result of her own actions? If the ability to
do the right thing for the right reasons builds in the categorical ability to do otherwise, then the Reason View becomes a species of incompatibilist view.

In support of the claim that Anne's understanding of the neighbors' pain and her desire to help alleviate it are the *reasons* for her
action, consider that these are the reasons Anne herself would give if
asked why she did what she did and that these are the reasons that
an observer would cite as explanations of her action. The fact that
there is a further causal explanation of Anne's having these reasons
does not make them any less her reasons, nor does it make them any
less *right* reasons. To heighten the point of the example, suppose
now that what I have been calling a cult is actually the World Justice
Committee, whose sole aim is to foster belief in the fundamental
human rights of all people. The committee's means for combating
racism, sexism, and other unjust attitudes is to work at the neigh-
borhood level, by inducing people to value befriending their neighbors. In this way, the committee thinks, the message of fundamental
human rights for all will best be spread.

What this example shows is that being compelled to do the right
thing for right reasons is just as objectionable, from the standpoint
of the sort of freedom required for moral responsibility, as being
compelled by anything else. The case of Anne shows the Reason
View to be faulty just in case one thinks that Anne acts from an appreciation of right reasons but that *genuine* reasons are required for
moral responsibility. Anne acts for right reasons, but the reasons are
not deeply *hers* because they were not acquired and endorsed by
way of an indeterministic mechanism of reflective evaluation; they
did not become the motivations for her act because of her asserting
herself into the world using her undetermined evaluative power. She
is the passive receptacle through which good works get done. Even
if she had wanted to, or begun to try to, find different reasons compelling, she could not have.

The Reason View is meant to be compatible with causal determinism. So a person's moral responsibility for an act is consistent,
on the view, with that person's life unfolding along a single determi-

nate path, along which there are causally necessary links between successive events and hence along which there are no forking paths. Whether a person is really praiseworthy for doing a good act when at no point in her life could she have done, decided, desired, or thought otherwise than she in fact did, is seriously questionable.[49] And that a person is really blameworthy for doing a wrong act when the sense in which he could have done otherwise at any point in the whole of his lifetime is only the conditional sense (such that, if things had been different—which they were not—he *would* have done otherwise) is likewise seriously dubious. For every bad-acting agent, the Reason View maintains that being blameworthy depends upon having the ability to do otherwise at the time of acting. But since the proponent of the Reason View is committed to its consistency with determinism, at every point in a person's life at which he does a wrong act, given the previous events, it was *physically impossible* for him at the time to have done a right act from an appreciation of right reasons.

Put another way, for each person at every instant of life, none of the alternate paths were accessible to him, given the path he was on. So, in the case of a person who does something wrong, given the commitment of the Reason View to causal determinism, although the view requires for the agent's blameworthiness that he have been able to take a different path—a path representing a right act—instead, at the time of the wrong act it was physically impossible for him to have done this. So if the proponent of the Reason View takes a sufficiently robust understanding of the ability to do otherwise, then, on the view, no one is ever blameworthy. I conclude that the Reason View of moral responsibility is unsuccessful.

The Reasons-Responsive Mechanism View

One recent compatibilist proposal regarding moral responsibility is John Martin Fischer's account of action on reasons-responsive mechanisms. According to Fischer, "The traditional assumption of the association of moral responsibility (and personhood) with control is quite correct."[50] But the sort of control required for moral responsibility does not require indeterminism, Fischer thinks. All the freedom that is required is what he calls "guidance control." On Fischer's view, guidance control is the agent control that is both necessary and sufficient for moral responsibility.[51]

On the account as set out in *The Metaphysics of Free Will*, "an agent exercises guidance control insofar as his action issues from a mechanism that is weakly responsive to reasons."[52] For an action to issue from a reasons-responsive mechanism is for it to be under the "control" of, since produced by way of, a mechanism that is sensitive to reasons. A mechanism's being sensitive to reasons is characterized counterfactually on Fischer's account. An agent acts from a reasons-responsive mechanism just in case, if the agent had had different incentives for acting and if the mechanism issuing in the action had been different in its particular details (while remaining of the same type), then the agent would have done otherwise. More precisely, "strong" reasons-responsiveness is distinguished from "weak" reasons-responsiveness. Strong reasons-responsiveness requires that, in all possible worlds most similar to the actual world in which the agent has sufficient reason to do otherwise (and in which the actual type of mechanism operates), the agent does otherwise.[53] Weak reasons-responsiveness, by contrast, requires only that there exist *some* possible world in which: there is a sufficient reason to do otherwise; the agent does otherwise; and the agent's actual mechanism operates. "For a mechanism to be weakly reasons-responsive," Fischer explains, "there must be a possible scenario in which the same kind of mechanism operates and the agent does otherwise."[54]

Given the fixity of the past, the fixity of the laws of nature, and the truth of determinism, it is not physically possible for an agent to do any act other than the one he does at each moment. (There are no forking paths in front of any person as he faces the future, if determinism is true.) But neither alternative possibilities for acting nor alternative possibilities for the operation of the actual particular type of mechanism leading to the act are needed to ground moral responsibility, Fischer claims. As he says, "Sameness of kind of mechanism need not require sameness of all details, even down to the 'micro-level.' . . . the scenarios pertinent to the reasons-responsiveness of an actual-sequence mechanism may differ with respect both to the sort of incentives the agent has to do otherwise and the particular details of the mechanism issuing in action."[55] An agent acting from a weakly reasons-responsive mechanism has a kind of control over his behavior, Fischer thinks, in that he is able to guide his behavior in acting by way of mechanisms that are attentive to reasons. He concludes, "Guidance control is *all* the freedom required for moral responsibility (and it is *not* also required that causal determinism fail to obtain)."[56]

While Fischer gives the start of a sophisticated and potentially promising compatibilist approach to analyzing the kind of freedom required for moral responsibility, the account as presently developed faces some significant difficulties. One challenge for the Reasons-Responsive Mechanism View is providing an account of the individuation of the relevant mechanisms, a difficulty analogous to the individuation problem for process reliabilism in epistemology.[57] Fischer admits that he has, in his presentation of the account of guidance control, left "extremely vague the crucial notion of 'same mechanism'."[58] But given its central role in the theory, spelling out the conditions of application for the notion of 'same mechanism' is critical.

An even deeper problem for Fischer's account remains. The account holds that acting from a weakly reasons-responsive mechanism is sufficient for guidance control. But from the fact that an act proceeds from *any* reasons-responsive mechanism, it does not follow that *the agent* has control over the action. This is because there is no requirement in the account that the mechanism be owned by, or be in an appropriate sense internal to, the actor. Thus there is no guarantee that the act produced by the mechanism will be an act that is self-determined by the agent, and self-direction, or self-determination, is central to the notion of agent control linked with moral responsibility.[59]

As Fischer's account stands, an act issuing from a reasons-responsive mechanism is supposed to be a free act and an act for which the agent may be held morally responsible, but that act can be one issuing from a mechanism that is imposed on the agent manipulatively. Eleonore Stump illustrates this difficulty using Robert Heinlein's story of the puppet masters, aliens who control a person's behavior by directing his thoughts in such a way that the mechanism on which the person acts is still responsive to reasons, although the mechanism is not one of the person's own. In this case, the action is under the control of the alien, not the human agent.[60] I think Stump is exactly right in arguing against Fischer. She points out that Fischer has not sufficiently appreciated the importance for moral responsibility of an act's being the agent's own, self-directed act (although Stump does not put it exactly this way), and she shows that a weakly reasons-responsive mechanism might not be one that should be identified as the agent's own mechanism. Thus Fischer's proposal is insufficient for freedom and responsibility, owing to its not providing strong enough conditions ensuring that the agent herself is behind, or is directing, the act. Indeed, Fischer admits with regard to this sort of problem that his account "needs to be filled in and refined substantially," for "it may be that the actual operation of this sort of mechanism occurs as a result of a responsibility-undermining process—direct stimulation of the brain, hypnosis, and so forth."[61] A requirement must, then, be added to Fischer's account regarding the ownership of the mechanism leading to the act, to ensure that it is internal to the self.

The weakly reasons-responsive mechanism account could be attacked from a different direction, as well. Not only does the account not include sufficiently stringent conditions ensuring self-direction or agent identification with the act, but further, the account does not include a sufficiently strong interpretation of the ability to do otherwise condition of the freedom required for moral responsibility.[62] This condition it analyzes counterfactually, such that, there is some possible world in which the agent has sufficient reason to do otherwise and does otherwise. But the *weak* reasons-responsiveness alleged to be sufficient for guidance control is too weak.

Imagine that a crazed killer attacks you. Suppose that he meets the legal definition of insanity and has killed twenty-two people before. While struggling with him for your life, you plead, "Please don't kill me; my family loves me!" He is unmoved. "Don't kill me," you try again. "Murder is immoral!" No hesitation comes into his murderous eyes. "Please don't," you try once more. "I'm getting married next week." No luck. Really desperate now, you cry, "My research team is on the verge of discovering a cure for cancer!" Unfortunately, those are your dying words.

Your killer was unresponsive to reasons. But suppose that in the case of this particular killer, there is exactly one possible scenario in which you would have succeeded in moving him to do otherwise than kill you. If you had thought to say, "Don't kill me; I have a pet blue lobster," he would have stopped in his tracks and changed his intent. As it turns out, your murderer was a fanatic fan of blue lobsters. Had he known you liked them, he would have embraced you as an immediate friend, rather than killing you. This killer acts from a mechanism that is "weakly responsive to reasons," in Fischer's sense. But it hardly seems that the mechanism is sufficiently responsive to reasons for the crazed killer to count as being *in control* of his action. Hence, weak reasons-responsiveness is not sufficient for guidance control. Or, if Fischer wants to continue to maintain that weak reasons-responsiveness is sufficient for guidance control, then the case shows that guidance control is not sufficient as the kind of control that grounds moral responsibility.[63]

Fischer's account in *The Metaphysics of Free Will* is, therefore, unsuccessful on a number of counts: In its reliance on the notion of weak reasons-responsiveness, it does not give an adequate account of the alternative possibilities condition for freedom of the sort required for moral responsibility. The view does not give an adequate account of the self-determination condition for responsible action, either, since it characterizes a responsible act as an act on a reasons-responsive mechanism without requiring that the mechanism be the agent's own and without giving an account of what it takes for a mechanism to be one's own. Finally, there are further problems regarding the individuation of mechanisms.

Conclusion

I have given grounds for rejecting each of the above versions of a compatibilist theory of moral responsibility. The traditional compatibilist Self-Direction View, as well as the newer Reason View and the Reasons-Responsive Mechanism View, face serious objections. This supports the judgment that an incompatibilist account of the freedom required for moral responsibility is the only sort of account that will do. The conclusion that *only* an incompatibilist account will do, however, has not been decisively supported, for the possibility remains that some other particular compatibilist account will be successful. This seems dubious, given the nature of several of the objections to the specific accounts I have considered above.

Nonetheless, the possibility remains that I have dismissed compatibilist accounts too quickly, as a result of not considering their primary source of *motivation*. Although each of the leading compatibilist accounts has difficulties, it may be that we ought to conclude that the accounts are at least in the right ballpark, if not satisfactory in all their details. A major motivation for compatibilist thinking about moral responsibility is the idea that a particular principle concerning moral responsibility has been shown to be false and that this result effectively *rules out* incompatibilist accounts. If this is correct, then we will have to look again at compatibilist accounts, since incompatibilist accounts will have been shown decisively to be faulty. Thus I turn in the following chapter to a discussion of the particular principle in question.

Notes

1. Susan Wolf, *Freedom Within Reason* (New York: Oxford University Press, 1990), p. 4.

2. Robert Audi makes a similar point against collapsing the notion of morally responsible action into the notion of free action. He complains that "sometimes philosophers assume that actions for which we bear moral responsibility are equivalent to free actions, and they often say little about moral responsibility beyond illustrating the equivalence claim and discussing the relation between free will and determinism" ("Responsible Action and Virtuous Character," *Ethics* 101, 1991, pp. 304–321). Although I do think that the problem of free will and determinism is connected to the problem of moral responsibility, as I explain below, I avoid the problem Audi notes by giving attention to competing accounts of moral responsibility itself.

3. Robert Nozick, *Philosophical Explanations* (Cambridge, MA: Harvard University Press, 1981), p. 291.

4. Fischer calls guidance control the *freedom-relevant condition*, allowing that there may be other conditions of moral responsibility than the freedom-relevant condition, such as epistemic and/or normative conditions. Fischer's account of guidance control is meant to give an accurate account of the freedom-relevant condition of moral responsibility. See John Martin Fischer, *The Metaphysics of Free Will: An Essay on Control*, Aristotle Society Series, vol. 14 (Cambridge, MA: Blackwell, 1994).

5. Moritz Schlick, "When Is a Man Responsible?" in *Problems of Ethics*, trans. David Rynin (New York: Prentice-Hall, 1939), pp. 143–156.

6. Ibid., p. 152.

7. Daniel Dennett, *Elbow Room: The Varieties of Free Will Worth Wanting* (Cambridge, MA: MIT Press, 1984), p. 165.

8. Ibid.

9. Ibid.

10. Ibid., p. 166.

11. A sustained defense of a pragmatic view of moral responsibility ascriptions is given in Marion Smiley's *Moral Responsibility and the Bound-*

aries of Community (Chicago: University of Chicago Press, 1992). Smiley's
theory is pragmatic in a sense more complex than the sense in which the
view I have articulated is a pragmatic view; her view is not a simple utilitar-
ian one, but rather is pragmatic in the sense of, in her words, taking "'the
practical' seriously in its efforts both to uncover the meanings of particular
concepts and to convey those meanings to others" (p. 23). Smiley argues
that "moral blameworthiness as now construed is essentially the Christian
concept of sin minus the authority of God, and that if we want to develop a
secular concept of moral responsibility, we will have to focus on our own
judgments of causal responsibility and blameworthiness in practice" (pp.
9–10). Her account aims to "underscore the dependence of our judgments
of responsibility on both the publicity of causal discoveries and the wield-
ing of political power among those with competing expectations of a particular individual or group" (p. 13). Because Smiley reconstructs moral responsibility as part of social and political practice, she maintains that "no
matter how sophisticated their logical analysis of free will and determinism
is philosophers are never going to be able to teach us anything about the
real nature of moral responsibility" (p. 21).

Smiley gives an intricately articulated defense of a conventional, rather
than metaphysical, account of moral responsibility. But I think the view is
too hasty in endorsing a skeptical conclusion regarding our abilities to discern genuine facts regarding individual moral responsibility, rather than
creating such "facts" in an assertion of interests and power. Also, in my
view, construing our values as wholly part of social and political practice
gives rise to a serious problem regarding their moral authority.

12. Peter Strawson classifies the reactive attitudes into the following
three types: the *personal* reactive attitudes, which are reactions to what one
perceives others' attitudes to be toward oneself, including, for instance,
gratitude, hurt, anger, and fear; the *impersonal,* or vicarious reactive, attitudes, which are reactions to others' attitudes toward others, such as moral
outrage at seeing someone treat another person poorly; and the *self-reactive*
attitudes, or reactions to one's own view of oneself, such as guilt, pride, and
shame. See Peter Strawson, "Freedom and Resentment," *Proceedings of the
British Academy* 48, 1962, pp. 1–25; reprinted in Gary Watson, ed., *Free
Will* (Oxford: Oxford University Press, 1982), pp. 59–80.

13. Hence I find puzzling Gary Watson's stated motivation of his project
in "Responsibility and the Limits of Evil: Variations on a Strawsonian
Theme," in Ferdinand Schoeman, ed., *Responsibility, Character, and the
Emotions: New Essays in Moral Psychology* (Cambridge: Cambridge University Press, 1987); reprinted in John Martin Fischer and Mark Ravizza,
eds., *Perspectives on Moral Responsibility* (Ithaca: Cornell University Press,
1993), pp. 119–148.

14. Fischer, *Metaphysics of Free Will*, p. 213.

15. Galen Strawson questions whether it is really impossible to give up the reactive attitudes and thereby questions the argument from the naturalness of the reactive attitudes to their justification. See Galen Strawson, "On 'Freedom and Resentment,'" in *Freedom and Belief* (Oxford: Clarendon Press, 1986); reprinted in Fischer and Ravizza, eds., *Perspectives on Moral Responsibility*, pp. 67–100.

16. John Martin Fischer takes this view; see *Metaphysics of Free Will*, p. 2.

17. Thomas Reid, *Essays on the Active Powers of the Human Mind*, Introduction by Baruch Brody (Cambridge, MA: MIT Press, 1969), p. 315.

18. Dennett, *Elbow Room*, p. 165.

19. Peter van Inwagen, *An Essay on Free Will* (Oxford: Clarendon Press, 1983), p. 209.

20. Ibid., p. 206.

21. Wolf uses the example of resentment to make the same point regarding the loss of distinctiveness of reactive attitudes on a nonmetaphysical approach to moral responsibility. See Wolf, *Freedom Within Reason*, p. 21.

22. Joel Feinberg, *Doing and Deserving: Essays in the Theory of Responsibility* (Princeton: Princeton University Press, 1970), p. 30.

23. This raises another way to put our criticism of the pragmatic theory. Imagine that your professor gives you an F on your exam. "But I don't deserve an F," you object. "I did the work on my own and the large bulk of it is correct." Your professor replies: "That doesn't matter. I can tell by my study of your personality that granting you an F on this exam will cause you to work very hard in this class during the remainder of the term. And I'm confident that when you work harder, not only will you produce excellent work, but you'll also spur the other students in the course to work harder. Students working harder and your producing excellent work are two worthwhile goals. Therefore, I am quite justified in giving you an F on this exam." It is unlikely that this explanation will leave you satisfied.

24. Smiley, in fact, takes this result to be a benefit of her pragmatic account of moral responsibility, since moral responsibility on a nonpragmatic account requires, she thinks, contra-causal freedom, which is, in her judgment, empirically unattainable. However, moral responsibility construed nonpragmatically may be shown to require freedom of a sort that is not contra-causal.

25. For a contrary opinion, see D. A. Carson, *Divine Sovereignty and Human Responsibility* (Grand Rapids, MI: Baker Books; London: Marshall Pickering, 1994). Carson takes an incompatibilist conception of freedom to be unbiblical. He does not dwell at great length, however, on the problems for compatibilist conceptions of freedom.

26. The *will* may be understood as a capacity for choice; or as the effective first-order desire, as Frankfurt and Hobbes define it; or as the capacity

for "going for something, starting on the path," trying to go down one path, as Watson characterizes it (Gary Watson, "Free Action and Free Will," *Mind* 46, 1987, p. 163, note 28). See also Brian O'Shaughnessy, *The Will*, vols. 1, 2 (Cambridge: Cambridge University Press, 1980).

27. David Hume, *A Treatise Concerning Human Nature*, ed. L. A. Selby-Bigge (Oxford: Oxford University Press, 1967; originally published in 1888), p. 407.

28. A. J. Ayer, "Freedom and Necessity," in Watson, *Free Will*, p. 20.

29. Ibid., p. 21

30. Thomas Hobbes, "Of Liberty and Necessity," in D. D. Raphael, ed., *British Moralists, 1650–1800*, vol. 1 (Oxford: Oxford University Press, 1969), p. 47.

31. I intend what I call the "compatibilist Self-Direction View" to represent the traditional compatibilist account of responsibility. But stating what exactly is the "traditional" compatibilist account is not perfectly straightforward. Perhaps we should take the "traditional" compatibilist to hold that an evaluation of the moral quality of the state of mind leading to the act is essential to assessing the agent's moral responsibility for his act. Martha Klein states that the traditional compatibilist maintains this (without citing any examples of compatibilists that count, on her view, as traditional): "The traditional compatibilist holds that it is sufficient for blameworthiness that when a person acted wrongly his act was the result of what can be called 'a morally reprehensible state of mind'. Roughly, he believes that if an agent has knowingly and willingly done the wrong thing then that agent deserves to be blamed and, possibly, punished" (*Determinism, Blameworthiness, and Deprivation*, Oxford: Clarendon Press, 1990, p. 1).

Filling in an account of Klein's sort of traditional compatibilism would require specification of "morally reprehensible states of mind" (and presumably also of "morally praiseworthy states of mind," if the account of praiseworthy action is taken by her traditional compatibilist to be structurally parallel to the account of blameworthy action). (For Klein's clarification of the notion of "a morally reprehensible state of mind," see *Determinism, Blameworthiness, and Deprivation*, pp. 27–29.) Adjudicating between Klein's and Wolf's characterizations of traditional compatibilism (as Wolf's is encapsulated in her description of the Real Self View) requires an answer to the question of whether we normally criticize an act in virtue of the bad state of mind that led to it, or rather because the act is bad and the person did the act intentionally or for his own reasons.

Klein recognizes the significant problem for the traditional compatibilist view that I go on below in the text to press and explain in detail. She writes regarding the traditional compatibilist account of responsibility (or, more precisely, of blameworthiness): "This approach to blameworthiness has seemed inadequate to me because it blatantly ignores an anxiety which comes naturally to us when we are asked to reflect on the conditions for moral responsibility and, in particular, when we are asked to reflect on . . . 'the problem cases.' . . . This anxiety can be summed up in the question: how can someone be morally responsible for his acts if he is not responsible for the desires and beliefs which motivate him?" (*Determinism, Blameworthiness, and Deprivation*, p. 1).

32. Jonathan Glover, *Responsibility* (London: Routledge and Kegan Paul, 1970), p. 66. Glover, as a compatibilist, of course holds that the attainment of the second condition is independent of the truth or falsity of determinism. It may be that an agent could have altered his intention, Glover claims, even if it is the case that, given the causal history of his intention, he could not have had a different one. This is because an intention is alterable depending on "whether or not reasons providing a fairly strong motive for doing so would have persuaded the person to change his course of action"(*Responsibility*, p. 136). For two incisive criticisms of Glover's compatibilist analysis of the second condition, see Klein, *Determinism, Blameworthiness, and Deprivation*, p. 21.

33. Wolf, *Freedom Within Reason,* chap. 2; reprinted as "The Real Self View" in Fischer and Ravizza, *Perspectives on Moral Responsibility.*

34. I am indebted to John Martin Fischer and Mark Ravizza, and to Gary Watson, for information regarding this case; they discuss it at length in Watson, "Responsibility and the Limits of Evil," and Fischer and Ravizza, "Introduction," in Fischer and Ravizza, *Perspectives on Moral Responsibility.*

35. Miles Corwin, "Icy Killer's Life Steeped in Violence," *Los Angeles Times,* May 16, 1982; as cited in Fischer and Ravizza, "Introduction," *Perspectives on Moral Responsibility,* p. 2.

36. As cited in Watson, "Responsibility and the Limits of Evil," in Fischer and Ravizza, *Perspectives on Moral Responsibility,* p. 131.

37. Robert A. Jones, "Lessons in the Making of a Demon," *Los Angeles Times,* March 27, 1990; as cited in Fischer and Ravizza, "Introduction," in *Perspectives on Moral Responsibility,* p. 3.

38. Fischer and Ravizza, "Introduction," in *Perspectives on Moral Responsibility,* p. 3.

39. Corwin, "Icy Killer's Life"; as cited in Watson, "Responsibility and the Limits of Evil," in Fischer and Ravizza, *Perspectives on Moral Responsibility,* pp. 135–136.

40. Watson, "Responsibility and the Limits of Evil," in Fischer and Ravizza, *Perspectives on Moral Responsibility*, pp. 135–136.

41. Charles Taylor, "Responsibility for Self," in Watson, *Free Will,* p. 112.

42. Ibid., p. 116.

43. Ibid., p. 126.

44. Ibid.

45. How would indeterminism help to secure her responsibility? If indeterminism were true, and indeterminism were located in the right places, then there would be alternative states of mind that she could choose to have as her own, and alternative decision outcomes regarding how to act, even given her bleak states of mind.

46. Wolf, *Freedom Within Reason*, p. 79.

47. However, there may be difficulties in assessing whether or not the agent actually acted *for* good reasons, or from a genuine appreciation of the True and the Good, as the case of Anne below shows.

48. Wolf, *Freedom Within Reason*, pp. 80–82.

49. Of course, the compatibilist will say that, even if determinism holds, the agent could have done, decided, desired, or thought otherwise in a conditional sense; but I have argued in Chapter 3 that the conditional analysis of the ability to do otherwise is inadequate.

50. Fischer, *Metaphysics of Free Will*, p. 133.

51. Ibid., p. 205.

52. Ibid., p. 205.

53. Ibid., p. 166.

54. Ibid., p. 179.

55. Ibid., p. 179.

56. Ibid., p. 205.

57. See Alvin I. Goldman, *Epistemology and Cognition* (Cambridge, MA: Harvard University Press, 1986); and Richard Foley, "What's Wrong with Reliabilism?" *Monist* 68, 1985, pp. 188–202.

58. Fischer, *Metaphysics of Free Will*, p. 244, note 16.

59. In "Free Action and Free Will," Watson points out that there are two conditions for freedom that all respectable theories must capture: self-determination, or ownership of the act; and alternative possibilities. In "A Coherence Theory of Autonomy" (*Philosophy and Phenomenological Research* 53, 1993, pp. 599–616), I stress the importance of the ownership, or self-determination, aspect of freedom and delineate a particular account of it.

60. Eleonore Stump, "Persons: Identification and Freedom," *Philosophical Topics* 24, 1996, pp. 183–214. I am grateful to Stump for making this paper available to me in typescript.

61. Fischer, *Metaphysics of Free Will*, p. 209.

62. Fischer relies heavily upon Frankfurt-type examples to prove that the freedom needed for moral responsibility is not the freedom to do or to decide otherwise. But if those cases can be undermined, then Fischer's case is also undermined. I take up this issue in the following chapter. Moreover, an

intuitively persuasive line of reasoning can be given supporting the conclusion that moral responsibility does, in fact, require alternative possibilities. This was given in countering the traditional compatibilist Self-Direction View above.

63. Fischer admits in a footnote that he has been made aware of this problem for his account of guidance control by a similar case posed by Ferdinand Schoeman (Fischer, *Metaphysics of Free Will*, p. 243, note 8). The difficulty could perhaps be remedied by Fischer's developing a notion of reasons-responsiveness midway between strong and weak.

In fact, since the writing of this chapter, Fischer has, with a coauthor, Mark Ravizza, published a book addressing this and other problems for the account of guidance control as weak reasons-responsiveness defended in *The Metaphysics of Free Will*. In the new book, *Responsibility and Control* (Cambridge Studies in Philosophy and Law, Cambridge: Cambridge University Press, 1998), Fischer and Ravizza conclude that, in order to be morally responsible for an action, the agent must act from a mechanism that is *his own* reasons-responsive mechanism, where the relevant notion of reasons-responsiveness is not "weak," but "moderate." Building on a distinction between *receptivity* to reasons and *reactivity* to them, the account of "moderate reasons-responsiveness" requires that an agent act on a mechanism that is regularly receptive to reasons, some of which are moral reasons, and at least weakly reactive to reason (*Responsibility and Control*, p. 82). For a mechanism to count as "regularly" receptive to reasons, it must be the case that, if asked about his actions, the agent would (if truthful and, I presume, self-aware—see *Responsibility and Control*, p. 90, note 35, for this clarification in the presentation of Fischer and Ravizza's view) produce a set of answers that exhibit an understandable pattern (from the point of view of some appropriate external observer), a pattern that includes some moral reasons and is minimally grounded in reality (*Responsibility and Control*, pp. 69–82, 85; p. 90, note 35). These new conditions move the reasons-responsiveness view closer to Wolf's Reason View (in requiring the agent's reasons to be "grounded in reality") and raise several interesting issues for further critical discussion that I will have to take up elsewhere, such as the accuracy of the proposed account of a mechanism's counting as "one's own." (See Fischer and Ravizza, *Responsibility and Control*, pp. 207–239.)

CHAPTER SIX

Responsibility and Alternative Possibilities

The structure of the argument in this chapter is as follows. Many philosophers are convinced that incompatibilist accounts of free action have been shown to be inconsequential, since moral responsibility has been shown not to require incompatibilist freedom. What shows moral responsibility not to require incompatibilist freedom, they think, is the defeat of a certain principle—the principle of alternative possibilities (PAP)—by "counterfactual intervener" cases.

But this widespread opinion is, in my view, wrong on two counts.[1] First, counterfactual intervener cases (known as "Frankfurt-type" cases) do not demonstrate the falsity of PAP. And second, even if they did, moral responsibility would not thereby be shown not to require incompatibilist freedom. For a principle other than PAP may well correctly link moral responsibility and alternative possibilities of a sort realizable only if indeterminism is true. Indeed, PAP is false. While Frankfurt's cases do not succeed in showing this, other cases—simpler, more straightforward cases—do show the falsity of PAP.

Hence, in the following sections in which I argue against Frankfurt's defeat of PAP, my aim is not to uphold PAP as a correct principle, but rather to counter the view that Frankfurt-type cases summarily undercut PAP. I find it surprising that so many philosophers have agreed that this is the case.

Since Frankfurt's examples do not show PAP to be mistaken, but other examples *do*, this leaves the task for the incompatibilist of formulating and defending an alternate principle showing the right relationship between alternative possibilities and moral responsibility. I undertake this task in the final sections of the chapter.

The Principle of Alternative Possibilities

Center stage in contemporary philosophical discussions of free will and moral responsibility is a certain controversial idea: that a person must have available to him alternatives for acting, in order for him to be morally responsible for what he actually does. Normally we would think, for instance, that a driver is morally responsible for rear-ending the car in front of him only if he could have done something different instead (only if, that is, he could have stopped his car in time). If we discover that, for some reason, the *only* thing the driver could have done at the time was to rear-end the other car (perhaps because his brakes failed), then the judgment that he is morally responsible for what he did seems rightfully suspended.

Recall our image of the future as a variety of forking paths, each path containing its own array of forking branches. Which path we take at any forking point determines what subsequent forks in the road we will face. Or so goes a common and natural way of thinking as we stand at a point in time and look forward into the future. Imagine yourself as walking down the path of your life and coming to a fork in the road. Two paths stretch before you: one veering ahead and to your left, the other angling toward the right.

According to the idea concerning moral responsibility sketched above, you can be said to be morally responsible for taking the path you take only if both of the two paths are genuinely open to you, and not if one of them is actually (but unbeknownst to you) blocked. Another way of looking at the idea is to put it this way: You cannot be held morally responsible for doing something that you do as you travel along a straight section of the path of your life, a section along which there are no forking branches. Whether standing at a point from which all apparently available alternative paths but one path are mere chimeras (such that, even if you tried to take them, you could not) or traveling along a straight section of your life from which there are not even apparently available forking branches, you are neither praiseworthy nor blameworthy for continuing down your path, since it is the *only* path in front of you, the only way you could possibly go. In order to be morally responsible for taking one certain path, you must have available to you at least one alternate path and choose your path from among the range of your alternatives. This natural thought concerning moral responsibility is captured in the following principle:

PAP: A person is morally responsible for what s/he has done only if s/he could have done otherwise.[2]

Most of us find this to be an intuitively plausible principle. To hold a person morally responsible for doing the single act he could have done at a time seems mistaken. Writes A. J. Ayer: "It is only when it is believed that I could have acted otherwise that I am held to be morally responsible for what I have done. For a man is not thought to be morally responsible for an action that it was not in his power to avoid."[3]

Since the publication of a certain influential paper, "Alternative Possibilities and Moral Responsibility," however, many philosophers have concluded that PAP is, in fact, false. By use of certain now well-known examples, Harry Frankfurt (1969) argues in this paper that, although PAP is initially attractive, it is, surprisingly, incorrect. The following section sets out examples that are taken by many philosophers to show the falsity of PAP.

Frankfurt-Type Cases

Frankfurt's alleged counterexamples to PAP are a series of variations of the case of Jones, who, by the setup of the case, is supposed to be unable to do otherwise than perform the action he performs. The most convincing of the cases against PAP is one involving $Jones_4$ (Frankfurt poses the case subsequent to examples involving $Jones_1$, $Jones_2$, and $Jones_3$) and another man, named Black. Black wants $Jones_4$ to perform a certain action and will go to considerable lengths to ensure that $Jones_4$ does what Black wants. Suppose that Black has set up a device for manipulating the processes of $Jones_4$'s brain and nervous system in a direct way, so that Black can determine that $Jones_4$ chooses to act and that he does act in one particular way and not in any other.

Black does not want to bother to intrude upon $Jones_4$ unnecessarily, so he waits until $Jones_4$ is about to make up his mind, and he does nothing unless it is clear to him that $Jones_4$ is going to decide in a way *contrary* to what Black wants him to do. If Jones₄ is about to decide to do something else, then Black will use his device to make Jones₄ decide to do, and to make Jones₄ do, what Black wants him to do. No matter what Jones₄'s initial preferences and inclinations are, Black's way will prevail.

Suppose that, as it actually happens, Jones₄ does decide *on his own* to perform, and does perform, just the act that Black wanted him to perform. So Black did not have to resort to using his device in order to get his way. It seems that Jones₄ had no alternative but to do what Black wanted him to do; whether he did it of his own accord or as a result of Black's intervention, he would have performed the action Black wanted. But if, as is supposed in the case, Jones₄ does it on his own, then he is apparently morally responsible for doing it. His responsibility is not affected by Black's lurking in the background ready to interfere, since that interference never comes into play. Writes Frankfurt:

> It would be quite unreasonable to excuse Jones for his action, or to withhold the praise to which it would normally entitle him, on the basis of the fact that he could not have done otherwise. This fact played no role in leading him to act as he did. . . . Indeed, everything happened just as it would have happened without Black's presence in the situation and without his readiness to intrude into it.[4]

We can construct any number of putative counterexamples to PAP on the basis of the Frankfurt prototype. Although cases like Frankfurt's are a bit bizarre, it is not to the point to argue that they are irrelevant since "things don't really happen like that" in the real world. For the cases are being used as an important philosophical tool to test a theoretical proposal: that a person's being unable to do anything different from what he actually does could be consistent with that person's being morally responsible for the act. If the cases succeed in describing a situation in which a person has no alternatives for acting, then by raising our intuitions regarding the person's moral responsibility, the cases may well lead to a significant philosophical conclusion.

In discussing the metaphysical sense of moral responsibility in the previous chapter, we noted that an agent's deserving a particular moral reaction (such as praise or blame) is grounded in that agent's *control* over his or her action. In the Frankfurt case, Jones₄ seems to possess some kind of control as he acts, but it is a kind of control that does *not* involve control over which of two (or more) alternate available actions he performs. If Jones$_4$ is morally responsible, then this apparently shows that the sort of control required for moral responsibility should be given a compatibilist analysis and not an incompatibilist one. Hence much is at stake in evaluating examples like Frankfurt's. The cases may decide the issue of whether the sort of freedom that is required for moral responsibility must be analyzed in a way that makes it consistent with causal determinism or in a way that makes it inconsistent with causal determinism.

Let us think about one case carefully. To make the case less abstract, I will fill in the details concerning the action desired by the counterfactually intervening agent and done by the actor.[5] Although the case I will describe presently is more specific than the previous case, it is just as fanciful; but, again, this is not a defect of the case for the purpose of testing PAP. The Frankfurt-type[6] examples may help us to understand more clearly what is required for moral responsibility in ordinary situations.

Consider the following case. Suppose that Sheila is thinking of sabotaging Caitlin's dance shoes in order to ensure that Caitlin will twist her ankle. A third dancer, Natascha, is delighted with Sheila's plan; she wants Caitlin injured so that she, Natascha, can be a member of the dance company in Caitlin's place. So Natascha wires a device in Sheila's brain that allows her to monitor and control Sheila's thought processes. (Natascha is not just an excellent dancer, but also a skilled neurosurgeon.) If Sheila is about to decide not to sabotage Caitlin's shoes after all, Natascha will use her device to intervene, causing Sheila to decide to sabotage the shoes. As it actually happens, Sheila decides on her own to sabotage the shoes. Natascha does not have to intervene. Sheila could not have done otherwise than sabotage Caitlin's shoes, for if she had been about to decide to do something different, Natascha would have caused Sheila to decide to commit the sabotage. In fact, Sheila does it on her own. Now the question is, is Sheila blameworthy for sabotaging Caitlin's dance shoes?

The most natural immediate response would seem to be that, indeed, Sheila is morally responsible for sabotaging Caitlin's shoes, since she did it "on her own." Natascha never used her device to intervene. The device was there, but Sheila was completely unaware of it, and it played no role in causing her decision. Hence, apparently, Sheila's decision is attributable to Sheila herself (and not to Natascha), and so Sheila is morally responsible for the act she decided to do.

But if Sheila is morally responsible for sabotaging Caitlin's dance shoes, then PAP appears to be false. PAP states that a person is morally responsible for doing something only if she could have done otherwise. But Sheila could not have done otherwise than sabotage Caitlin's shoes, since the presence of the counterfactual intervener, Natascha, ensures that Sheila will sabotage them. (If Sheila had been about to decide to back down and not sabotage the shoes, then Natascha's device would have kicked in to make Sheila decide to sabotage them. So in the circumstances, Sheila could do no other than sabotage the shoes.)

The Received Lesson of Counterfactual Intervener Cases

Cases like this one have thus convinced many philosophers that PAP is incorrect. And if PAP is false, then moral responsibility seems not to require alternative possibilities after all. If moral responsibility does not, in fact, require alternative possibilities, then apparently the kind of freedom involving alternative possibilities—incompatibilist freedom—cannot be necessary for moral responsibility. Thus, many philosophers take arguments against PAP based on Frankfurt-type examples to demonstrate a significant result: that incompatibilist accounts of freedom are off track and irrelevant—they are irrelevant, at least, to moral responsibility, since the kind of freedom those accounts depict is not the sort that is required for moral responsibility at all. Fischer writes, "Moral responsibility does not depend upon the existence of *any* sort of alternative possibilities. In my opinion, this is the natural, straightforward lesson of the Frankfurt-type cases."[7]

Although the view voiced by Fischer is widespread, I think it is mistaken. I will argue that, contrary to initial appearances, Frankfurt-type cases do *not* show the falsity of PAP. Furthermore, even if arguments based on Frankfurt-type examples did succeed in defeating PAP, this would not entail that moral responsibility does not depend upon the existence of *any* sort of alternative possibilities. My aim is not to defend PAP. I think the principle is shown false by other considerations, as I go on to explain below. But I believe that

Frankfurt does not *show* PAP to be false. Of course, since Frankfurt-type cases seem to so many people clearly to show the falsity of PAP, my claim that they do not do so will require some elaboration and defense. But before undertaking this defense, I would like to first set out several other important recent lines of response to Frankfurt and explain where I think they go wrong.

Strategies Against Frankfurt-Type Cases

Compatibilist philosophers have, of course, endorsed Frankfurt's conclusion, and, indeed, the argument of Frankfurt's paper has been a major motivation for many in adopting a compatibilist position regarding determinism and the sort of freedom required for moral responsibility. As for incompatibilists, in responding to the argument against PAP based on Frankfurt-type cases, many have, in my view, made a misstep. Nearly universally, incompatibilist respondents have granted to proponents of Frankfurt-type counterexamples the judgment that the agent in question is morally responsible for what he does.[8] Van Inwagen, for instance, agrees that Jones is morally responsible in Frankfurt's case, and thus he concedes that Frankfurt has shown PAP to be false.[9] Nonetheless, van Inwagen maintains, there are other principles concerning moral responsibility and alternative possibilities that are immune to Frankfurt-type counterexamples and that thus uphold incompatibilism.[10]

But if PAP is shown false by Frankfurt-type counterexamples, then it is arguable that van Inwagen's proposed principles are defeated by such examples, as well. For the perspective that encourages our taking Jones to be morally responsible in the Frankfurt case also encourages our taking the agents in analogous counterexamples to van Inwagen's principles to be morally responsible. I will focus on just one of van Inwagen's three principles in order to illustrate this point, although a good case can be made against the other two principles also, to the effect that those principles are likewise vulnerable to Frankfurt-type counterexamples.[11]

According to proponents of Frankfurt-type counterexamples, Sheila is morally responsible for willfully sabotaging the dance shoes of Caitlin, even if Sheila could not have done otherwise, given that Natascha monitored Sheila's decision process by way of the device implanted in Sheila's brain and would have made Sheila carry out the sabotage if Sheila had been about to do otherwise. One of

the three principles with which van Inwagen replaces PAP is the
principle of possible action (PPA):

> *PPA:* A person is morally responsible for failing to perform a
> given act only if s/he could have performed that act.[12]

PPA is an intuitively plausible principle. Applied to an instance of
Sheila's failure to act in a certain way, for instance, the principle
gives the following result: Sheila is morally responsible for failing to
appear onstage at her appointed time to dance only if she could have
appeared onstage at that time (and not if, say, she was tied up backstage by a gangster). Suppose that Sheila stays backstage by will, refusing in a temper tantrum to appear onstage at her appointed time
to dance. Then PPA gives the result that Sheila may be held morally
responsible for failing to show up onstage. (We can add that her failure has moral significance, since the entire show comes to an awkward halt without Sheila's entrance, which leads to a bad review in a
prominent arts journal, causing embarrassment and financial loss to
other dancers and to the producers of the show.)

But now suppose that, unbeknownst to her, if Sheila *had* begun to
try to go onstage, Natascha would have crushed her knee with a
stick. Natascha did not, in fact, intervene to make Sheila stay backstage. As it actually happened, Sheila decided to do so on her own.
Thus by way of the same sort of reasoning that supports Frankfurt-
type counterexamples to PAP, Sheila is morally responsible for failing to appear onstage at her appointed time to dance, even though
she could not have performed that act. Hence PPA falls to Frankfurt-type counterexamples, if PAP does.

Other incompatibilists have not, as van Inwagen does, conceded
Frankfurt's defeat of PAP. But they have made what I see as a significant mistake: They have granted the moral responsibility judgment
on which Frankfurt's attack against PAP is based. This mistake leads
James Lamb, for instance, to argue for the unappealing view that
there is nothing in Frankfurt's account that warrants the belief that
Jones could not have done otherwise than he did.[13] But Jones could
not have done otherwise, since by virtue of the case, if he had tried
(or begun to try, or wanted to do otherwise, or whatever precisely is
conceived to be the triggering event for Black's intervention), Black
would have made Jones commit the desired action.[14]

The erroneous move of granting the agent's moral responsibility in Frankfurt-type scenarios has sent other incompatibilists scurrying to find some different alternative possibility—what Fischer dubs a "flicker of freedom"[15]—available to the agent even in such scenarios. Thus, for instance, one line of incompatibilist response to the case I have described is that, although Sheila could not have done otherwise and although she could not have decided otherwise than to sabotage Caitlin's dance shoes (by virtue of the elaborate setup of the case), still she could have *tried* to decide otherwise. In saying that she could have tried to decide otherwise, we might mean that she could have gone some way toward deciding not to sabotage the shoes: She could have begun a process with the aim of a certain outcome. After all, presumably the intervention of the counterfactual intervener Natascha's device is triggered by the occurrence of some event, an event that could be described as Sheila's trying to decide, or beginning to decide, in an alternate way than as Natascha desires. And the presence of indeterminacy, or a "flicker of freedom," at this point—whether to begin to decide to sabotage the shoes or to begin to decide otherwise—shows that Sheila's being morally responsible for her act does not conflict with the truth of PAP.[16]

A related "flicker of freedom" response is based upon a certain kind of libertarian picture of agency (an agent-causation type of account), according to which an agent performs a free act by way of standing in a direct agent-causal relation with a volition to perform that act. In the actual case, Sheila sabotages the shoes as the result, at least apparently, of a volition that she herself agent-caused. But Sheila could have done otherwise than agent-cause the volition to sabotage the shoes. Even in the scenario involving Natascha, Sheila has a significant power: the power not to agent-cause the volition to sabotage the shoes. In the alternate case, if Natascha had intervened, then Sheila would have sabotaged the shoes "of Natascha's accord"—that is, as the result of a volition, albeit in Sheila's head, that Natascha caused. So Sheila's ability either to agent-cause her volition or not to agent-cause the volition to sabotage Caitlin's shoes secures the alternate possibilities needed for her to be morally responsible for what she does.[17]

I have given two examples of a general "flicker of freedom" strategy for rebutting Frankfurt-type counterexamples, a strategy that begins by conceding the agent's moral responsibility in such cases.

Fischer's complaint against all such flicker strategies is that the alternative possibility granted to the agent on *any* flicker account is "not sufficiently *robust* to ground the relevant attributions of moral responsibility."[18]

This is not my complaint. I think it is a mistake on Fischer's part to take all incompatibilists, or even all flicker strategists, to hold that the alternate scenarios themselves *ground* responsibility attributions.[19] For the strongest incompatibilist view concerning responsibility and determinism does not rest its case upon the "robustness" of alternative actions available to the agent at the time of acting, but rather upon the requirement for moral responsibility of an indeterministically generated self.

Perhaps some incompatibilists have given the impression that moral responsibility ascriptions are *grounded in* robust alternative possibilities for acting. This is not my view, however. In my view, moral responsibility requires indeterminism so that an agent is not pushed by previous events into preferring and acting exactly as she does at each moment. A free act is one done deliberately from a preference of the agent's such that the preference was not coercively imposed and such that it was not causally determined by previous events that the agent would have precisely that motivation for action. Moral responsibility requires indeterminism in the construction of the self, such that the reasons for acting and desiring that one adopts as one's own are independently acquired, not acquired of necessity in a way that is fully explicable by reference to the laws of nature and events in one's past, including genetic and neurophysiological events.

Once granting the moral responsibility of the agent, both of the flicker strategies described above seem to me adequate. If we *were* in some way to know that, for instance, Sheila is morally responsible in the case of her sabotaging the dance shoes, then a plausible way to save PAP would be to specify that what she is morally responsible for is not precisely the act of sabotaging the shoes, but rather beginning to try to sabotage the shoes or being the agent-cause of the volition to sabotage the shoes, so that, since Sheila *could* have done otherwise than either of these, PAP has not been shown to be false.[20] Since I think PAP is shown false by other considerations, as I explain below, both of these particular flicker strategies to protect PAP seem misguided. But they are still adequate strategies for showing that PAP is not shown false by Frankfurt-type cases.

Where I do think that both of the described flicker strategies go fundamentally wrong is in taking for granted the agent's moral responsibility. For—and this is the key point I want to stress—the arguments against PAP based on Frankfurt-type counterexamples do not demonstrate the agent's moral responsibility, but only assume it. More precisely, to return to the case of Jones, the implicit premise taken over from arguments against PAP based on Frankfurt's case seems to be the following: If Black does not intervene and Jones decides to do X, and subsequently does X on the basis of this decision, then Jones is morally responsible for doing X. What drives the flicker strategist's need to find alternative possibilities even in Frankfurt-type scenarios is the granting of this problematic premise. In the following section, I give reasons to question it.

The Failure of Frankfurt-Type Cases to Show the Falsity of PAP

It is not hard to argue against the premise in question. Notoriously an act X can be done in circumstances that undermine the agent's moral responsibility for doing X, even when the agent decided to do X and did X on the basis of this decision. Such circumstances include deciding to do X and doing X under serious threat or as the result of posthypnotic suggestion. One might grant this point but respond that an implied premise in the argument against PAP is that Jones is not in any such unusual circumstances involving the present manipulation of another agent. The inference stated in the problematic premise is, however, undermined not only by manipulative circumstances. Perhaps Jones was the victim of severe emotional deprivation in his childhood of a sort that undermines his responsibility.[21] Or, more pertinent from my point of view, perhaps the thesis of causal determinism is true.

The metaphysical presuppositions in Frankfurt-type examples are unstated. And whether or not causal determinism holds is relevant to our intuitions concerning Jones's moral responsibility. Or, at least, whether or not determinism is true *ought* to be relevant—this is precisely what incompatibilist arguments are designed to show.

According to incompatibilists, our everyday notions concerning our own and others' freedom and moral responsibility in acting can be shown to be, upon reflection, in need of revision if the thesis of causal determinism is true. So to maintain from the outset that Jones is morally responsible in Frankfurt's example begs the question against incompatibilists. It fails to take into account all of the potentially relevant information. Since we are not given the information of whether indeterminism or determinism is to be assumed true in the Frankfurt-type cases, we really ought to be agnostic about whether or not the agents in such cases are morally responsible for what they do.

It is surprising that so many people find it unproblematic to pronounce upon Jones's responsibility in Frankfurt's case, despite a serious lack of information about Jones. I do not deny that the intuition that the protagonists in Frankfurt-type cases are morally responsible is a common intuition. Since I want to bring into question the idea that this intuition is the right one, I will provide a diagnosis of the widespread judgment that this intuition is appropriate. Three explanations appear especially likely.

Diagnoses of the Widespread Intuition

One of these is implicit or explicit commitment to a nonmetaphysical account of the function of moral responsibility ascriptions. To take the case of Jones: Let us specify Jones's action as killing Smith. One might say that Jones is morally responsible for his act of killing Smith, since he killed Smith deliberately. Either the pragmatic or the expressive theory of moral responsibility ascriptions could make sense of this statement. But since I argued in the previous chapter that the nonmetaphysical conceptions of moral responsibility are impoverished, I set aside this sort of support for the common intuition.[22]

A different explanation is that the intuition is generated in the process of taking a perspective inappropriate for assessing an agent's moral responsibility. Specifically, in thinking about Frankfurt-type cases, we often, I believe, project ourselves into the position of the actor. In considering the case of Jones killing Smith in the presence of Black, for example, we focus on Jones in the moments prior to his decision about what to do, and we envision him as believing himself to have alternatives for deciding and acting. Presumably, Jones takes it to be within his power to decide to kill Smith and within his power to decide not to kill Smith, and he takes it to be within his power actually to kill Smith and within his power to refrain from killing Smith. We make similar assumptions in our own practical deliberations, and we often take ourselves to be morally responsible for what we do. Thus in a mental act of extension of the first-person perspective to the case of Jones, perhaps we identify with Jones's belief that he has available options, and we take his consequent decision to kill Smith to be made under this assumption. Jones *thought* he could have done otherwise (even though he could not have, in fact), and still he decided in the particular way he did. Jones would believe his act to satisfy PAP, if he thought about it, and hence he would hold himself morally responsible for the act.

But whether or not Jones takes himself to be morally responsible for killing Smith does not settle the question of whether or not he is, in fact, rightly held morally responsible for it. Jones can be wrong about the issue of whether or not what he does meets the requirements for morally responsible action. Furthermore, Jones's subjective perception of available options is irrelevant. For if determinism is true, then, given the past and the laws of nature, at every moment there is exactly one physically possible future. Then Jones *has* no available options, even for deciding what to do. His belief that he does have them is simply false. A perfect predictor—a being with knowledge of all of the relevant facts about the past and of the laws of nature—could tell us with certainty what Jones will decide, based on her knowledge of the past and the laws. Given determinism, every decision that Jones has *ever* made in his lifetime was, at the time, the only decision he could have made, given the past and the laws. As to what Jones could have done, the judgment that is relevant to assessing his moral responsibility is not the mistaken first-person one.

A third possible explanation for the widespread intuition regarding Frankfurt's case is this: In judging Jones to be morally responsible for killing Smith, we reason that Jones is responsible because he decided to kill Smith and because he decided to do so not as the result of Black's intervention, but rather "on his own." In other words, perhaps we think that Jones committed his act freely, of his own accord, if he was not *pushed* into killing Smith by anything or anyone. And since, by hypothesis in this case, Black did not inter-

vene (that is, Black did not push Jones into killing Smith), we conclude that Jones committed his act freely, and hence we conclude
that Jones is morally responsible for killing Smith.

But our confidence that Jones decided "on his own" makes a
metaphysical assumption. We assume in making this judgment concerning Jones that he made his decision in a spontaneous way not
determined by prior factors. *But this is not so, if determinism is true.*
Rather than focusing attention on Jones in the moments of deliberation prior to acting, focus instead on the possibility of the truth of
causal determinism. If determinism is true, then past events together
with the laws of nature are jointly sufficient for Jones's making the
particular decision he makes. Any person with a Black-type device
in his brain who chooses X (but is prevented by the device from
choosing Y) *must* choose X if determinism is true. Determinism is
an "invisible controller," and so we neglect it when making intuitive
judgments about a person's responsibility for choosing X. The device in Frankfurt's examples does not force Jones to choose X. It
simply prevents him from choosing Y. But the truth of determinism
entails that, given the past and the laws of nature, Jones chooses X.
It is primarily this "pushing" or compelling feature of determinism,
in my view, that rules out morally responsible agency. The problem
is that, if determinism is true, then one is necessitated at each moment to make one particular decision (or to do one particular act),
and that does not leave any "elbow room" for free agency.

Thus, rather than granting the agent's moral responsibility in
Frankfurt-type cases, what the incompatibilist ought to argue is the
following: If determinism is true, then (again taking the case of
Jones killing Smith) Jones was, in fact, *pushed* into killing Smith. He
was pushed by the past and the laws of nature to kill Smith, since
the past and the laws, being what they are, causally necessitated
Jones's action of killing Smith; and this undercuts Jones's responsibility. In the actual circumstances, given the truth of determinism,
Jones could do no other than kill Smith. Hence, Jones does not have
available alternatives for action in the Frankfurt case if determinism
is assumed to hold, yet Jones is not morally responsible; so PAP is
not defeated.

Whether or not one finds these arguments from determinism
against Jones's moral responsibility ultimately persuasive, one must
at least admit that the considerations—considerations that have

moved many intelligent individuals to endorse incompatibilism— deserve *a hearing*. And it is precisely this hearing that arguments based on Frankfurt-type examples against PAP shamelessly fail to grant. For the arguments *begin* with the assumption of the agent's moral responsibility, in isolation from the consideration of meta- physical issues. Hence, the arguments may lead us to think about PAP, but they do not demonstrate its falsehood.

Objections and Replies

In this section, I consider and respond to two important objections to the position of agnosticism that I have advocated regarding the moral responsibility of agents in Frankfurt-type cases.

Manner of Walking Down Life's Path.   In arguing against the justification of the common intuition, I relied upon the idea that a person's moral responsibility for acting as she did might be under- mined by her being pushed by the past and the laws of nature into doing just that act. A compatibilist certainly will reply that one is not objectionably *pushed* by the past when the factors doing the pushing are certain events internal to the agent, such as the occur- rences of particular beliefs, desires, and decisions. Is not being pushed by one's own considerations exactly what we *want* in valu- ing our own agency? The use of the term 'pushed' suggests that an agent, in this case Jones, is moved by factors outside of him, as in a person's being forcefully pushed by another person, or as in a train car's being pushed along a track by an engine car. These cases are quite different, the compatibilist points out, from being moved by reasons that one finds compelling. The incompatibilist ought to ap- preciate the difference, says the standard compatibilist objection, between chains of causal determination that run external to one and chains of causal determination that run "through one's head."

However, the model of a person as chugging along on a certain line of straight train tracks, without any forks in the path, is the an- tithesis of a deep-seated and pervasive image of ourselves as free agents. The idea that we can direct our behavior by our thoughts (preferences, beliefs, intentions) is welcome, but it is only superfi- cially comforting. It comforts until we think about the possibility that even our thoughts are driven to be what they are by previous neurophysiological events, which themselves stand in a chain of events (between which there are deterministic causal links), a chain going backward through events in our childhood brains and to events prior to our birth. The compatibilist picture of free and responsible agency incorporates the assumption of determinism, such that free agents have available to them only one path into the future at every moment of their lives. But whether pushed by another person from the outside or pushed by my own past including internal events, on the compatibilist picture I am pushed nonetheless: The next state of mine at any instant is completely determined. It remains incomprehensible to one with incompatibilist sympathies how a person could legitimately be held morally responsible for walking down the path that he has to walk.

In answer to this concern, Fischer contends that although, given determinism, there is just one available path before him into the future, still he is free and responsible in choosing his *manner of walking* along that path. Fischer writes: "Even if there is just one available path into the future—I may be held accountable for *how I walk down this path*. I can be blamed for taking the path of cruelty, negligence, or cowardice. And I can be praised for walking with sensitivity, attentiveness, and courage."[23] But Fischer's "how I walk" language is vague and unconvincing. It does not succeed in upholding a compatibilist conception of the sort of freedom required for moral responsibility. For what does it mean to "walk with sensitivity"? To do sensitive acts? But they are determined, if determinism is true. Does it mean to have sensitive thoughts? But they also are determined, if determinism is true. Whether Fischer takes the path of cruelty or kindness, whichever path he takes was the only path available to him at the time, given the past, if determinism is true. To speak as if one has options about what sort of attitude to take as one walks along the only path available to one is misleading, since whatever attitude one has at a time is the only attitude it is physically possible for one to have, given the past and the laws.

The most natural conception of freedom rests on the idea of forking paths into the future. In Frankfurt-type cases, the counterfactual intervener rules out the alternative scenarios. But so does determinism. Thus the situation in Frankfurt-type cases is overdetermined, if determinism is true. The alternative pathways are doubly blocked. It is physically impossible for Jones to take an alternative pathway, given determinism. And it is physically impossible for Jones to take an alternative pathway, given Black and his device. If we focus on the presence of Black and on the nonactivation of his device, then it seems that Jones is morally responsible for his act, since he did the act deliberately, unaware that alternative pathways were blocked. Suppose that determinism is true. Then only one event is physically possible at each moment, given the past and the laws of nature. Then, arguably, Jones does not have freedom in acting sufficient to ground his moral responsibility.

Therefore, what ought to be said concerning Frankfurt-type cases is the following: Whether or not Jones is morally responsible for killing Smith cannot be ascertained as simply as proponents of these cases as counterexamples to PAP would have us believe. Rather, Jones's responsibility depends upon whether or not causal determinism is true. If it is true, then Jones cannot do otherwise than kill Smith, but Jones is not morally responsible for killing Smith. Because killing Smith was the physically necessary outcome of the laws of nature and past events, Jones is not the fit subject of such reactive attitudes as moral indignation, outrage, and hatred. Alternately, suppose that determinism is not true. Then, Jones could not have done otherwise than kill Smith, by hypothesis, yet there may be indeterminism in an appropriate place or places to ground Jones's moral responsibility for the act of killing. He may be responsible for killing Smith in virtue of the fact that he could have decided otherwise, or could have tried to decide otherwise, or could have formed a different preference concerning what to do in the circumstances. Depending upon how the case is constructed, the case and the truth of indeterminism may leave room for indeterministic causal links to be located in the appropriate places for Jones to count as acting freely according to the right indeterminist account, saving Jones's moral responsibility. The point is that more investigation than a moment's thought needs to go into reaching a conclusion as to Jones's moral responsibility for his act.[24] Since we are not told in the Frankfurt case whether indeterminism or determinism is assumed to be true, we simply do not know enough about Jones to rest securely on any particular judgment concerning his moral responsibility for his act.

The Status of Ordinary Initial Judgments. Let me consider a second important objection to this position. Some philosophers will object to the idea I have proposed—that we do not know whether or not Jones is morally responsible for his action (until we know whether or not causal determinism is true)—by claiming that this is a highly unnatural and counterintuitive position. Surely we know whether or not he is responsible; we know this by briefly consulting our intuitions about whether or not Jones's is a case in which we would readily apply the term 'morally responsible', a term for which we have learned appropriate and inappropriate uses as speakers of our language. If a person who intentionally kills another person, not as a result of insanity or coercion of any kind, does not count as a free and responsible agent, then who does? To count Jones as morally responsible is a matter of common sense, and so any philosopher who tries to convince us that we do not know whether or not he is morally responsible holds a view that is unnatural and unpersuasive.

This position has some appeal. But consider that our ordinary initial judgments are often subject to revision, upon the consideration of further information that we come to see as relevant. For instance, I might at one time think that it is perfectly appropriate to order veal at a restaurant because it is tender and it tastes delicious but subsequently come to view it as inappropriate to order veal once learning of and reflecting on the inhumane treatment of calves used to produce veal for human consumption.

But, one might object, the example concerning veal involves a change in ethical judgment based upon receiving new information relevant to the ethics of the situation, whereas the issue under discussion is the right use of a particular term in the English language: the term, 'morally responsible'. We have learned as speakers of the language when to, and when not to, use this term; the job of philosophers is simply to set out the principles systematizing our normal usage.

However, just as we come with reflection and maturity to revise our practices of applying the terms 'good' and 'appropriate' (a child might think it is good to paint with his finger paints on the living-room wall), so too we might be led by certain theoretical considerations to revise our views concerning what counts as an act for which a person is to be held morally responsible. The possibility of the truth of the thesis of scientific determinism is not a consideration that immediately occurs to unreflective common sense as it considers cases of responsibility or nonresponsibility, and so unreflective commonsensical judgments concerning moral responsibility in particular cases should not be taken as conclusive. Those intuitions are proved accurate only by surviving a process of rational examination. The incompatibilist alleges that such examinations will reveal the ordinary initial judgments to be mistaken and in need of revision.

Frankfurt gets us to take a commonsensical view toward Jones in judging his moral responsibility, a view that simply assumes that the question of determinism's truth or falsity is irrelevant. But this makes us miss the incompatibilist's deeper concern. As Richard Double aptly expresses the situation, "Frankfurt has gotten us to put on our compatibilistic spectacles, and these spectacles make us myopic concerning the incompatibilist's more radical challenge."[25] Thus the reasoning in support of taking Frankfurt-type cases as counterexamples to PAP is superficial. It is superficial in a way similar to the superficiality of the introductory philosophy student who purports to defeat epistemic skepticism concerning the external world by producing a pen in front of his face and claiming to know that it is there. In both cases, the reasoning fails to engage all of the relevant considerations. Double draws this analogy, comparing the situation to Peter Unger's analysis of the debate between the skeptics and G. E. Moore. In claiming to know of the existence of his hand, Moore did not refute, or even address, the skeptical worry that drives our placing the requirements for epistemic justification at a high level.[26]

In granting that Jones is morally responsible in response to Frankfurt-type cases, in sum, an incompatibilist puts himself into the compatibilist's territory and then has to battle his way out. But a perfectly plausible response to Frankfurt is a more radical one of insisting to see no good reason to grant the initial premise. When Frankfurt states regarding his original example that "Jones$_4$ will bear precisely the same moral responsibility for what he does as he would have borne if Black had not been ready to take steps to ensure that he do it,"[27] he may be right, depending upon further details of the situation. But since it is not specified in Frankfurt's case or others like it whether or not we are to assume the thesis of causal determinism to be true, we do not know whether or not Jones is morally responsible in the cases, and thus we can conclude nothing about the truth or falsity of PAP.[28]

Arguments against PAP based upon Frankfurt-type cases are, thus, inconclusive. The arguments depend upon one's having a particular intuition about the agent's moral responsibility for his or her act in the presence of the counterfactual intervener, and Frankfurt's intuition is not universally shared. And even if Frankfurt's intuition is *widely* (albeit not universally) shared, this can be explained in a number of ways, including, most fundamentally, by a widespread failure to think seriously about the possibility of the truth of determinism when forming initial judgments of moral responsibility concerning the Frankfurt-type cases. We can conclude that Frankfurt-type cases do not show that PAP is false. Hence, moral responsibility has not been shown by Frankfurt-type examples to be consistent with a lack of available alternatives.

Why PAP Is False

Let's turn to the matter of whether PAP *is* true or false. We actually do not need elaborate Frankfurt-type cases to lead us to question the principle. PAP, as traditionally stated, is imprecise, in that it is not sufficiently temporally indexed. The most natural reading of the principle would suggest that a person is morally responsible for doing something at a time only if she could have done otherwise *at that time*. Suppose, then, we understand PAP as follows:

PAP_1: A person is morally responsible for doing X at t only if s/he could have done otherwise than X at t.

But it is clear on a little reflection that PAP_1 is false. For a person may be *only* able to do X at t (and not able to do other than X at t) because of free actions of her own, while retaining her moral responsibility for doing X.

For instance, consider a variation on a case of Dennett's.[29] Suppose that Howler knows that he suffers a condition making him likely to murder the first person he sees under a full moon, so he freely submits himself to being locked into a windowless room on the night of the full moon. Howler is praiseworthy for not murdering the first person under the full moon at midnight, although at the time he is unable to do so. It seems clear that Howler retains his praiseworthiness despite his inability to do otherwise at the time because of his freely making himself, at a previous time, unable to do otherwise at the later time. Now Dennett takes the case of a person's being praiseworthy in not running out and murdering the first person under a full moon (while locked in a windowless room) to show that moral responsibility does not require alternative possibilities of any sort. But I think Dennett draws the wrong conclusion. For the locked-in person does not deserve praise for not doing something he is unable to do, where his inability is not due to any free actions of his own.

Let's suppose that the agent in question was, instead, *thrown* into the locked room at 7 P.M., not that he entered it by his own free choice. To say that the agent, in this case, is praiseworthy for refraining from killing someone at midnight is akin to claiming that you are praiseworthy for not, with a twitch of your nose, turning your enemy's delectable food into poisonous snakes. This latter is a highly implausible claim (unless you have some quite unusual powers), since (I am presuming) you cannot do that, and your inability is not due to your own free actions. By contrast, Howler may be praised for not killing the first person under the full moon at midnight, where his praiseworthiness is dependent on the fact that, since he knew he was likely to kill someone, he freely put himself into the locked room in order to prevent it.[30]

Here is another case indicating the falsity of PAP: A woman is walking down the street, carrying her infant daughter. A man suddenly grabs the child from her mother, holds a gun to the child's head, and threatens to kill the child unless the mother hands over her wallet. Given the woman's past, including free choices she has made to have and care for her daughter, to love and cherish her, and the woman's beliefs concerning the relative unimportance of money, suppose that it is, at the time of the threat, physically and psychologically impossible for her to do anything other than form and act upon the preference to hand over the wallet, whether it contains five dollars or her life's savings. I take it that we would agree that the woman is praiseworthy for handing over the money in exchange for the life of her daughter, although at the time, she was unable to do otherwise. Whereas determinism entails for each person a lack of available alternatives at each and every moment of life, this case does not show that moral responsibility for action is consistent with such a lack. The mother's praiseworthiness at the time of handing over the money is made sense of in part by our understanding her to be a self-made woman—a person who has freely chosen from among alternatives to make herself into a certain sort of person, namely, one who loves and values her daughter more than money. Thus the mother's inability to do otherwise at the time in question is due in part to past free actions making her into the sort of person that she is.

Consider another case. Suppose that it is very important that I get on the 10 A.M. flight to New York. Suppose that if I do not get on it, I will miss the baptism service of my brother's son, which I have promised to attend. So I would be morally blameworthy for deliberately missing the 10 A.M. plane. Now suppose that I do not own a car or live near any public transportation that could take me to the airport. Further suppose that at 9 A.M. I phone the friend scheduled to take me to the airport and say that I do not need a ride after all. I do not call a cab. Instead, I sit in front of the television on my couch at home for the next hour. Now, at 10 A.M., I cannot do otherwise than miss the plane to New York, but it seems that I am still morally blameworthy for doing so.[31]

This case is similar to one described by James Lamb as an instance of "getting oneself into an impossible position."[32] Peggy Sue deliberately gets herself arrested, and so, at the time when she should go to the function she promised to attend, she cannot go. Peggy Sue is morally responsible for breaking her promise to attend the function, even though at the time appointed to attend, she cannot do otherwise than *not* attend. Let us add to Lamb's description of the case that Peggy Sue deliberately got herself arrested by flashing a police officer. Suppose that she was dreading attending her sister's piano performance as she had promised and that she flashed the police officer hoping precisely to make herself unable to attend the performance. Peggy Sue seems morally responsible for not attending the performance as she had promised to do, although at the time of the performance, she could not have.[33] Thus Lamb takes the case of Peggy Sue to show PAP false.

Actually, although this case seems to be a clear violation of PAP, it is indeterminate without some added stipulations. That is, even in this apparently straightforward case, we do not really know whether or not Peggy Sue is ultimately morally responsible for not attending the function she promised to attend (when she got herself arrested and so made herself unable to attend) until we know whether or not she freely got herself arrested (by flashing the police officer). And we do not know whether or not she freely got herself arrested until we know whether or not everything she has ever thought and done has been causally determined by the past and the laws of nature. Perhaps Peggy Sue's flashing the officer was a causally determined event in a chain of events tracing backward through events of her being sexually abused in her childhood. Those childhood events may have left their mark on her personality, not in the form of a constraining mental illness, but in such a way that, while she remains a sane and rationally capable person, Peggy Sue's desire for physical self-exposure can be traced through deterministic causal links between events back into the past to the events of sexual abuse. In seeing Peggy Sue's moral responsibility to be undermined, we need not view her as irrevocably damaged to the point of insanity, but only as an agent pushed along on a course of life that does not involve any forking branches—as an agent whose life unfolds along a single deterministic path. Thus the Peggy Sue case is unclear as a counterexample to PAP as most naturally construed (as PAP_1) until we know whether or not causal determinism is true. The case *is* a counterexample to PAP, given the stipulation that indeterminism is true and that Peggy Sue's flashing the officer was a free act in virtue of its having causal indeterminism at the appropriate place in its history.

There are many cases of freely getting oneself into a situation such that, once in it, one cannot do otherwise than what one does. For example, consider the case of an inebriated alcoholic flying into a violent rage against his wife and children. Suppose that his violence is the deterministic outcome of events in his alcohol-affected brain. So, given his personality, his past and his drunkenness, his flying into a violent rage is, at the time, inevitable. According to PAP_1, he would *not* be morally blameworthy for his acts of violent raging, since he could not do otherwise at the time. But this is counterintuitive. If the facts about the world leave room for him to have freely begun to drink in the first place, in full awareness of his past violent outbursts when intoxicated, then it seems that his moral responsibility for his violence persists, derivative from his having freely gotten himself into such an inebriated state.[34] This case is parallel to that of honest Abe, discussed in the previous chapter. Abe may have so habituated himself into telling the truth that he is at some point literally unable to tell a lie. But his telling the truth is still praiseworthy, given his own undetermined construction of the honest character from which his truth telling derives. So PAP$_1$ is false.[35]

These are fairly ordinary sorts of examples. At least, they are more ordinary than Frankfurt-type cases, in not involving the presence of a counterfactual intervener such as Black or Natascha. Moreover, I think that the several cases in this section succeed where Frankfurt-type cases fail: They show that PAP (as most naturally construed: PAP$_1$) is false.

Incompatibilism Without PAP

The task of the final sections of this chapter will be to settle upon a principle with which to replace PAP, a principle more accurately specifying the alternative possibilities condition for morally responsible action. I have argued above that it is only if persons have the ability sometimes to act freely, on an incompatibilist construal, that they are the sorts of beings who can legitimately deserve praise and blame for some of their behavior. If the outcomes of our decision processes are never undetermined by the past and the natural laws, then we are not responsible for being the sorts of people that we are or for the acts that follow from our character. The following is a further argument for the position that determinism and responsibility are incompatible.

If events involving agents are links in completely deterministic causal chains (and there is no such thing as agent-causation), then sense cannot be made of holding agents deeply responsible for their choices and actions. This is because picking out one event rather than another in a chain of deterministic causes and effects, and taking *that* event as the one deserving of moral responsibility, is arbitrary. Each event in a deterministic causal chain leading to event x is *one* cause of x. But which event is properly held morally responsible for x? Surely not the most proximate cause, since, in the case where x is an action, the most proximate cause of x is the movement of some group of muscles, and muscles are not deeply responsible for actions. Neither are mental events; agents are.

Perhaps one will explain that agents are sufficiently complex thinking organisms to be named the morally responsible parts of causal chains. The complexity of agents and their ability to act for reasons is what makes the ascription of moral responsibility to them sensible. The compatibilist might put this by saying that what makes persons morally responsible is their ability to set ends for themselves and to give reasons for those ends being better than others. The crucial question for the compatibilist is this one: Why would the two classes of beings, the 'morally responsible beings' and the 'beings who can set ends for themselves', perfectly correspond? Exactly what about being able to act for reasons explains the (alleged) fact that such beings are to be held morally responsible?[36]

What makes us think, in assigning moral responsibility, that "the buck stops" with the agent? I think this is because we consider an agent as a center of control. We have reviewed various accounts of agent control over action, accounts that make that control compatible with determinism. But I have argued that the sort of control depicted by each of these compatibilist theories—the Self-Direction View, the Reason View, and the Reasons-Responsive Mechanism View—are unsatisfactory as accounts of the kind of control needed to ground moral responsibility.

The reason we take agents to be deeply responsible for their choices and the actions resulting from them is, I believe, because we think that there is some indeterminism involved in the outcomes of their deliberative processes, such that what makes the difference in whether a causal chain proceeds one way or another from some point in time is the undetermined deliberative faculty of the agent. Given the past and the laws of nature, if determinism is false, then at some points in time there is *more than one* physically possible future, and what makes the difference in settling *which* of these becomes actual is the deliberative power of an agent himself. An agent is, again, a center of control, and it is this control—control over *which* among a range of physically possible futures becomes actual—that grounds the moral responsibility of, and makes sense of the ascription of moral responsibility to, agents.

If determinism and moral responsibility *are* incompatible, then what principle regarding alternative possibilities and moral responsibility is correct? We have seen that is not the case that, in order for an agent S to be morally responsible for performing act A at a time t, S must have been able to do otherwise than A at t, since S may be unable to do otherwise than A at t in part *because of* S's own free act at a time other than t committing her to do A at t. That is, PAP has been ruled out. I will examine several alternative principles: an in-compatibilist principle proposed by Lamb, which I will argue is unilluminating; a second principle derived from one proposed by van Inwagen concerning moral responsibility for facts, which I be-lieve falls to Frankfurt-type counterexamples given the stipulation of properly located indeterminism; and, finally, two new disjunctive principles, one of which, I believe, is a correct principle concerning moral responsibility for action.

Weak PAP

Lamb distinguishes three versions of PAP—a strong version, a moderate version, and a weak version—and ultimately endorses the weak version.[37] According to Lamb's weak version of PAP:

> *Lamb's Weak Version of PAP:* A person is morally responsible for doing something only if at some time there is *something* he could have avoided doing.[38]

Writes Lamb, "I have argued that there is at least one formulation of the principle of alternative possibilities—the weak principle—which is reasonable to believe."[39] Unfortunately, in fact, Lamb gives no argument whatsoever for the claim that the weak version of PAP is reasonable to believe. He simply poses the weak version of the princi-ple and claims that, by way of it, purported counterexamples to the necessity of the ability to do otherwise for moral responsibility can be shown to be unsuccessful. How exactly Frankfurt-type examples are undercut by the weak PAP, Lamb does not make clear.

Is it reasonable, at any rate, to believe Lamb's formulation of the weak version of PAP? Consider the following case. Suppose that the only thing that Carl could have avoided in his lifetime was using the tissue in the box to the right of his bed when suffering a flu at the age of ten. He could have, instead, used a tissue from the box to the left of the bed. But during the rest of his life, *each action* of his is one that he could not have avoided. Why think that it is a necessary condition of Carl's moral responsibility for some act that he commits at age thirty-five—say, lying to his neighbor concerning the attractiveness of her new hairstyle—that Carl was able to have avoided, at some point earlier in his life, using the tissue in the box to the right of the bed? Of course, the avoidability of this one act of tissue use is not being alleged to be a sufficient condition for his moral responsibility for lying to his neighbor, but only a necessary condition. But why should we think it is necessary? Why is it relevant at all? Further argument in support of the necessity of the proposed condition would be useful.

The *something* italicized in the weak version of PAP needs further specification. Would not the *something* have to be *something relevant* to the act in question in order reasonably to affect the judgment concerning the agent's moral responsibility for that act? For free action of the sort required for moral responsibility, there has to have been indeterminism somewhere crucial in the causal processes leading to the act. The indeterminism cannot be located just anywhere. It certainly is not sufficient to ground free and responsible agency that there be some indeterminism somewhere in the universe or that there be one instance of indeterminism at some—any—point in a person's life. The weak version of PAP may well be a true principle in stating only a necessary condition for morally responsible action, yet it is so weak as to be rather unilluminating.

Van Inwagen's Principle: Responsibility for Facts

Van Inwagen has recently defended a rather straightforward principle concerning responsibility for facts. Ginet defends one nearly identical to it.[40] Van Inwagen asserts regarding his principle: "however many *other* principles relating free will and moral responsibility there may be that can be shown false by Frankfurt-style examples, if this principle is true, then no agent who is unable ever to act otherwise is morally responsible for any fact."[41] His proposed principle is as follows:

> *van Inwagen's Principle:* If it is a fact that *p*, an agent is morally responsible for the fact that *p* only if that agent was once able to act in such a way that it would not have been the case that *p*.

According to this principle, a necessary condition for a certain person's being morally responsible for the fact that *p*, is that the obtaining or nonobtaining (of the fact that *p*) depends upon the action of that person. For example, the fact that Jim is fired is something for which Meredith can be held morally responsible only if Meredith is in a position to do something that impacts whether or not Jim is fired. More precisely, the principle tells us that, if it is a fact that Jim was fired, then Meredith is morally responsible for this fact only if she was once able to have acted in a way that would have made it the case that Jim was not fired. Perhaps Meredith could have refrained from firing Jim herself. Or perhaps she could have given a positive report concerning Jim's performance to his superior, rather than the negative report she in fact gave. But if Meredith does not have it within her power to act in any way that would make it the case that Jim is not fired, then she cannot be held morally responsible for the fact that Jim is fired.

Van Inwagen considers the question of whether or not a counter-factual intervener scenario of the sort considered earlier in this chapter overturns his proposed principle. He concludes that it does not. Suppose, van Inwagen writes:

> Cosser wanted Gunnar to shoot and kill Ridley, which Gunnar seemed likely to do; he intended to, and he had the means and the op-portunity. But if Gunnar had changed his mind about killing Ridley, Cosser would have manipulated Gunnar's brain in such a way as to have re-established his intention to shoot Ridley. In the event, Cosser's "insurance policy" turned out not to have been necessary, for Gunnar did not change his mind, and shot and killed Ridley "on schedule." Cosser played no causal role whatever in the sequence of events that led up to the killing.[42]

Suppose further that Ridley is a widower, so that his children, once Ridley is killed, are orphans. Now take 'Ridley's children are now orphans' to replace 'p', in order to test van Inwagen's proposed principle. Van Inwagen says we are to assume that there was no sec-ond gunman or heart attack or accident in nearby logical space, so that if Gunnar had not shot Ridley, then Ridley's children would not now be orphans. Given the setup of the case, van Inwagen con-cludes, Gunnar was *not* able to act in such a way that, if he had, Rid-ley's children would not now be orphans. For even if Gunnar had decided not to kill Ridley, "Cosser would have 'changed his mind back,' and he would have killed Ridley anyway."[43] The fact that p— the fact that Ridley's children are now orphans—would have ob-tained "no matter what." Since Gunnar was not able to act in such a way that it would not have been the case that p, Gunnar is *not*, according to the proposed principle, morally responsible for the fact that *p*, and this, van Inwagen thinks, is just the right result.

But given a certain way of filling in the metaphysical conditions of the case, I think that this is *not* the right result. Suppose that Gunnar was able to have formed a different preference as the outcome of his deliberations over what to do but that, in fact, he formed the preference to kill Ridley anyway. Van Inwagen allows such a filling in of the case: "If you think that something special has to be added to the truncated story [e.g., subtracting Cosser] to ensure that Gunnar is responsible for this fact—indeterminism, 'agent causation'—feel free to add it."[44] But if the metaphysics of the situation allow for Gunnar's deliberations to go either way, and yet he decisively forms the preference for shooting Ridley, without any interference from Cosser, then it seems incontrovertible that Gunnar is self-directed in what he does and is morally responsible for the fact that Ridley's children are now orphans. Thus it seems that van Inwagen has not specified the correct principle concerning alternative possibilities and moral responsibility for facts.

Acts themselves are often the objects for which we seek to discern agent moral responsibility or nonresponsibility. Normally, for instance, we ask whether or not Sam is morally responsible for betraying Nancy, rather than whether Sam is morally responsible for the fact that Nancy was betrayed by Sam. Furthermore, talk of responsibility for action is in keeping with discussions stemming from Frankfurt's original presentation of PAP. Therefore, a principle formulating the truth about moral responsibility for action is desirable.[45] Substituting '*S*' for 'the agent' and '*S* does *x* at *t*' for '*p*' in van Inwagen's principle concerning moral responsibility for facts generates the following principle:

> *Derived van Inwagenian Principle:* If *S* does *x* at *t*, then *S* is morally responsible for doing *x* at *t* only if *S* was once able to act in such a way that it would not have been the case that *S* did *x* at *t*.

This principle gives the result, first, that no one is morally responsible if determinism is true. Second, it gives the result that agents in counterfactual intervener (Frankfurt-style) cases are *not* morally responsible for what they do, even if indeterminism is true and indeterministic links are appropriately located in the causal chains leading to the acts.[46] According to the derived principle, Sheila is not responsible for sabotaging Caitlin's shoes, for instance, and Jones is not responsible for killing Smith. For, given the existence of the counterfactual intervener, Black, it is false that Jones is ever able to act in such a way that it would not have been the case that Jones killed Smith at t. Black's presence ensures that Jones will kill Smith at t. But suppose that indeterminism is present in Jones's deliberative process and that he decides for reasons that incline, but do not necessitate, his decisive formation of a preference concerning what to do. And suppose that Black never interferes and that Jones acts on his preference, with undefeated authorization, to kill Smith. And suppose that Jones meets whatever other conditions there are for being morally responsible for an act (besides the freedom condition), such as being an agent of a certain age and possessing some minimal degree of normative competence. Then it is clear that Jones is rightly held morally responsible for killing Smith. Hence derivation from van Inwagen's proposed principle concerning facts gets us a principle concerning acts that initially seems adequate. But counterfactual intervener cases remain sufficiently problematic to warrant the formulation of an alternate proposal.

Two Disjunctive Principles: Responsibility for Acts

The examples we have seen to overturn the original principle, PAP_1 (cases of freely getting oneself into an impossible position), have a certain feature in common: In each, the agent's *inability* to do otherwise at the time in question is causally traceable to past free acts of his or her own. Reflection on such cases thus leads one to formulate the following principle regarding moral responsibility for action and alternative possibilities:

> *Disjunctive Principle 1 (DP-1):* A person S is morally responsible for doing X at t only if *either* S could have done otherwise than X at t *or* S's inability to do otherwise than X at t is causally explicable at least in part by S's own act(s) at some time(s) other than t, such that S could have done otherwise at that (those) other time(s).[47]

This principle seems to account accurately for the moral responsibility of the agents in the counterexamples I described to PAP. Assuming indeterminism is true, the principle makes sense, for instance, of Peggy Sue's moral responsibility for not attending the function as promised: Although she could not have attended at the time of the function (given that she was being held by the police), her inability to attend then is causally explicable at least in part by her own actions, which were such that she could have done otherwise when she performed those acts. (She could have formed and acted upon a different preference than the preference to get herself arrested by flashing the police officer.) The principle also makes sense, for instance, of the alcoholic's blameworthiness for his violent attack on his wife and children.

However, DP-1 does not work for agents in indeterministically specified counterfactual intervener cases. Assume determinism is false. Then, in my view, we should allow for the possibility that agents in counterfactual intervener scenarios, such as Jones and Sheila, are morally responsible for what they do. The placement of the indeterminism may allow for either agent to form preferences with undefeated authorization. But neither can *do* otherwise than perform one particular overt action at the time of acting,[48] due to the presence of the counterfactual intervener, and their inability to do otherwise is *not* due to acts of their own, but rather is due to a counterfactual intervener's device. Consider alternatively, then, the following principle:

> *Disjunctive Principle 2 (DP-2):* A person S is morally responsible for doing X at t only if *either* S could have done otherwise than X at t *or* S could have at some time done something other than what s/he did, something that would be reasonably expected to have the result that S would do otherwise than X at t.[49]

It is reasonable to expect the absence of Frankfurt-type counterfactual interveners. So when S at t_1 decisively forms a preference to do Y at t_2, it is reasonable to expect that S will do Y at t_2. If S is in a counterfactual intervener scenario that allows S the possibility of forming a preference for doing something other than X, yet S forms and acts on the preference for doing X, then S is morally responsible, according to DP-2, for doing X, even though she could not have done otherwise than X at the time, given the presence of the noninterfering potential intervener. And this is just the right result. Her moral responsibility for her act is preserved by her having been able to have done something that "normally" would have led, or would reasonably be expected to have led, to her doing other than X. Since she could have taken this alternate path but did not, she is morally responsible for what she does.

I believe DP-2 gives the right results for all of the cases we have examined in this chapter. Consider the case of my missing the flight: I could not have done otherwise at the time of the flight's departure, but I am blameworthy only if I could have called a cab in time to make the flight. In the case in which Peggy Sue does not attend the function as promised, she is morally responsible for failing to attend only if she could have refrained from flashing the officer by, for instance, continuing to walk peacefully down the sidewalk. When Sheila sabotages the dance shoes, she is blameworthy only if she could have decisively preferred not to sabotage them. Howler is praiseworthy in refraining from murder only if he could have stayed outside on the night of the first full moon. Honest Abe, who cannot at present tell a lie, is praiseworthy in telling the truth at a time t only if he could have done something at a time earlier in his life that would be reasonably expected to have the result that he would do otherwise at t, such as adopted the policy that lying is the best course of action. And the alcoholic in his violent raging is blameworthy only if he could have, for instance, refrained from drinking any alcohol at all earlier in the evening.

Now, suppose that we try to construct a "global" Frankfurt-style intervener case as a test of this principle. Call the actions that would lead to the reasonable expectation of the person doing otherwise with respect to the target action the 'alternative precursors' (APs). Now suppose that the person chooses none of the APs but that *had* she ever attempted to do so, she would have been prevented by the "agent in the wings" (the counterfactual intervener). That is, extend the Frankfurt scenario to the APs as well. Now, is the person morally responsible for what she does at t, given that she could not have done otherwise at t and given that she could not have done anything (because of the counterfactual intervener) that would reasonably be expected to have the result that she would do otherwise at t? If so, DP-2 is violated.

Let us take the case of Sheila (the jealous dancer) and Natascha (the counterfactual intervener—dancer and neurosurgeon). There are two ways to imagine the proposed extension of the case. In one, Natascha waits until Sheila in some way begins to commit an AP and then prevents Sheila from doing it. In this case, Sheila can begin to perform an AP and, in effect, that is a kind of minimal AP itself. So this account of the scenario leaves an AP of some sort open to Sheila. Thus Sheila is morally responsible when she sabotages the shoes, and DP-2 is not violated. Consider a second account. Natascha has infallible knowledge of what Sheila will do, begin to do, prefer to do, and so forth, and Natascha would prevent any AP she knew that Sheila would perform. On this scenario, there is not any minimal AP available to Sheila. In this case, however, given the infallibility of Natascha's knowledge, Natascha's inaction is part of the cause for Sheila's not adopting any AP. It is causally determined by the past, circumstances, and the natural laws that Sheila will not even begin to prefer doing otherwise, since the presence of Natascha is part of the circumstances. In the case of Natascha as an infallible predictor, the fact that Natascha has not acted at t_1 to prevent Sheila from adopting an AP at t_2 means that it is already settled at t_1 that Sheila will not adopt the AP at t_2. Thus Sheila is not morally responsible for sabotaging the dance shoes.[50]

I conclude that DP-2 ought to replace PAP as the principle formulating the right relation between moral responsibility for action and alternative possibilities.

Conclusion

The fact that someone had no alternatives for action at the time of acting does initially alter our intuitions about praise and blame. Further thought reveals, however, that open alternatives to a certain action need not be available at the time of that action in order for an agent to be morally responsible for performing it. We have seen that arguments from Frankfurt-type scenarios fail to overturn PAP, since they posit the agent's moral responsibility from the beginning without considering relevant metaphysical questions. But, in fact, we do not need Frankfurt-type counterfactual intervener cases to lead us to doubt PAP, as other sorts of more ordinary cases call the principle into question. Examples include cases of "getting oneself into an impossible situation," such as the case of Peggy Sue and that of Howler in freely putting himself into a locked room. Even these cases turn out not to lead as straightforwardly as we might initially think to the correct conclusion regarding the relation between the availability of alternative possibilities and moral responsibility. I have considered several candidate principles and proposed DP-2 as a reasonable principle describing a necessary condition for moral responsibility, a condition that cannot be met if there is at every moment exactly one physically possible future.

Notes

1. Actually, I think the above reasoning is wrong on a third count, as well: Even if moral responsibility *were* shown not to require incompatibilist freedom, it would not follow that incompatibilist accounts of freedom are inconsequential, for freedom of an incompatibilist sort might be required—indeed, I think, *is* required—to undergird our considered intuitions concerning human dignity, our standing in genuine personal relationships, and our sense of ourselves as practical deliberators facing an open future.

2. In the paper at the center of contemporary philosophical controversy on this issue, "Alternative Possibilities and Moral Responsibility," Frankfurt states PAP as follows: "A person is morally responsible for what he has done only if he could have done otherwise" (Harry Frankfurt, "Alternate Possibilities and Moral Responsibility," *Journal of Philosophy* 66, 1969, pp. 829–839; reprinted in John Martin Fischer, ed., *Moral Responsibility*, Ithaca: Cornell University Press, 1986).

3. A. J. Ayer, "Freedom and Necessity," in *Philosophical Essays* (London: Macmillan, 1954), pp. 271–284; reprinted in Gary Watson, ed., *Free Will* (Oxford: Oxford University Press, 1982), p. 15.

4. Frankfurt, "Alternate Possibilities,"; reprinted in Fischer, *Moral Responsibility*, p. 150.

5. Sometimes the Frankfurt case is filled in by describing Jones as deciding between two candidates for whom to vote (e.g., in John Martin Fischer, *The Metaphysics of Free Will: An Essay on Control*, Aristotle Society Series, vol. 14, Cambridge, MA: Blackwell, 1994); or as deciding whether or not to kill another man, Smith (e.g., in Daniel Dennett, *Elbow Room: The Varieties of Free Will Worth Wanting*, Cambridge, MA: MIT Press, 1984), such that, whether Jones does it "on his own" or as the result of Black's intervention, the unfortunate Smith ends up dead.

6. In the original paper presenting his counterexamples to PAP, Frankfurt notes: "After thinking up the example that I am about to develop I learned that Robert Nozick, in lectures given several years ago, had formulated an example of the same general type and had proposed it as a counterexample to the principle of alternative possibilities." ("Alternative Possi-

bilities"; reprinted in Fischer, *Moral Responsibility*, p. 148, note 2). None-theless, I call counterfactual intervener cases against PAP "Frankfurt-type," in keeping with the large body of philosophical literature following Frank-furt's article.

7. Fischer, *Metaphysics of Free Will*, pp. 207–208.

8. The one exception of which I am aware is Carl Ginet, who reports re-garding Frankfurt's intuition in favor of Jones's responsibility, "I do not share that intuition" ("In Defense of the Principle of Alternative Possibili-ties: Why I Don't Find Frankfurt's Argument Convincing," in James Tomberlin, ed., *Philosophical Perspectives* 10, 1996, p. 406.)

9. Peter van Inwagen, *An Essay on Free Will* (Oxford: Clarendon Press, 1983), pp. 164, 179–180.

10. Ibid., pp. 165–171. The alternate principles van Inwagen calls PPA, PPP1, and PPP2.

11. For more fully elaborated defenses of the claim that van Inwagen's principles fall to Frankfurt-type counterexamples, see Robert Heineman, "Incompatibilism Without the Principle of Alternative Possibilities," *Aus-tralasian Journal of Philosophy* 64, 1986, pp. 266–276; and Martha Klein, *Determinism, Blameworthiness, and Deprivation* (Oxford: Clarendon Press, 1990).

12. Both Frankfurt's original formulation of PAP and van Inwagen's for-mulation of PPA are changed here only by my use of gender-inclusive pro-nouns. See van Inwagen, *Essay on Free Will*, p. 165.

13. James Lamb, "Evaluative Compatibilism and the Principle of Alter-native Possibilities," *Journal of Philosophy* 90, 1993, pp. 517–527; see espe-cially p. 521.

14. I am aware that one might use the type-token distinction, along with a certain theory of the individuation of events, to argue that the action Jones commits in the alternate scenario (in which Black intervenes) would not be the same action particular, only an action of the same type, since event par-ticulars are individuated (wholly or in part) by their causal histories. (See van Inwagen, *Essay on Free Will*, pp. 166–180, for a development of this sort of line in defense of his proposed principles concerning moral respon-sibility and alternative possibilities. Van Inwagen says that he is unable to formulate a precise notion of 'act-universal' as opposed to 'act-particular'; he prefers to see agents as morally responsible for events or states of affairs, rather than for actions. Therefore, his defense of his principles rests, in-stead, on the notion of a 'state-of-affairs universal'.) Thus, one might argue that, precisely speaking, Jones *can* do otherwise in the Frankfurt-type cases: The event particular that occurs in the case of his killing Smith without Black's intervention is distinct from the event particular that occurs in the case of his killing Smith by way of Black's intervention. But this line of re-sponse to Frankfurt I do not find particularly compelling, both because it

relies for its success in defeating Frankfurt-type counterexamples to PAP on their proponents' accepting a certain theory of event individuation and, more importantly, because the sort of alternative possibility granted to the agent does not seem to be the right sort to be crucial in accounting for his moral responsibility.

15. Fischer, *Metaphysics of Free Will*, p. 134.

16. Actually, on this line of response, Sheila's moral responsibility for her act *does* conflict with PAP as it is formulated by Frankfurt, since Sheila cannot *do* otherwise than sabotage Caitlin's shoes. The incompatibilist endorsing this line of response to Frankfurt-type cases must *either* defend an alternate PAP-like principle *or* say that what Sheila is responsible for is not sabotaging the shoes, but rather *trying to decide to sabotage the shoes*.

17. William Rowe attributes this kind of position to Thomas Reid in *Thomas Reid on Freedom and Morality* (Ithaca: Cornell University Press, 1991); see, in particular, pp. 75–93. In order to save PAP exactly as it is formulated by Frankfurt, a flicker strategist taking this line would have to say that what Jones is morally responsible for is not killing Smith, but *killing Smith on his own*, where by this the strategist means killing Smith as the result of a volition that he himself agent-caused.

18. Fischer, *Metaphysics of Free Will*, p. 140.

19. Alfred Mele agrees and defends the point against Fischer in his "Soft Libertarianism and Frankfurt-Style Scenarios," *Philosophical Topics* 24, 1996, 123–142.

20. A problem arises as to whether either of these (e.g., beginning to try to kill Smith or being the agent-cause of the volition to kill Smith) is *an act*.

21. See Klein, *Determinism, Blameworthiness, and Deprivation* for a development of this sort of position.

22. It is inaccurate to say that Jones did his act with sufficient control to ground his being *deserving* of blame, since the notion of freedom underlying desert involves an openness in the future that is ruled out by determinism. There is an intuitively natural and pertinent question concerning the fairness of holding responsible a person for deciding in the only way it was physically possible for him to decide in the circumstances. (Fischer, in maintaining incompatibilism with respect to freedom and determinism, but compatibilism with respect to freedom and responsibility, seems in thinking about moral responsibility to take insufficiently seriously considerations of fairness.) A compatibilist may well assert that this sense of fairness is a relic of outmoded theological doctrines and that there is no such thing as, in Dennett's words, "before-the-eyes-of-God Guilt." But the assertion remains just that; and as it stands, it bears no logical force whatsoever in overturning a deeply felt and pervasive sense of fairness, a sense of fairness that supports an incompatibilist freedom requirement for moral responsibility.

23. Fischer, *Metaphysics of Free Will*, p. 216.

24. Another way of putting the bottom line about Frankfurt-type cases is this: Either indeterminism is true or determinism is true. If indeterminism is true, then there may be indeterminism between successive events located at right points in the production of Jones's decision and act in order to save his genuine free agency. If there is indeterminism (and hence alternative possibilities) in the appropriate place or places, then Jones is morally responsible for his decision and act. The intuitive immediate judgment that Jones is responsible for his act in the presence of the counterfactual intervener, Black, is saved, and there are shown to be alternative possibilities of some sort in Frankfurt-type cases. Then moral responsibility has not been shown to be consistent with determinism, although PAP as traditionally stated (if it requires having available options for acting at the moment of acting) is false. (For this solution, a PAP-like principle would need careful formulation in order to spell out exactly what sort of alternatives must be available to preserve moral responsibility. I undertake formulation of an alternate principle below.) Alternately, determinism holds. If so, then no person can ever do or decide otherwise than he in fact does; and at each moment, one particular outcome is causally necessitated by prior factors. Then Jones is not morally responsible for what he does.

25. Richard Double, *Metaphilosophy and Free Will* (Oxford: Oxford University Press, 1996), p. 88.

26. G. E. Moore, "A Defence of Common Sense" and "Proof of the External World" in *Philosophical Papers* (London: George Allen and Unwin, 1959).

27. Frankfurt, "Alternate Possibilities,"; reprinted in Fischer, *Moral Responsibility*, p. 150.

28. Robert Heineman ("Incompatibilism") defends this same conclusion by distinguishing two senses of the phrase 'could have done otherwise'. The sense in which an agent who is not responsible because of an inability to do otherwise according to PAP is different from the sense in which an agent is unable to do otherwise in Frankfurt's case, Heineman argues. While I agree with Heineman's conclusion that Frankfurt-type cases do not show the falsity of PAP (since arguments resting on them make a bare assertion of the agent's responsibility for his act given his decision to do it, rather than providing an argument for this claim), I do not think that distinguishing between two senses of the term 'could have done otherwise' is the most compelling way, or even the right way, of showing this. To say that an agent is able to do otherwise at a time is to say that, when standing at that point in time, the agent faces more than one genuine alternative for the future: It is physically possible for him to do something or to do something else. In the Frankfurt-type scenarios, the alternate pathways are blocked, so it is physically possible for the agent to do only one act. If determinism is true, then it is at every time for every agent physically possible for him to do only one

act. Thus the sense in which the agent in a deterministic scenario is unable to do otherwise and the sense in which the agent in a Frankfurt-type scenario is unable to do otherwise are the same: It is physically possible for him to do only one act. What we do not know in the Frankfurt-type scenarios is whether the agent is *pushed* by the past and the laws into taking his course of action, or whether indeterminism leaves room for him freely to have chosen to do the act that is the only one physically possible for him at the time. Hence, on my view, we do not know whether or not the agent is morally responsible.

29. Dennett, *Elbow Room*, p. 134.

30. In another case, Dennett contends that, although he could not torture an innocent person for $1000, he is still praiseworthy for not doing it (*Elbow Room*, p. 133). (And he takes this to show that moral responsibility does not require alternative possibilities.) Here is one line of response: Although it is not now possible for Dennett to agree to torture an innocent person for $1000, given his rational and volitional state, his being morally responsible for not agreeing to do so is dependent upon the fact that he could have had a different character (or a different rational and volitional state). We assume, I believe, in judging Dennett praiseworthy that he constructed his character in an undetermined way, such that he was not necessitated to become the sort of person he is, but could have made himself to be a different sort of person if he had made different choices. So perhaps Dennett is morally responsible for refraining from torture; but if so, then this is derivative from his being responsible for being the sort of person who cannot torture, since he could have constructed a different character. One might expand on this idea by arguing that Dennett is morally responsible for refraining from torture, even though he could not have done otherwise at the time, only if the preference that led to his act of refraining was indeterministically acquired in the right sort of way.

31. Actually, I think it is unclear whether or not I should be blamed for deliberately missing the plane until it is known whether or not I freely undermined all of my ways of getting to the airport on time to make the flight. This case is a counterexample to PAP if we add to it the assumption of the truth of indeterminism and stipulate that indeterministic causal links were located in the appropriate places to enable my freely undermining all of my ways of getting to the airport on time. I discuss these issues explicitly in the text below. There remains a problem with this example concerning whether or not "missing the 10 A.M. flight" counts as an action or, rather, as an omission. Ginet holds that agents in Frankfurt-style examples cannot be held responsible for nonactions, where the agent does not try to act in a certain way but could not have acted in that way in any case. See Ginet, "Principle of Alternative Possibilities," p. 413.

32. Lamb, "Evaluative Compatibilism," p. 518.

33. The principle that *ought* implies *can* is saved, provided that we do not require that one can, *at the time,* commit the act one ought to do. The principle may be taken instead to require that one *could* have done the act one ought to do at the appropriate time *had* one done certain acts in the past that one could have done then. So Peggy Sue *ought* to attend the party as promised only if she *can* attend, and she can attend if her attending or not attending is up to her actions (at some time or another), not causally necessitated by circumstances external to her.

34. Even if there is a genetic predisposition to alcoholism, the condition cannot be triggered without acts of drinking alcohol, acts that may be, depending in part upon metaphysical conditions, free.

35. Eleonore Stump gives a similar case ("Intellect, Will, and the Principle of Alternate Possibilities," in John Martin Fischer and Mark Ravizza, eds., *Perspectives on Moral Responsibility,* Ithaca: Cornell University Press, 1993, pp. 246–248). Ruth is praiseworthy for remaining with her mother-in-law, Naomi, rather than returning to her own homeland, although, given the way in which Ruth has freely constructed her character, she could at the time have done nothing other than accompany Naomi. Aristotle, as well, argues that a person can be blameworthy for being a certain sort of person now, even if he cannot now change himself, if earlier in life he had a chance to become a different sort of person (*Nicomachean Ethics,* bk. 3, chap. 5; see Richard McKeon, ed., *Introduction to Aristotle,* 2nd edition, Chicago: University of Chicago Press, 1973). And Anselm, in *Cur Deus Homo* (bk. 1, chap. 24), gives an example showing the falsity of PAP_1: A slave throws himself into a ditch out of which he cannot climb, thereby making himself unable to do the work required of him. Sure enough, once in the ditch, he cannot do otherwise than fail to do the work. But since the slave is responsible for being in the ditch in the first place, Anselm concludes that he is responsible for failing to do his work.

36. See Susan Wolf, "The Real Self View," in *Freedom Within Reason* (New York: Oxford University Press, 1990) for a development of this question.

37. Lamb, "Evaluative Compatibilism." According to Lamb's strong version of PAP, "a person is morally responsible for doing something only if *at the time* he could have refrained" (p. 518). Lamb rightly rejects this principle.

According to Lamb's moderate version of PAP, "a person is morally responsible for doing something only if *at some time*—past, present, or future—he could have avoided doing it" (p. 519). The moderate principle is problematically stated, since the act at issue might not have been available *at the other (past or future) times.* So the moderate principle needs to be formulated differently, perhaps as follows: A person is morally responsible for doing something at *t* only if at some time—past, present, or future—he could have avoided his having to do it at *t.* Or perhaps the following is better: A person is morally responsible for doing something at t only if he could have done something at some time other than t to make it the case that the act did not inevitably occur at t.

38. Lamb, "Evaluative Compatibilism," p. 527.

39. Ibid.

40. Ginet, "Principle of Alternative Possibilities," p. 403.

41. Peter van Inwagen, "Fischer on Moral Responsibility," *Philosophical Quarterly* 47, 1997, p. 376.

42. van Inwagen, "Fischer on Moral Responsibility," p. 376.

43. Ibid., p. 377.

44. Ibid.

45. van Inwagen says that he insists on taking agents to be morally responsible not for actions, but for the consequences of these—events or states of affairs. (See van Inwagen, *Essay on Free Will;* and "Fischer on Moral Responsibility.") But ordinarily we *do* ask about responsibility for acts, and I have not seen any good reasons for thinking that this is not a legitimate question.

46. That is, it gives this result *unless* one calls the act done on one's own a *different* act than the one done by way of interference from the counterfactual intervener; and on this basis one argues that the condition of the derived principle is met. But I decline to make this move for reasons discussed in note 14.

47. In usual circumstances, cases of agents being able to act in only one particular way due to their own free acts are cases in which their options are minimized by their own *past* free actions. But I do not stipulate that the free acts that (at least partially) explain a person's only being able to do X at t must be past acts, in order not to rule out cases of time travel in which a person makes himself only able to do X at t by virtue of some free acts of his at times later than t.

48. Unless, that is, one claims that the act done by way of intervention and the act done without intervention are two *different act tokens* (even though acts of the same type). One might allege that in virtue of the availability of each of these alternatives, the agent who acts without intervention is able to do otherwise at the moment of action. Again, I reject this move.

49. The time other than t need not be prior to t.

50. I am grateful to Keith Lehrer for helpful correspondence concerning the extended Frankfurt-type scenario. Compare my treatment of such a scenario with Robert Kane's discussion of an ever-present nonintervening Frankfurt-style controller in Robert Kane, "Freedom, Responsibility, and Will-Setting," *Philosophical Topics* 24, 1996, pp. 67–90; see especially pp. 85–88.

Anglin, W. S. 1990. *Free Will and the Christian Faith*. Oxford: Clarendon Press.

Anscombe, G. E. M. 1981. "Causality and Determination." In *The Collected Philosophical Papers of G.E.M. Anscombe*, vol. 2. Minneapolis: University of Minnesota Press.

———. 1963. *Intention*. Ithaca: Cornell University Press.

Aristotle. 1973. *Nicomachean Ethics*. In Richard McKeon, ed., *Introduction to Aristotle*, 2nd edition. Chicago: University of Chicago Press.

Audi, Robert. 1991. "Responsible Action and Virtuous Character." *Ethics* 101, pp. 304–321.

———. 1973. "Intending." *Journal of Philosophy* 70, pp. 387–403.

Augustine. 1964. *On the Free Choice of the Will*. Indianapolis, IN: Bobbs-Merrill.

Austin, J. L. 1961. "Ifs and Cans." In *Philosophical Papers*. Oxford: Oxford University Press.

Ayer, A. J. 1954. *Philosophical Essays*. London: Macmillan.

Beaty, Michael D., ed. 1990. *Christian Theism and the Problems of Philosophy*. Library of Religious Philosophy, vol. 5. Notre Dame, IN: University of Notre Dame Press.

Benson, Paul. 1987. "Freedom and Value." *Journal of Philosophy* 84, pp. 465–486.

Bishop, John. 1989. *Natural Agency: An Essay on the Causal Theory of Action*. Cambridge: Cambridge University Press.

Brand, Myles. 1984. *Intending and Acting*. Cambridge, MA: MIT Press.

Bratman, Michael. 1996. "Identification, Decision, and Treating as a Reason." *Philosophical Topics* 24, pp. 1–18.

———. 1987. *Intention, Plans, and Practical Reason*. Cambridge, MA: Harvard University Press.

Broad, C. D. 1962. "Determinism, Indeterminism, and Libertarianism." In Sidney Morgenbesser and J. H. Walsh, eds., *Free Will*. Englewood Cliffs, NJ: Prentice-Hall.

Campbell, C. A. 1957. "Has the Self 'Free Will'?" In *On Selfhood and Godhood*. London: George Allen and Unwin.

Carson, D. A. 1994. *Divine Sovereignty and Human Responsibility*. Grand Rapids, MI: Baker Books; London: Marshall Pickering.

Chisholm, Roderick M. 1976. "The Agent as Cause." In Myles Brand and Douglas Walton, eds., *Action Theory*. Dordrecht, Holland: D. Reidel.

221

_____. 1964a. "Human Freedom and the Self." The Lindley Lecture, University of Kansas. Reprinted in Gary Watson, ed., *Free Will*. 1982. Oxford: Oxford University Press.

_____. 1964b. "J. L. Austin's Philosophical Papers." *Mind* 73, pp. 1–26.

Christman, John, ed. 1989. *The Inner Citadel: Essays on Individual Autonomy*. New York: Oxford University Press.

Churchland, Paul. 1970. "The Logical Character of Action-Explanations." *Philosophical Review* 79, pp. 214–236.

Clarke, Randolph. 1993. "Toward a Credible Agent-Causal Account of Free Will." *Nous* 27, pp. 191–203.

Davidson, Donald. 1980. *Essays on Actions and Events*. New York: Oxford University Press.

_____. 1973. "Freedom to Act." In Ted Honderich, ed., *Essays on Freedom of Action*. London: Routledge and Kegan Paul. Reprinted in Donald Davidson, 1980, *Essays on Actions and Events*. New York: Oxford University Press.

Dennett, Daniel. 1984. *Elbow Room: The Varieties of Free Will Worth Wanting*. Cambridge, MA: MIT Press.

_____. 1978. "On Giving Libertarians What They Say They Want." In *Brainstorms*. Montgomery, VT: Bradford Books.

Double, Richard. 1996. *Metaphilosophy and Free Will*. New York: Oxford University Press.

_____. 1992. "Two Types of Autonomy Accounts." *Canadian Journal of Philosophy* 22, pp. 65–80.

_____. 1991. *The Non-Reality of Free Will*. New York: Oxford University Press.

Dretske, Fred. 1988. *Explaining Behavior*. Cambridge, MA: MIT Press.

Dummett, Michael. 1964. "Bringing About the Past." *Philosophical Review* 73, pp. 338–359.

Dupre, John. 1996. "The Solution to the Problem of Free Will." *Philosophical Perspectives* 10, pp. 385–402.

Dworkin, Gerald. 1988. *The Theory and Practice of Autonomy*. Cambridge: Cambridge University Press.

Eels, Ellery. 1991. *Probabilistic Causality*. Cambridge: Cambridge University Press.

Ekstrom, Laura Waddell. Forthcoming. "Keystone Preferences and Autonomy." *Philosophy and Phenomenological Research*.

_____. 1998a. "Freedom, Causation, and the Consequence Argument." *Synthese* 115, pp. 333–354.

_____. 1998b. "Protecting Incompatibilist Freedom." *American Philosophical Quarterly* 35, pp. 281–291.

_____. 1995. "Causes and Nested Counterfactuals." *Australasian Journal of Philosophy* 73, pp. 574–578.

_____. 1993a. "A Coherence Theory of Autonomy." *Philosophy and Phenomenological Research* 53, pp. 599–616.

_____. 1993b. Review of *The Theory and Practice of Autonomy*, by Gerald Dworkin. *Philosophical Review* 102, pp. 616–619.

Feinberg, Joel. 1970. *Doing and Deserving: Essays in the Theory of Responsibility*. Princeton: Princeton University Press.

Fine, Gail. 1981. "Aristotle's Determinism." *Philosophical Review* 90, pp. 561–579.

Fischer, John Martin. 1996. "A New Compatibilism." *Philosophical Topics* 24, pp. 49–66.

_____. 1994. *The Metaphysics of Free Will: An Essay on Control*. Aristotle Society Series, vol. 14. Cambridge, MA: Blackwell.

_____. 1983. "Incompatibilism." *Philosophical Studies* 43, pp. 127–137.

_____. 1982. "Responsibility and Control." *Journal of Philosophy* 79, pp. 24–40.

Fischer, John Martin, ed. 1986. *Moral Responsibility*. Ithaca: Cornell University Press.

Fischer, John Martin, and Mark Ravizza. 1998. *Responsibility and Control*. Cambridge: Cambridge University Press.

Fischer, John Martin, and Mark Ravizza, eds. 1993. *Perspectives on Moral Responsibility*. Ithaca: Cornell University Press.

Flint, Thomas P. 1987. "Compatibilism and the Argument from Unavoidability." *Journal of Philosophy* 84, pp. 423–440.

Frankfurt, Harry. 1992. "The Faintest Passion." *Proceedings and Addresses of the American Philosophical Association* 66, pp. 5–16.

_____. 1987a. "Identification and Wholeheartedness." In Ferdinand Schoeman, ed., *Responsibility, Character, and the Emotions: New Essays in Moral Psychology*. Cambridge: Cambridge University Press. Reprinted in Harry Frankfurt, 1987b, *The Importance of What We Care About*. Cambridge: Cambridge University Press.

_____. 1987b. *The Importance of What We Care About*. Cambridge: Cambridge University Press.

_____. 1977. "Identification and Externality." In Amelie Rorty, ed., *The Identities of Persons*. Berkeley: University of California Press.

_____. 1971. "Freedom of the Will and the Concept of a Person." *Journal of Philosophy* 68, pp. 5–20.

_____. 1969. "Alternate Possibilities and Moral Responsibility." *Journal of Philosophy* 66, pp. 829–839.

Ginet, Carl. 1996. "In Defense of the Principle of Alternative Possibilities: Why I Don't Find Frankfurt's Argument Convincing." *Philosophical Perspectives* 10, pp. 403–417.

_____. 1990. *On Action*. Cambridge: Cambridge University Press.

_____. 1966. "Might We Have No Choice?" In K. Lehrer, ed., *Freedom and Determinism*. New York: Random House.

Glover, Jonathan. 1970. *Responsibility*. London: Routledge and Kegan Paul.

Goetz, Stewart. 1997. "Libertarian Choice." *Faith and Philosophy* 14, pp. 195–211.

Goldman, Alvin I. 1986. *Epistemology and Cognition*. Cambridge, MA: Harvard University Press.

_____. 1970. *A Theory of Human Action*. Englewood Cliffs, NJ: Prentice-Hall.

Good, I. J. 1980. "Some Comments on Probabilistic Causality." *Pacific Philosophical Quarterly* 61, pp. 301–304.

_____. 1961–1962. "A Causal Calculus I–II." *British Journal for the Philosophy of Science* 11, pp. 305–318; 12, pp. 43–51; errata and corrigenda, 13, p. 88.

Gorovitz, Samuel. 1964. "Leaving the Past Alone." *Philosophical Review* 73, pp. 360–371.

Harre, R., and E. H. Madden. 1975. *Causal Powers: A Theory of Natural Necessity*. Oxford: Blackwell.

Heineman, Robert. 1986. "Incompatibilism Without the Principle of Alternative Possibilities." *Australasian Journal of Philosophy* 64, pp. 266–276.

Hempel, C. G. 1965. "Aspects of Scientific Explanation." In *Aspects of Scientific Explanation and Other Essays in the Philosophy of Science*. New York: Free Press.

Hitchcock, Christopher. Forthcoming. "Contrastive Explanation and the Demons of Determinism." *British Journal for the Philosophy of Science*.

_____. 1993. "A Generalized Probabilistic Theory of Causal Relevance." *Philosophy of Science* 43, pp. 290–292.

Hobart, R. E. 1934. "Free Will as Involving Determination and Inconceivable Without It." *Mind* 43, pp. 1–27.

Hobbes, Thomas. 1962. *The English Works of Thomas Hobbes*. Vol. 5, ed. W. Molesworth. London: Scientia Aalen.

Hobbs, Jesse. 1991. "Chaos and Indeterminism." *Canadian Journal of Philosophy* 21, pp. 141–164.

Honderich, Ted, ed. 1973. *Essays on Freedom of Action*. London: Routledge and Kegan Paul.

Horgan, Terence. 1985. "Compatibilism and the Consequence Argument." *Philosophical Studies* 47, pp. 339–356.

Horwich, Paul. 1987. *Asymmetries in Time*. Cambridge, MA: MIT Press.

Hume, David. 1977. *An Inquiry Concerning Human Understanding*. Indianapolis, IN: Bobbs-Merrill. Originally published in 1748.

Humphreys, Paul. 1989. *The Chances of Explanation*. Princeton: Princeton University Press.

Jeffrey, Richard. 1974. "Preferences Among Preferences." *Journal of Philosophy* 71, pp. 377–391.

_____. 1971. "Statistical Explanation vs. Statistical Inference." In Wesley C. Salmon, J. G. Greeno, and Richard Jeffrey, eds., *Statistical Explanation and Statistical Relevance*. Pittsburgh, PA: University of Pittsburgh Press.

Kane, Robert. 1996a. "Freedom, Responsibility, and Will-Setting." *Philosophical Topics* 24, pp. 67–90.

_____. 1996b. *The Significance of Free Will*. New York: Oxford University Press.

_____. 1985. *Free Will and Values*. Albany, NY: SUNY Press.

Kant, Immanuel. 1960. *Religion Within the Bounds of Reason Alone*. Trans. T. Greene and H. Hudson. New York: Harper and Row.

_____. 1959. *Foundations of the Metaphysics of Morals*. Trans. L. W. Beck. Indianapolis, IN: Bobbs-Merrill.

Kapitan, Tomis. 1996. "Modal Principles in the Metaphysics of Free Will." *Philosophical Perspectives* 10, pp. 419–445.

Kim, Jaegwon. 1973. "Causes and Counterfactuals." *Journal of Philosophy* 70, pp. 570–572.

Klein, Martha. 1990. *Determinism, Blameworthiness, and Deprivation*. Oxford: Clarendon Press.

Lamb, James. 1993. "Evaluative Compatibilism and the Principle of Alternative Possibilities." *Journal of Philosophy* 90, pp. 517–527.

_____. 1977. "On a Proof of Incompatibilism." *Philosophical Review* 86, pp. 20–35.

Lehrer, Keith. 1997. *Self Trust: A Study of Reason, Knowledge, and Autonomy*. Oxford: Clarendon Press.

_____. 1990a. *Metamind*. Oxford: Clarendon Press.

_____. 1990b. *Theory of Knowledge*. Boulder: Westview Press.

_____. 1989. *Thomas Reid*. New York: Routledge.

_____. 1980. "Preferences, Conditionals and Freedom." In Peter van Inwagen, ed., *Time and Cause*. Dordrecht, Holland: D. Reidel.

_____. 1976. "'Can' in Theory and Practice: A Possible Worlds Analysis." In Myles Brand and Douglas Walton, eds., *Action Theory*. Dordrecht, Holland: D. Reidel.

_____. 1968. "Cans Without Ifs." *Analysis* 29, pp. 29–32.

Lehrer, Keith, ed. 1966. *Freedom and Determinism*. New York: Random House.

Leibniz, G. W. 1982. *New Essays on Human Understanding*. Trans. Peter Remnant and Jonathan Bennett. Cambridge: Cambridge University Press.

_____. 1973. *Philosophical Writings*. Trans. Mary Morris and G. H. R. Parkinson. London: J. M. Dent and Sons.

Lewis, David. 1986a. *On the Plurality of Worlds*. Oxford: Blackwell.

_____. 1986b. *Philosophical Papers*, vol. 2. New York: Oxford University Press.

_____. 1981. "Are We Free to Break the Laws?" *Theoria* 47, part 3, pp. 113–121.

_____. 1973. "Causation." *Journal of Philosophy* 70, pp. 556–567. Reprinted in David Lewis, 1986, *Philosophical Papers*, vol. 2. New York: Oxford University Press.

_____. 1970. "Anselm and Actuality." *Nous* 4, pp. 175–188.

Locke, John. 1975. *An Essay on Human Understanding*. Ed. Peter Nidditch. Oxford: Clarendon Press.

McCann, Hugh. 1995. "Divine Sovereignty and the Freedom of the Will." *Faith and Philosophy* 12, pp. 582–598.

_____. 1974. "Volition and Basic Action."*Philosophical Review* 83, pp. 451–473.

McIntyre, Alison. 1994. "Compatibilists Could Have Done Otherwise: Responsibility and Negative Agency." *Philosophical Review* 103, pp. 453–488.

McKay, Thomas, and David Johnson. 1996. "A Reconsideration of an Argument Against Compatibilism." *Philosophical Topics* 24, pp. 113–122.

Mele, Alfred. Forthcoming. "Goal-Directed Action: Teleological Explanations, Causal Theories, and Deviance." *Philosophical Perspectives*.

_____. 1997. "Agency and Mental Action." *Philosophical Perspectives* 11, pp. 231–249.

_____. 1996. "Soft Libertarianism and Frankfurt-Style Scenarios." *Philosophical Topics* 24, pp. 123–142.

_____. 1995. *Autonomous Agents: From Self-Control to Autonomy*. New York: Oxford University Press.

_____. 1992. *Springs of Action: Understanding Intentional Behavior*. New York: Oxford University Press.

Morgenbesser, Sidney, and J. H. Walsh, eds. 1962. *Free Will*. Englewood Cliffs, NJ: Prentice-Hall.

Moya, Carlos. 1991. *Philosophy of Action*. Oxford: Blackwell.

Murray, Michael J. 1993. "Coercion and the Hiddenness of God." *American Philosophical Quarterly* 30, pp. 27–38.

Murray, Michael J., and David F. Dudrick. 1995. "Are Coerced Acts Free?" *American Philosophical Quarterly* 32, pp. 109–123.

Nagel, Thomas. 1986. *The View from Nowhere*. New York: Oxford University Press.

Nozick, Robert. 1981. *Philosophical Explanations*. Cambridge, MA: Harvard University Press.

O'Connor, Timothy. Forthcoming. *Persons and Causes: The Metaphysics of Free Will*. Oxford: Oxford University Press.

_____. 1996. "Why Agent Causation?" *Philosophical Topics* 24, pp. 143–158.

_____. 1993. "Indeterminism and Free Agency: Three Recent Views." *Philosophy and Phenomenological Research* 53, pp. 499–526.

O'Connor, Timothy, ed. 1995. *Agents, Causes, and Events.* New York: Oxford University Press.

O'Shaughnessy, Brian. 1980. *The Will.* 2 vols. Cambridge: Cambridge University Press.

Perry, John. 1979. "The Problem of the Essential Indexical." *Nous* 13, pp. 3–21.

Pike, Nelson. 1965. "Divine Omniscience and Voluntary Action." *Philosophical Review* 74, pp. 27–46.

Piper, Adrian. 1985. "Two Conceptions of the Self." *Philosophical Studies* 48, pp. 173–197.

Plantinga, Alvin. 1990. "Advice to Christian Philosophers." In Michael D. Beaty, ed., *Christian Theism and the Problems of Philosophy.* Notre Dame, IN: University of Notre Dame Press.

_____. 1974. *God, Freedom, and Evil.* Grand Rapids, MI: Eerdmans.

Pollock, John. 1986. *Contemporary Theories of Knowledge.* Totowa, NJ: Rowman and Littlefield.

Railton, Peter. 1981. "Probability, Explanation, and Information." *Synthese* 48, pp. 233–256.

_____. 1978. "A Deductive-Nomological Model of Probabilistic Explanation." *Philosophy of Science* 45, pp. 206–226.

Reichenbach, Hans. 1957. *The Philosophy of Space and Time.* New York: Dover Publications.

_____. 1946. *Philosophic Foundations of Quantum Mechanics.* Berkeley: University of California Press.

Reid, Thomas. 1983. *The Works of Thomas Reid.* Ed. W. Hamilton. Hildeshein: George Ulm.

_____. 1969. *Essays on the Active Powers of the Human Mind.* Introduction by Baruch Brody. Cambridge, MA: MIT Press.

Rowe, William. 1993. *Philosophy of Religion.* Belmont, CA: Wadsworth.

_____. 1991. *Thomas Reid on Freedom and Morality.* Ithaca: Cornell University Press.

Salmon, Wesley C. 1998. *Causality and Explanation.* New York: Oxford University Press.

_____. 1984. *Scientific Explanation and the Causal Structure of the World.* Princeton: Princeton University Press.

_____. 1971. "Statistical Explanation." In Wesley Salmon, J. Greeno, and R. C. Jeffrey, *Statistical Explanation and Statistical Relevance.* Pittsburgh: University of Pittsburgh Press.

Schlick, Moritz. 1939. "When Is a Man Responsible?" In David Rynin, trans., *Problems of Ethics*. New York: Prentice-Hall.

Schoeman, Ferdinand, ed. 1987. *Responsibility, Character, and the Emotions: New Essays in Moral Psychology*. Cambridge: Cambridge University Press.

Schopenhauer, Arthur. 1960. *Essay on the Freedom of the Will*. Trans. Konstantine Kolenda. Indianapolis, IN: Bobbs-Merrill.

Shatz, David. 1986. "Free Will and the Structure of Motivation." *Midwest Studies in Philosophy* 10, pp. 451–482.

Slote, Michael. 1982. "Selective Necessity and the Free-Will Problem." *Journal of Philosophy* 79, pp. 5–24.

_____. 1980. "Understanding Free Will." *Journal of Philosophy* 77, pp. 136–151.

Smiley, Marion. 1992. *Moral Responsibility and the Boundaries of Community*. Chicago: University of Chicago Press.

Sorabji, Richard. 1983. *Necessity, Cause and Blame*. Ithaca: Cornell University Press.

Strawson, Galen. 1986. *Freedom and Belief*. Oxford: Clarendon Press.

Strawson, Peter. 1962. "Freedom and Resentment." *Proceedings of the British Academy* 48, pp. 1–25. Reprinted in Gary Watson, ed., 1982, *Free Will*. Oxford: Oxford University Press; also reprinted in John Martin Fischer and Mark Ravizza, eds., 1993, *Perspectives on Moral Responsibility*. Ithaca: Cornell University Press.

Stump, Eleonore. 1996. "Persons: Identification and Freedom." *Philosophical Topics* 24, pp. 183–214.

_____. 1990. "Intellect, Will, and Alternative Possibilities." In Michael D. Beaty, ed., *Christian Theism and the Problems of Philosophy*. Notre Dame, IN: University of Notre Dame Press.

_____. 1988. "Sanctification, Hardening of the Heart, and Frankfurt's Concept of Free Will." *Journal of Philosophy* 85, pp. 395–412.

Suppes, Patrick. 1970. *A Probabilistic Theory of Causality*. Amsterdam: North-Holland.

Swanton, Christine. 1992. *Freedom: A Coherence Theory*. Indianapolis, IN: Hackett Publishing.

Taylor, Charles. 1982. "Responsibility for Self." In Gary Watson, ed., *Free Will*. Oxford: Oxford University Press.

Taylor, Richard. 1992. *Metaphysics*, 4th Edition. Englewood Cliffs, NJ: Prentice-Hall.

Thalberg, Irving. 1978. "Hierarchical Analyses of Unfree Action." *Canadian Journal of Philosophy* 8, pp. 211–226.

_____. 1976. "How Does Agent Causality Work?" In Myles Brand and Douglas Walton, eds., *Action Theory*. Dordrecht, Holland: D. Reidel.

van Inwagen, Peter. 1997. "Fischer on Moral Responsibility." *Philosophical Quarterly* 47, pp. 373–381.

_____. 1993. *Metaphysics*. Boulder: Westview Press.

_____. 1983. *An Essay on Free Will*. Oxford: Clarendon Press.

_____. 1980. "The Incompatibility of Responsibility and Determinism." *Bowling Green Studies in Applied Philosophy* 2, pp. 30–37.

_____. 1978. "Ability and Responsibility." *Philosophical Review* 87, pp. 201–224.

_____. 1975. "The Incompatibility of Free Will and Determinism." *Philosophical Studies* 27, pp. 185–199.

Velleman, J. David. 1992. "What Happens When Someone Acts?" *Mind* 101, pp. 461–481. Reprinted in John Martin Fischer and Mark Ravizza, eds., 1993, *Perspectives on Moral Responsibility*. Ithaca: Cornell University Press.

Vihvelin, Kadri. 1995. "Causes, Effects, and Counterfactual Dependence." *Australasian Journal of Philosophy* 73, pp. 560–573.

_____. 1991. "Freedom, Causation, and Counterfactuals." *Philosophical Studies* 64, pp. 161–184.

Warfield, Ted A. 1996. "Determinism and Moral Responsibility Are Incompatible." *Philosophical Topics* 24, pp. 215–226.

Watson, Gary. 1987a. "Free Action and Free Will." *Mind* 46, pp. 145–172.

_____. 1987b. "Responsibility and the Limits of Evil: Variations on a Strawsonian Theme." In Ferdinand Schoeman, ed., *Responsibility, Character, and the Emotions: New Essays in Moral Psychology*. Cambridge: Cambridge University Press. Reprinted in John Martin Fischer and Mark Ravizza, eds., 1993, *Perspectives on Moral Responsibility*. Ithaca: Cornell University Press.

_____. 1975. "Free Agency." *Journal of Philosophy* 72, pp. 205–220.

Watson, Gary, ed. 1982. *Free Will*. Oxford: Oxford University Press.

Wiggins, David. 1973. "Towards a Reasonable Libertarianism." In Ted Honderich, ed., *Essays on Freedom of Action*. London: Routledge and Kegan Paul.

Williams, Bernard. 1995. *Making Sense of Humanity*. Cambridge: Cambridge University Press.

Wolf, Susan. 1990. *Freedom Within Reason*. New York: Oxford University Press.

_____. 1987. "Sanity and the Metaphysics of Responsibility." In Ferdinand Schoeman, ed., *Responsibility, Character, and the Emotions: New Essays in Moral Psychology*. Cambridge: Cambridge University Press..

_____. 1981. "The Importance of Free Will." *Mind* 90, pp. 386–405. Reprinted in John Martin Fischer and Mark Ravizza, eds., 1993, *Perspectives on Moral Responsibility*. Ithaca: Cornell University Press.

_____. 1980. "Asymmetrical Freedom." *Journal of Philosophy* 77, pp. 151–166.

INDEX